The Idea of Authorship
in America

Kenneth Dauber

The Idea of Authorship in America

Democratic Poetics from Franklin to Melville

The University of Wisconsin Press

The University of Wisconsin Press
114 North Murray Street
Madison, Wisconsin 53715

3 Henrietta Street
London WC2E 8LU, England

5 4 3 2 1

Printed in the United States of America

Library of Congress Cataloging-in-Publication Data
Dauber, Kenneth, 1945–
    The idea of authorship in America: democratic poetics from
Franklin to Melville / Kenneth Dauber
    288 pp.   cm.
    Includes bibliographical references.
    1. American literature—19th century—History and criticism.
2. American literature—18th century—History and criticism.
3. Authors and readers—United States—History. 4. Authority
in literature. 5. Authorship—History. I. Title.
PS201.D38   1990
810.9—dc20   89-40530
ISBN 0-299-12480-0   CIP
ISBN 0-299-12484-3 (pbk.)

To my father, z'l, and to my mother,
a good writer and a good teacher

Let it be with me that when I read a book it should be as if the book were written especially for me and spoke to me of what I know and all that befalls me.

From a prayer of the Chassidim of Breslau

Contents

Acknowledgments

My thanks to a number of people whose aid and encouragement have been indispensable in the course of this project. Allen Fitchen at The University of Wisconsin Press saw the beginning, promoted the middle, and trusted in the end. Aaron Rosen, Marcus Klein, and Joe Fradin gave me sage and sensitive advice about the Introduction. Baruch Hochman, Richard Brodhead, and Edgar Dryden offered selfless readings at a time when it meant the most to me. For permission to reprint versions of the chapters on Benjamin Franklin and Hawthorne, thanks to the editors of *Criticism* and *The Thoreau Quarterly*. For knowing what work is and providing an atmosphere in which it may flourish, thanks to my colleagues at the State University of New York at Buffalo. And most of all, as ever, for valuing what is valuable, thanks to my wife, Antoinette.

Buffalo, New York
January 1990

Introduction

Books are hard to write. They are hard to write for familiar technical reasons—it is difficult to fashion an elegant whole. And they are hard to write for substantive reasons—it is difficult to get the thought precisely right. But books are hard to write for yet another reason and one which the sympathetic reader to whom this work, according to what Hawthorne calls an "antique fashion," is addressed will recognize as founding for the others. It is the difficulty of sympathy itself, of that agreement about what constitutes elegance or rightness in the first place and without which it is impossible to proceed. To put it in question form, what, after all, authorizes a book? If a long Western tradition of skepticism had not already taught us the lesson, certainly the last decade of literary criticism should have, that, ultimately, nothing does. And yet we do write nevertheless, and that we do testifies to a certain faith in writing, a certain faith in each other that we may make of that nothing something, after all. Let us call this faith a democratic faith. It is a peculiarly American faith and the subject of the work that follows.

My starting point is the issue of an author's authority. How does a writer justify his presumption in intruding himself on our notice? What kind of reading does a reader owe a writer? "I desire to speak . . . like a man in a waking moment, to men in their waking moments," says Thoreau in *Walden,* evidently aware of how human it is to fall asleep over even a good book.[1] But why should we not fall asleep? What does a writer have to say that is so important that we need read? Claims vary according to time and place. To confine ourselves to the nineteenth century, the realist novelist writing in order to imitate is, in a sense, the opposite of the romantic poet singing his inspiration. The first puts forth a faithful objectivity, the second a powerful subjectivity. The one claims accurate observation, the other insight. Whatever the case, however, some foundation is supposed in a truth that justifies observation and insight and that the reader will miss unless he take the work up. A sort of transcendental authority is claimed, offering security, but at the cost of a coercion too great, at least for the early American temperament, to bear. It is an authority compelling writer and reader to observe or to be inspired and to which, accordingly, no democrat—certainly no democrat of the first years of American democracy—could very happily wish to submit.

As Benjamin Franklin puts it in the opening lines of his *Autobiography*, "this may be read or not as any one pleases." For all its modesty, the statement sounds a revolutionary American note. The prose is casual. There is no radical stridency. Franklin, easy and self-possessed, does not need to attack any established authority in order to justify himself. Indeed, he does not even justify himself by establishing some new authority in its stead. All the more, however, he thus exhibits a self-determination, as it were, prior to justification. He exhibits the independence of selfhood as a sort of inalienable right and guaranteed by the right to such selfhood that he grants others as well. What is there to recommend the writer's work? He recommends it only as it is the product of a man whom other men may choose to read. He has no special vision. He knows no truth his readers must know. His readers do not have to read. For that matter, he does not have to write. And yet, writing and reading after all, they rather assert their own truths. They assert that the work is true *because* they write and read it.

American writing, we should say, is democratic rather than truthful. Its poetics, in effect, is a rhetoric. It is "making"—poesis—

conceived of as neither imitating nor creating, but negotiating. We might say, addressing the problems of current theory, that an American poetics is immune to the "deconstruction" of poetry into rhetoric, because it is rhetorical from the start. Or, to put it more broadly, constructed as it is quite openly, built and rebuilt continuously according to nothing it does not establish at the moment of its building, American writing is immune to theory, as it is usually conceived, altogether. It is pragmatic rather than theoretical. It is political rather than philosophical. And, indeed, in a skeptical age, when philosophy could provide itself with no theory it might regard as legitimate, Americans were writing free of the need for legitimation, on the basis of that freedom, in fact, which Kant called practice's absolute.[2]

Of course, it should be needless to say, such freedom was not without its burdens. Thoreau fearing and Franklin, as it almost seems, courting the reader's sleep exhibit different temperaments in regard to freedom. They offer different responses to their rhetorical situations. Freedom from established truths, after all, means the labor of establishing them, and such labor is often difficult. I would not, therefore, imagine that the turn to practice solved, rather than altered, all difficulties. It has become far too usual among opponents of theory to assume that the political nature of writing is guaranteed by a polity more fixed than it really is.[3] Ostensibly commonsensical notions like "interpretive communities" have been proposed, designed to sustain writing with a stability that philosophy, under the onslaught of deconstruction, cannot seem to supply.[4] Still, American writers did not expect to escape the uncertainty of negotiation, for their freedom meant, rather, that they would engage it. The appeal to fixed truths is what they wished to avoid at all costs. They would avoid it in itself as denying their writing any self-motivation, and they would avoid it in its consequences as inevitably it would be undermined. The writer knew he was no independent "I." He was no transcendent self, but achieved his selfhood in the context of other nontranscendent selves, in the context of the community of "we." And yet to promote that "we" as a substitute transcendence, to fix the relationship between "I's" instead, would have been only to reintroduce the very problem that "we" was invoked to solve. As we might put it, it thus is perfectly true that without a "we" nothing we might call an "I" could emerge. Yet this was an issue not to be resolved, only to be navigated. Who "we" are was the problem exactly, and it was to do something about it that the writers wrote in the first place.

"This may be read or not as any one pleases." Writer and reader are thrown on each other. What have they, but each other? And yet, as well, it is just in the context of the possibility of *not* having each other that the having becomes possible. Franklin's statement must be read in a certain light. From only a slightly altered perspective its self-assurance appears like bravado. On the one hand, it is a simple declaration of fact. Undoubtedly, a work *may* be read or not. On the other hand, to read it or not is what Franklin specifically enjoins us to do. Franklin turns the declarative into an imperative. The statement becomes a dare. He challenges us to read or not to read, raises the fact to consciousness in order to turn consciousness into fact in its place. This is how things are, he seems to say. Yet things thus are only as we make them, and we make them, indeed, only because we might not.

Franklin's relationship to his reader is, if we may put it this way, the empirical condition produced by his faith. Finally, as he trusted, his reader was someone on whom he could count, and so the individuals he writes for are already his readers. His community is sustained by individuals disposing their individuality toward each other. Franklin trusts to politics, which is why he regards even honesty as policy. "Dear Son," he addresses his work, certain that strangers too, though they are not his son, will be interested in what he says. But such certainty is never guaranteed, and that it is not is what gives it its ethical force. Many of the writers after Franklin whom we will discuss did not have sons, while those who did could not be sure that even they might not be strangers. Hawthorne conceives of his reader as lying under some mossy gravestone. Melville dedicates *Pierre* to a mountain. How can the writer continue to write if the reader, like Bartleby, "prefer not to" read?

We may be tempted toward mystification, toward justifying

writing on some basis other than simple "pleasing to," after all. Writing which ought, simply, to be read becomes independent of reading, a work referring to itself or a truth beyond itself and soon, as a result, a work seemingly independent of writing, as well. A reversal threatens. The community authorizing what its truths should be comes to assume an authority based on truths hypostatized as revealed in advance. Or rather, since no such revelation is ever evident at the present, the community's goal becomes the recapture of some lost revelation. As Perry Miller interprets American literature, the history of American writers is their attempt to reconstitute the Puritan relation of their words to spirit in secular terms. Or as Sacvan Bercovitch has seen it, they attempted to project such spirit-words onto the language of the world. Or as Charles Feidelson sees it, they progressively discovered the impossibility of reconstitution or projection.[5] The dream of an originary language dies hard. "In the beginning was the Word." In the beginning, word and thing were one. God, naming things, knew them, and the curse of tongues at Babel, it is supposed, was the fall from the possibility of such knowing. And yet, as we might point out, men's first words were never God's. Naming the animals, Adam named, for all mankind, rather, his relation to things. He named but what man would count *as* knowledge. The curse of Babel was a fall from consensus, rather than from knowledge, and it was brought about precisely by the attempt to render such consensus as immutable as God's knowledge, nevertheless. It is a fall whose history in American literature we shall trace, as Americans, resisting such an attempt, struggled to maintain their relations despite increasing pressure.

My first chapter, on Benjamin Franklin's *Autobiography*, develops the idea that autobiography is the "epic" mode of a democracy. That is, in a democracy, every man's life is "true." Everyone is an author, and writing, though belonging to the community, belongs also to each of its members, who, in writing themselves, authorize everyone else to write as well. The author need appeal to nothing beyond his writing. A "second Edition" of his life, as Franklin said his autobiography was, it does not refer to living, but is at one with it. Consciousness is not *of* living, but is living itself. The consequences for literary form are discussed. The *Auto-biography*'s openness, the looseness of its construction yet its coherence, is explored as a model of American writing in general.

The second chapter, on Charles Brockden Brown, discusses what happens when authorship becomes a profession. The institutionalization of writing hierarchizes authority. All men are no longer authors. Writing does not justify itself, and the writer must appeal to a life anterior to his writing to which he claims a special access. Rhetoric is replaced by poetics. Autobiography becomes fiction or, in the case at hand, romance—the tradition of the so-called American romance—which I see as fiction in the process of a constant return to its lost autobiographical origins. Brown's lack of concern about integrating his novels is investigated as writing which refuses the alienation of formalization in a work. His presumed wildness and inconsistency are rehabilitated as the struggles of an author against authorship as his age was defining it.

The third chapter is on Fenimore Cooper and his "myth" of Leatherstocking. The related issues of myth, convention, and the idea of a "national" literature are raised. Cooper's career is followed through a progressive alienation he never quite fully understands. The "representative" American writer, as he was universally considered, he "others" his life in Cooperstown in order to cast it authoritatively as the life of the nation. Yet as what he writes becomes too much the life of the nation, Cooper attempts to recapture it as his life, after all. He refuses to subordinate himself to the other, refuses "transcendence" in the folk—in the manner recommended by Bakhtin and Leslie Fiedler, say[6]—and insists on his independence from the folk instead. The result is his well-known aristocratic brand of democracy, his impossible partisanship of culture *and* nature, and his simultaneous position as first among American authors who yet is only an imitator of the Englishman Walter Scott.

The fourth chapter, on Edgar Allan Poe, develops further Cooper's problem of otherness and independence. The central issue here is Poe's plagiarism. His unsuccessful borrowing from other authors is compared with Coleridge's successful borrowing. His formalism, a sort of reification of his distance from his reader, is investigated and its mystification as "symbol" analyzed. For "romantic" though he was, Poe could be inspired by another's poetry only by playing romantic as in a masquerade. Inspiration meant not life in the larger poetic spirit, but the death of his own spirit. In his necrophiliac representations of lovers of death and the dead, he quite precisely portrays his own dilemma. Poe comes as close to a poetics of transcendence as any American of the period could. But his very Americanness, despite himself, kept redefining transcendence as a bizarre joke, beauty as an "effect," poetry as a rhetoric after all.

The fifth chapter, on Hawthorne, engages the power of what I would call his "outsidedness" rather than otherness. By temperament reclusive, not unhappy to spend a decade after college quietly in his mother's attic, he yet approaches the reader more directly than any other writer under discussion. "Though disinclined to talk overmuch of myself and my affairs at the fireside, and to my personal friends," as he says in "The Custom-House," "an autobiographical impulse" has yet "taken possession of me, in addressing the public." Barred from autobiography, condemned to fiction, as it were, even in the presence of his "personal friends," Hawthorne yet manages autobiography in the very condition of fiction. In effect, he domesticates his alienation. Caught in conventionality, he raises it to the level of a consciousness in which it becomes conventional no more. Hawthorne's allegory is discussed as a self-conscious appropriation of convention, and his persistent refusal to symbolize is explained.

The concluding chapter, on Herman Melville, extends much of what we will have been studying. Melville's early novels of adventure among the cannibals are Franklin's autobiography or Brown's romance as fiction returning to autobiography. His *Moby-Dick* is Cooper's national myth. His *Pierre* is Poe's plagiaristic grotesquerie. In the progress of his career from popular novelist to writer of the unpublished *Billy Budd,* he even recapitulates Hawthorne's progress, only reversing it. Yet perhaps because of his initial popularity, defining his writing as rhetorical from the start, Melville is committed to a democratic poetics even as he engages what in other writers threatens it. "Call me Ishmael," as *Moby-*

Dick begins. Allegory, allusion, the traditions and transcendences which the name "Ishmael" invokes, are already inscribed within the give-and-take, what we have called the negotiations, of Melville's address to the reader, which is not quite fictive after all. I believe even Melville's anonymity at the end is such a negotiation. It is not an abandonment of his readers for some private wisdom or skepticism. But in the face of his not being listened to—in the face of America, on the eve of the Civil War, not listening to itself—it is a writing as dumb as his readers are deaf. Melville's "silence" is a speaking silence, and as his increasingly opaque and, then, his posthumous writing demonstrates, Melville, offering his audience "unreadable" works, extends democratic poetics about as far as it can go.

The Idea of Authorship
in America

1   Benjamin Franklin and the Idea of Authorship

At the threshold of America stands "B. Franklin, Americain." This is the inscription on one of the popular medallions struck in Franklin's honor on the occasion of his ambassadorship to France, and it is especially appropriate.[1] Franklin, abroad and at home, for better and for worse, has been our most enduring exemplar. The picture on the medallion represents the general sense of him well. Here is Franklin, perfectly attired in studded shirt and closed collar—and with a fur cap on his head! The tensions of American culture, that natural paradise that yet aspires to the vanguard of Western civilization, appear together in one figure. Down-home earthiness meets urbane sophistication, native sagacity cosmopolitan wit. Franklin spans America's diversity. He gave it electricity, daylight savings time, a new stove, its first public library, the idea for the union of its colonies, a university, a fire department, government borrowing from the people, bifocals, and on and on. "One might enumerate the items of high civilization," says Henry James in a famous passage, "which are absent from the texture of American life," and there follows a list ranging from "sovereign," "church," and "army," to "novels," "Epsom," and "Ascot."[2] Franklin, then, would seem to have gone far toward providing such items himself, to have created America's civilization single-handedly, and all of it, from "high" to low, with everything in between. Businessman, scientist, statesman, man of let-

3

ters, his genius was in no one field above any other, but in his having worked so many fields, in his having *been* America in all of its variousness.

This identification of Franklin with his nation is remarkable, and I take it to be the beginning of any uniquely American studies. Both personal and national, "American" appears before us undivided, referring equally to the general and to the particular. No division need, or even should, be undertaken. No a priori objection that we confuse different senses of American should be raised. Indeed, it is only by refusing to raise it that we can really investigate what "American," in Franklin's sense, means. We must resist the seductions of presumably more rigorous analysis. We must not separate out independent elements of our identification, even if only to put them together again in some deeper resolution. If we speak of Franklin as American, it is as describing neither the fortuitous circumstance of his having lived in America, nor yet some idea of a fundamental characteristic he shares with others who lived with him. American, in Franklin, means neither something accidental nor something essential. For, in the wide range of his national activities, Franklin is not a part of America's variety and not its principle, but variety at its very level.

Here, we must not be misled by a habit of what we take to be disinterested investigation. Too typically we place Franklin at a kind of arm's length away from us. We eye him skeptically, afraid of being taken in. We remove ourselves from our own observations of him, as if disinterest would not affect observation with interests of its own. We insist, for example, that an individual cannot really be his community except in some too near view from which we must be careful to distance ourselves. But we do not see that, for Franklin, only a community of individuals would even be an American community and that our distance, accordingly, displaces Americanness from the very perspective in which it signifies. Let us not be so ready to assume, a priori, such an ostensible objectivity that we would do better to interrogate. If our failure to divide "American" appears to be naive, if it is parochial or, even, ideologically motivated, at least it is the ideology of

America itself. Let us render our subject in its own language. Let us develop our reflections in the terms of what we reflect about. Or, if reflection itself means division, separating ourselves from what we reflect about, we may even admit the inescapability of terms of separation. But let us, reflecting not only *on* America, but *as* American, give our very division, as it were, an "undivided" account.

We have said that Franklin had no preeminent genius, that he is given to us as dispersed across his nation. And yet, since this Franklin is given to us primarily through his own writings, we cannot help suspecting that he was preeminently the writer through whom we learn of his other eminences, author of a self too designedly American and concealing the real man behind the model we have thus far accepted. *The Autobiography of Benjamin Franklin* is a work of art, we usually say. It is a fiction its author would foist upon us out of some ulterior, however benevolent, motivation, an artifact to be rejected or, even, accepted. As we should note, however, it would thus fill the gap of some divide between us which it simultaneously begets. It would resolve only such an opposition of Franklin to his world which consideration of it as art actually creates. Here would be the equivalent at a formal level of the a priori approach, but registered for us, now, in the order of its generation. It is a descent from "American" in its irreducibility, from an identity of American writing with American reading. It is a departure from a certain simultaneity of producing and processing American works—a "fall," let us call it, whose significance we must undertake to evaluate.

I. The Idea of Authorship

I can remember, when I was a little boy, my father used to buy a scrubby yearly almanac with the sun and moon and stars on the cover. And it used to prophesy bloodshed and famine. But also crammed in corners it had little anecdotes and humorisms, with a moral tag. And I used to have my little priggish laugh at the woman who counted her chickens before they were hatched, and so forth, and I was convinced that honesty was the best policy, also a little priggishly. The author of these bits was Poor Richard,

and Poor Richard was Benjamin Franklin, writing in Philadelphia well over a hundred years before.

And probably I haven't got over those Poor Richard tags yet. I
rankle still with them. They are thorns in young flesh.

Because although I still believe that honesty is the best policy, I
dislike policy altogether; though it is just as well not to count your
chickens before they are hatched, it's still more hateful to count
them with gloating when they *are* hatched. It has taken me many
years and countless smarts to get out of that barbed wire moral
enclosure that Poor Richard rigged up. Here am I now in tatters
and scratched to ribbons, sitting in the middle of Benjamin's
America looking at the barbed wire, and the fat sheep crawling
under the fence to get fat outside and the watchdogs yelling at the
gate lest by chance anyone should get out by the proper exit. Oh,
America! Oh, Benjamin! And I just utter a long loud curse
against Benjamin and the American corral.

Moral America! Most moral Benjamin. Sound, satisfied Ben![3]

These are D. H. Lawrence's words, in a well-known passage whose
sentiments are shared by many of us. Franklin's moralisms are
absurdly simplistic. His conventional virtues are a falsification of
life. Our presumed identity of "American" is roundly denied, for
Franklin stands condemned as the representative of just that public America that, privately at least, Americans have always opposed. It is the opposition of the romantic in us to the formalism of
neoclassicism, of a certain warm idealism to cold, practical cal-
culation. It is the classic division of self and society, the individual
and rules in general. It is the historic division in the renaissance of
transcendentalist and Yankee, earlier of heart and head, and earlier still, as scholars of the colonial period tell us, of antinomian
and Puritan orthodoxy. What is particularly significant about
Lawrence's formulation of the division, however—where he offers
us something beyond the standard formulation—is the opportunity he provides us to see it in the making. For Lawrence,
unmistakably the partisan, does not assert the division so much as
he reenacts it. He intentionalizes the American division, removing it from the plane of ostensibly disinterested statement and
placing it inside a context it creates for itself.

This creativity is nowhere more evident than in Lawrence's virulence. He insists on taking everything Franklin says as a personal affront. His hostility seems so much in excess of what Franklin warrants that it is manifestly self-generated. It is not a response to some prior hostility, the result of an attempt by Franklin to tyrannize him. But it is read back into, in order to deny, Franklin's utter obliviousness to the Lawrence for whom his work was proving so tyrannical. It is Franklin's "satisfaction" that Lawrence cannot stand, his "priggishness" or "gloating," which are but aggressive terms for what, to an indifferent observer, might just as easily appear as an innocent or, at worst, naive contentment. Franklin's disinterest looms everywhere as a silent rebuke. His monumental imperturbability, his almost divine detachment in the face of Lawrence's mere mortal's struggles, are unbearable. For Franklin does not so much oppose Lawrence's aspirations as he fails to understand or, for that matter, even care to understand them, and it is this that Lawrence cannot abide. "Benjamin" and "Benjamin's America" were ignoring him, and they were doing so successfully, were building a literature and a nation based upon ignoring him. Writing in another age and with another temperament, writing, most of all, as a European between the wars at a period when the balance of world power seemed to be shifting across the Atlantic, Lawrence could not but see in Franklin the negation of everything he hoped to achieve. Here was success, mastery, a man with a command of himself and his art that Lawrence, striving romantic and suffering Englishman, could never really hope for. By inscribing Franklin within a context motivated by his private pains, therefore, Lawrence turns Franklin's very completeness inside out. Independence becomes arrogance, simple self-sufficiency an act of aggression against others. Franklin, as he claims later, cut a "hole in the side of England," inventing, for that purpose, what Lawrence calls a "dummy" American, a crude, almost invulnerable mechanical soldier against which the more natural and human European could not hope to stand.[4] Lawrence's opposition *to* Franklin is thus successfully transferred. It becomes the opposition *of* Franklin.

More important for our purposes, however, as Lawrence continues, the opposition becomes, finally, opposition actually *in* Franklin. This is a critical development evident in Lawrence's focus, in the passage we quoted, on the proposition that honesty is the best policy. For such a proposition need not be construed, as Lawrence construes it, hypocritically. To a sympathetic reader, indeed, to an audience, let us say, before the "fall" to which we have alluded, sharing the writer's presuppositions and, in a sense we will elaborate later, written into the work from the start, it expresses but a simple democratic faith. Policy, no calculating means to an end, might be seen as the functioning of man in a society where power is disseminated universally, as the operation of a citizen of a nation in which the operation of all the citizens is what determines events. But Lawrence is not a sympathetic reader, and so, unable to join with the work in agreement, he projects his opposition to it onto it, where it appears as a putative opposition of honesty to policy. Alienated and objectifying his alienation from Franklin in Franklin, he makes all but inevitable paradox, contradiction, the binary oppositions of formal analysis. He creates, simultaneously, a method of analysis and the work as object to be analyzed, which, however, no matter how much analysis may then explain it, will enshrine forever its separateness from him. Indeed, he creates the *Autobiography* as a classic, which it has become all the more for Americans, and even for those who rather follow than struggle against it.

Accordingly, we may freely note that Franklin was from the beginning America's glorious achievement, the *Autobiography* its indisputably great work of art. Even Emerson could admire Franklin, and Melville, who did not completely trust him, seemed to be fond of him nevertheless.[5] Yet the axis of Lawrence's bias, if not the bias itself, was the axis of American writers of the nineteenth century as well. As an Englishman, Lawrence inverts things, but the terms are the same. This is why, in fact, *Studies in Classic American Literature* was so important to a generation rediscovering itself and why it remains so popular. For hostility to America we must substitute hostility to Europe, for insecurity about the continued significance of an English fiction substitute insecurity about an emergent American fiction. The bind in which American writers found themselves after the War of 1812 has been well documented.[6] Called upon, in a burst of nationalism at the new country's "victory," to produce at last works of art representative of what was uniquely American, they struggled to free themselves of the forms of an English fiction which was their inevitable literary model. Here, and even more intensely than in Lawrence, is a literature asserting itself only in opposition to another literature. It is writing striving for self-determination but dependent by definition, writing in a love-hate relationship under the shadow of writing which has not yet learned to love or to hate, which is innocent of designs against it or of the need of designing itself. Thus Americans, too, though they did not oppose Franklin, mistook him in striving toward him. They would reproduce him in a world and in a medium that inescapably transform him. The *Autobiography* is, as it were, a part of American literature's prehistory. It is what American writers were after all along but could never achieve precisely because they were after it.

It is important to insist on the literary formulation of the problem here. For although what is at issue is a cultural shift, yet Lawrence's use of textual terms folds literature back onto culture, making it integrated with, rather than a representation of, culture. The significance of this will become apparent as we continue. But we may note here, at any rate, Lawrence's description of Franklin's presence as a function of his dispersion throughout his materials. Franklin is inescapable. He appears all over, even in almanacs Lawrence's father picks up thousands of miles away from America over a hundred years after Franklin lived. Lawrence's attempt to set Franklin up as legislator of tyrannies thus takes the form of setting him up as an "author," as he calls him. And yet the fact remains that Franklin does not seem to authorize anything. In the maxims he repeats there is articulated but a conventional wisdom without voice, sentiments arising from no person and no passion, which always were and always will be and which, accordingly, cannot be effectively resisted. The would-be maker of books cannot escape the retailer of old saws, and he must struggle desperately to hold Franklin accountable, to fix his responsibility for what he says so that he has someone and something from which he can escape. Behind the maxims is Poor Richard, and behind Poor Richard is Benjamin Franklin, as if behind Franklin there were not the folklore in which all—Franklin, Poor Richard, and maxims—was properly dissolved.

The result is the emergence as a problem of a question never raised until after Franklin, the idea of authorship itself. It is a death and a birth, the end of writing continuous with reading and the beginning of the work as an object. Literature as process, we may say, becomes literature as a series of artifacts—models if one is partial to them, constraints if one is not. They are things independent, unities susceptible of formal analysis. And both writer and reader must struggle with them, writer and reader who are no longer one in the activity of producing and receiving meaning, but eternally at odds, striving to assert either their ownership of or independence from works which resist them both.

II. Epic

Let me state my thesis plainly. *The Autobiography of Benjamin Franklin* is America's primary epic. It is like the *Iliad* in Greek culture, by which I mean not that the *Autobiography* and the *Iliad* share any thematic or even, necessarily, structural elements, but that they exist in comparable relationships to their audiences. The *Autobiography* is an epic as Lukács has best defined it, a work continuous with its readership, neither inferior to it as representing it nor superior as holding out an ideal to which it may aspire.[7] In a manner to be elaborated in the course of this chapter, rather, it is, at least from the point of view of its rhetoric, its culture itself: coextensive with it, showing no marks of a world outside it or, insofar as such marks may appear, assimilating them back into it in a way that abolishes the world's independent existence. The *Autobiography* is, thus, a true original. It does not, in a Lawrentian sense, propose anything personal, anything new, but, in the sense of Poor Richard's maxims, it re-presents as its own whatever propositions are available. It begins with its culture and ends with it, effectually obliterating all beginnings and endings before itself and itself as a beginning or ending. It presents itself as being, it presents itself as having always been, and it is impossible, except with hindsight, to see how it might ever cease to be. This is an almost theological conception of originality, a conception of some primal All out of which everything emerges. And, indeed, the *Autobiography,* I am maintaining, would be just such an original, except that, since it is an original writing rather than an original Being, an action and not an existence, rhetoric rather than metaphysics is involved, words and not the Word. This is a point to which we shall return later in greater detail, but what should be made clear here is that, whatever the truth of the matter concerning the *Autobiography's* place in some objective history, whatever our knowledge of its particular context, the language of the work itself does not permit us to inquire into anything outside the work to explain it. We know that Franklin began writing the *Autobiography* at some particular point and stopped writing it at another. We are certain that he selected some things to include in it and left others out and, given our best documentary evidence, that he either misremembered many events he does record or even deliberately altered them. And yet, because there are no signs within the text itself of such discontinuities between it and the world, we must either forsake such external knowledge or risk misinterpretation. The world exists but in the terms in which he writes it. Or, as we have put it, the work becomes the world and meaning wholly a rhetorical matter.

Two letters from friends, traditionally printed at the beginning of part 2 of the *Autobiography,* may serve to clarify the situation. These are letters urging Franklin to continue his story of himself. They argue the usefulness of the project and set forth its value to the general well-being. Yet though Franklin, as the editors of the Standard Yale Edition tell us, meant to include them in the completed work,[8] we should not make the mistake of attributing to him the motives they espouse. There is a pietism about the letter of Abel James, for example, a too insistent high-mindedness, that would turn the *Autobiography* into an agent of a transcendent morality: "I know of no Character living nor many of them put together, who has so much in his Power as Thyself to promote a greater Spirit of Industry and early Attention to Business, Frugality and Temperance with the American Youth" (p. 134). The virtues enumerated are all Franklinian virtues, but the tone is not, the superciliousness, the smugness of the didact betraying a habit of imposing himself quite dissimilar to the sufficiency of a Franklin content simply to relate his beliefs. Hence, as in "Spirit of Industry" and "American Youth," we see the hypostatization, by a true believer in the Virtues as gods, of what in Franklin are but qualified human attributes.

In the letter of Benjamin Vaughan, on the other hand, there is an apocalypticism, the reverse of smugness, but which turns the *Autobiography* equally into an instrument of what transcends it, into a stay against some primal Hobbesian chaos:

> For the furtherance of human happiness, I have always maintained that it is necessary to prove that man is not even at present a vicious and detestable animal; and still more to prove that good management may greatly amend him; and it is for much the same reason, that I am anxious to see the opinion established, that there are fair characters existing among the individuals of the race; for the moment that all men, without exception, shall be conceived abandoned, good people will cease efforts deemed to be hopeless, and perhaps think of taking their share in the scramble of life, or at least of making it comfortable principally for themselves. (P. 139)

Here is a fundamental pessimism at odds with Franklin's benignity, an intensity, a pressure, simply incompatible with the even, almost unmotivated style of the *Autobiography,* written with the expectation of "a Weeks uninterrupted Leisure in my present Country Retirement" (p. 43). It is not that Franklin writes only for amusement. There is *utile* as well as *dulce* in his work, as he states in the opening pages. But all purposes are, finally, subordinated to the fundamental nonpurpose of restating his life: "since such a[n actual] Repetition is not to be expected, the next Thing most like living one's Life over again, seems to be a *Recollection* of that life; and to make that Recollection as durable as possible, the putting it down in Writing" (p. 44). We shall return to the issue of "writing," too, as well as to that of rhetoric, later in this chapter. But we should note, here, that "Recollection," so far from presenting us with the psychological cause of the *Autobiography,* reconstitutes all causes, psychological or otherwise, within the *Autobiography* as part of its manifest content. Thus where Vaughan writes, "you are ashamed of no origin; a thing the more important, as you prove how little necessary all origin is to happiness, virtue, or greatness" (p. 137), Franklin admits, "I would not however insinuate that my Ambition was not flatter'd by all these Promotions. It certainly was. For considering my low Beginning they were great Things to me" (p. 197). Franklin need not "prove" anything. Motives of all sorts, even the motive of concealing motives, become simple facts. And this is why Franklin may include the two exhortatory letters in his text in the first place. Nothing Franklin writes about exists outside his text, not his friends, not his culture, not the influences on him, not even himself. This is true epic status, and alongside it all autobiographies, all narratives for that matter, autobiographical or not, with which we might be tempted to compare it are reduced to the status of either the personal alone, or more dangerously, the personal eliding itself in the impersonal.

The Puritan autobiographies of Franklin's era and before are, perhaps, the clearest example. For the sake of comparison we may take, as representative, *A Personal Narrative* of Jonathan Edwards, Franklin's opposite number in what we have called the standard division of American intellectual history. For Edwards, as Perry Miller, for example, would have it, is a protoromantic, an explorer, albeit in religious terms, of inwardness and of that universal truth which resides within.[9] Presumably, he thus represents a concern wholly at odds with Franklin's neoclassic outward interests, as manifested in, say, Franklin's argument, in connection with the death of his son from smallpox, of the importance of inoculation where we would expect some mention of private grief (p. 170), or in his discussion of his marriage from its financial side to the almost complete exclusion of matters of the heart (p. 129). The difference between the men, however, lies not in the fact that one emphasizes insides and the other outsides, as if those terms were objectively specifiable and we could assign writers to the rule of one or the other, but in their acceptance of those terms in the first place, in their construction of the work in such a way as to admit or deny the possibility of anything existing outside it. In Edwards' *A Personal Narrative,* a self anterior to the work journeys through the length of the work to find itself. The work is not wholly an instrumentality, as it is for Abel James and for Vaughan. Indeed, in the course of Edwards' search, the instrument becomes an end. Edwards becomes a searcher, a man defined by the very progress he has set out upon. He lives the life of his means to discover his life, self and work becoming, in the progress of the work, coextensive. But self and work do not begin so, and the resulting difference between where Edwards begins and where he ends allows for a mystification impossible in the Franklin who begins and ends in the same place.

To some extent this is because all endings tend to become theological. As Frank Kermode has explained so well, they provide teleologies for events which, read sequentially, are experienced in a far different way.[10] The course of events is recreated, the substantiality of any particular destroyed by the structuralization of the final cause in which it is dissolved. But in Edwards, the difficulty is compounded because the progress toward a telos is his subject. Precisely the discrepancy between first and second readings, as it were, is at issue:

> My affections seemed to be lively and easily moved, and I seemed to be in my element when engaged in religious duties. And I am ready to think, many are deceived with such affections, and such a kind of delight as I then had in religion, and mistake it for grace.[11]

One senses, here, an immersion in the particularity of events, in the search itself, rather than in its goal, so that it is all the more poignant when what the text itself leads us to be interested in observing is taken away as unworthy of interest. The work fades from view. The unity achieved is projected beyond it. The progress toward unity creates the illusion that more is united than really is. Before the work is the self; at its end is the self at one with its world. Forgotten is the fact that the self's world is only the work, the only world Franklin ever admits. The self becomes a typological self, the work "symbolic." Language as words becomes language as the Word. The community that language began by consolidating is dissolved into a visionary unity transcending community, transcending writing, destroying the stability of the very rhetoric from which Franklin will not let us extricate him.

Franklin stands opposed to Edwards, then, not because he is a neoclassical denier of self and Edwards a romantic explorer of it, but because he refuses even to admit a self discontinuous with his denials or explorations and so obviates the very terms which Edwards finds so problematic. Indeed, Franklin opposes neoclassicism equally with romanticism, as a look at a true neoclassical autobiography will make clear. No such American work of quality comparable to Franklin's or Edwards' exists, but Gibbon's *Autobiography,* written at very nearly the same time as Franklin's, should serve just as well.

In Gibbon, too, we find discontinuity, though of a somewhat more difficult sort to get at. Gibbon, as well as Edwards, seeks unity. He would explain himself as a man like other men. But rationalist, child of the Enlightenment that he is, he cannot combine what is peculiar to him and general to humanity in the typological mode of an Edwards. Presumably, he would proceed to write on the basis of what he shares with us all: "A lively desire of knowing and of recording our ancestors so generally prevails, that it must depend on the influence of some common principle in the minds of men." But such a procedure denies the very individuality he wishes to integrate with "common principle":

> I shall not expatiate more minutely on my economical affairs which cannot be instructive or amusing to the reader. It is a rule of prudence, as well as of politeness, to reserve such confidence for the ear of a private friend, without exposing our situation to the envy or pity of strangers. . . . Yet I may believe and even assert that in circumstances more indigent or more wealthy, I

should never have accomplished the task, or acquired the fame, of an historian; that my spirit would have been broken by poverty and contempt; and that my industry might have been relaxed in the labour and luxury of a superfluous fortune. Few works of merit and importance have been executed either in a garret or a palace. A gentleman, possessed of leisure and independence, of books and talents, may be encouraged to write by the distant prospect of honor and reward: but wretched is the author, and wretched will be the work, where daily diligence is stimulated by daily hunger.[12]

Unity, here, is possible only at the level of the norm, the abstract, even the statistical average. Only by maintaining himself there can Gibbon succeed, and he must, as a result, keep out by conscious effort such portions of his life as are of purely personal concern. The result is a gap between self and world and a work that fills the gap, but fills it by denying such parts of Gibbon or his world as are not normalizable. The rhetoric of Gibbon's *Autobiography* is a rhetoric of exclusion. It is never in danger of mystification, for what lies beyond it is held always in view. But it is in constant danger of trivializing itself and can never be an epic. Self and work neither begin together nor end together, but *extend* together in a middle which exists by virtue of its place between a beginning and an end that are never, as they are in Franklin, obliterated. To use the term we have already introduced, if the mode of Franklin is "recollective," the mode of Gibbon is retrospective. It exists in the context of a priority to which it must always refer. The lessons in it are all, already, learned. The work is past, or, at least, refers to incidents in the past, and it is, as a result, a constant reminder of limitation, of incompleteness, of the failure to fulfill all that its author desires. Franklin's recollection, on the other hand, is a constant success. It exists in a continuous present that can never admit of limitation. Neither pointing beyond his life nor a mere record of it, it is his life itself, at once the fulfillment of what, accordingly, may never even become his desire.

III. Writing

Franklin's way of indicating this, as we have seen, is to refer to his life quite overtly in literary terms, calling it, as in the passage quoted above, his "Writing." As numerous critics have noted, this is, in fact, one of his most striking stylistic habits. The regrettable actions of his youth he terms "errata." The epitaph he composes for himself refers to his body as "the Cover of an old Book" with "Its contents torn out" (p. 44n). Even a repetition of his life, were he to be given the chance of it, would be but a "second Edition to correct some Faults of the first" (p. 43). As we now can see, however, more than metaphor is involved here, more than the employment of a "natural figure of speech for the former printer" (p. 43n), as the Yale editors put it. Franklin means quite literally what he says, and in particular, his insistence on the printed nature of his *Autobiography,* on the fact that it is not a story told but one inscribed on paper, more than confirming the epic unity of life and work for which we have been contending points to the difference of Franklin's epic, its particularly American way of uniting terms united quite otherwise in Homer. For by giving us his life in writing, to continue quoting,

> I shall indulge the Inclination so natural in old Men, to be talking of themselves and their own past Actions, and I shall indulge it, without being troublesome to others who thro' respect to Age might think themselves oblig'd to give me a Hearing, since this may be read or not as any one pleases. (P. 44)

Franklin distinguishes writing from speaking, here, for the openness of choice it provides, the freedom of "as any one pleases." Thus although we have been arguing that the author and audience of the *Autobiography* are continuous, yet the dependence of that continuity on deliberation needs to be insisted upon. The immediacy of Homer's oralness, its necessity—prior to compulsion, it is true, but precisely, therefore, beyond either authorial or audience control—is casually, perhaps, but categorically rejected. Franklin's work *is* a work after all, to modify somewhat our earlier position. And yet it remains a work which is still no object, a work, rather, because it is made. Never natural, it is sustained by the decision to write it and the decision to read it which Homer's song, rather performed than made, simply cannot admit.

Such a work, it remains true to say, does not at all intrude itself *between* writer and reader. It does not admit the possibility of alienation, say, that independent of it stands another world which is its boundary, which, even initially, defines it as a romantic inside or a neoclassical outside, as something that may be compared with an objective or subjective reality not included in it. But in a purely positive way, excluding nothing, Franklin's work is founded on choice. The community it embraces is the product of willed association. It is a community of readers and writers freely assenting to each other, bound by a sort of secular covenant differing from theological or romantic covenants because not compelled by truth, and differing from neoclassical social "contracts" because not based upon natural law. At its heart is not even rational self-interest, as the Enlightenment theorists of contracts would have it, but nonrational choice, devotion based on a purely arbitrary predilection, "as any one pleases." To put this in yet a different way, to triangulate Franklin's position on yet another plane, though he is not innocent in the manner of traditional oral epics, he is not self-conscious in the manner of traditional written ones, either. Franklin's epic is innocent and self-conscious both. Neither assuming the continuity of oral communities nor attempting in writing to restore to a community the continuty it has forever lost, Franklin's *Autobiography* is created by a community which thereby creates itself. Franklin's world is wholly rhetorical, as we have said. But as we may now see, neither the Homeric extension of rhetoric to the status of what we might call the natural, nor yet the Virgilian and Miltonic restriction of it to the mechanics of mere suasion, will do for Franklin. Franklin's rhetoric is sufficient unto itself, and it embraces a community, accordingly, neither assumed nor cajoled but agreed upon, a community which, reading itself, makes itself.

Let us consider, by way of comparison, three great invocations in the three sorts of epic we are discussing. "Sing, O goddess," Homer begins, simply, directly, the author in perfect agreement with an audience he need not even, therefore, address.[13] And yet, properly speaking, no author and no audience exist in Homer, for the collective memory in which they proclaim themselves, invited but uncontrolled, has been exalted above the level of culture to become the voice of the god. Choice, here, can never be more than a secondary phenomenon, a sort of resistance to or acquiescence in inevitability. Assent, so complete as to have suffered, as it were, a repression by generalization, appears in such places to which it manages a return as but a bowing to destiny. The single exception, perhaps the only chink in Homer's armor, will be recalled as proving the rule, the objection of Thersites to Agamemnon's conduct of Greek affairs. For Thersites' animadversions are reiterated later by Achilles, by the always reliable Nestor, and by Odysseus, who rebukes Thersites by beating him. Yet Thersites, speaking "idly and in no orderly wise," asserts himself while all others, even the heroes, "sat them down and were stayed in their places." Speaking not, as does, say, Achilles, the mere division of Greek culture against itself, he speaks outside the culture altogether and as refusing to authorize it. He is the one example in the *Iliad* of a man who "pleases"—merely because he is, selfishly, arbitrarily, *not* pleased—not to listen to Agamemnon, and Homer can understand him but as unnatural, "ill favored . . . bandy-legged . . . lame . . . warpen." The ugly violence in Homer, lurking beneath the heroic violence, surfaces in Thersites' beating, the negation of enemy by conqueror, the assimilation of Trojan to Greek culture that is at bottom the absolute refusal to admit of difference. The potential tyranny of "good order," the coercion necessary if all are to be "stayed in their places," emerges, a denial of culture by promoting it to nature, where difference is a meaningless term.

On the other hand, "Of Arms and the Man I Sing. . . . Help me, O Muse," writes Virgil.[14] As Lukács has noted, only a memory of Homer's continuity is present in the *Aeneid,*[15] and this is implicit already in the necessity Virgil finds of writing what Homer did, indeed, "sing." For the "voice" of the *Aeneid* is not the Muse's but Virgil's who in invoking the Muse's assistance would, though but a man, yet claim a god's power. Authorship, as we move from Homer to Virgil, has become a problem, a burden. It is evident biographically in Virgil's dissatisfaction with his epic and in the epic itself, as it strains after an authority it can never quite achieve. The labor of the *Aeneid* is a labor of justification, of aligning what is felt as an ultimately irreconcilable difference. Less direct, perhaps, than Milton's attempt to justify the ways of God to man, it is an attempt to justify the ways of man, Roman ways, *as* God's. Culture is precisely *not* nature, here, and choice, threatening to remind us of this, is so threatening that it must be denied even Homer's secondary operation. Heroes are not allowed even to seem to decide, but ask the gods in advance what has been decided for them. The readers, upon whose assent culture's elevation to nature depends, must be persuaded to deny themselves. This is why, in fact, the absence of direct appeal to the reader in Virgil's invocation is something other than the similar absence in Homer. For while Homer as it were honestly takes his audience for granted, Virgil attempts to make his audience take itself for granted. Rhetoric has become propaganda, the criticism traditionally offered against the *Aeneid,* and with reason.

How different from both Homer and Virgil is Franklin's "Dear Son." For however trivial the words may seem, they constitute as genuinely epic an invocation as either of the two more heroic openings we have discussed. What is invoked in an epic is its sustaining force, the source of its truth, and Franklin's readership is precisely such a source, though sustaining the *Autobiography* as much by its limits as by its extent. The audience overleaped in Homer and denied in Virgil is given full play. Instead of the god we have a man. In place of vision we have social exchange. Presenting the *Autobiography* as a letter, Franklin assures that the experience he relates will remain never more than a cultural transaction.

Of course the manifest fictiveness of the letter form, the fact that Franklin is not "really" writing to his son, needs to be considered. Yet this no more than any other fiction of the *Autobiography* presupposes a nature on which the *Autobiography,* because a fictionalization of it, thereby covertly depends. For what is fictionalized is not, in fact, reality, but the work itself, the "real" letters which, as we have discussed, are included within the work. "Dear Son," accordingly, but exposes more clearly the *Autobiography*'s status as its own reality. It is part of the *Autobiography*'s epic rhetoric. Indeed, the presence of both real *and* fictive letters is but a more striking example of what we called earlier the *Autobiography*'s originality. An epic which does not imitate prior epics, it rather stands in for them, as in this case by its use of a conventional invocation whose conventionality is derived from itself. In the *Autobiography* the major problem of composing an epic in modern times is thus solved. The fall of epic discourse into conventionality is internalized. The fate of the *Iliad,* its socialization, which, after all, is what enabled us to see its invocation as a mystification in the first place, is precluded because accepted from the start. The *Autobiography* becomes the foundation of a new literature forever free of the myth of a fall. Or, rather, the literature proceeding from the *Autobiography* is fallen from a union of man with men instead of the gods. Its paradise is the wholly rhetorical one of writer and readers in agreement, of a culture of perfect assent.

"Call me Ishmael"; "It is a little remarkable that—though disinclined to talk overmuch of myself and my affairs at the fireside, and to my personal friends—an autobiographical impulse should twice in my life have taken possession of me, in addressing the public"; "I should not obtrude my affairs so much on the notice of my readers if very particular inquiries had not been made by my townsmen concerning my mode of life"; "You don't know about me without you have read . . .":[16] these are rhetorical openings, attempts to recapture that perfect agreement with a reader that in Franklin is not yet lost and which constitute retrospectively, as it were, another demonstration of the significance for the American tradition of Franklin's letter form. And yet, though we cannot analyze these openings in detail here, a view of the works in which they appear, rather, as attempts to recapture truths somehow prior to their rhetoric is so prevalent as to warrant a note, however brief. It is a view, as we may now see, arising from a misunderstanding of Franklin's letter form, from a naturalization of it, a promotion of it to nature. It is a misunderstanding visible already in Franklin's day.

IV. Nature and Culture

We may begin as early as Crèvecoeur and his own description of the American experience in *Letters from an American Farmer*. For Crèvecoeur, no less than for Franklin, the first problem is his own authority. How shall he justify what he is to write? What status can he claim for his notion of "What Is an American?" His initial answer, much the same as Franklin's, is to submit his ideas to the provisionality of social exchange in the letter. In his long defense of his presumption to write to an English gentleman, however, he falls back on a nature which necessitates an abandonment of writing altogether. Doubtful of his skill with the pen, he is comforted with the reflection that "writing letters is nothing more than talking on paper," that "a letter is only conversation put down in black and white." The "scientific rules" of letter writing may be violated, the style will be "incorrect," but because "the only line I am able to follow, [is] the line which nature has herself traced for me," the correspondence will be valuable.[17] Crèvecoeur, at least in his pose of American, is no master of rhetoric as suasion. Accordingly, he opts for a rhetoric which is natural, and he was received, and has since been read, as a sort of American Rousseau, applauded for the naturalistic descriptions that bulk so large in the rest of his book.

And yet a less preconceivedly romantic view of Crèvecoeur makes it hard to credit his appeal to nature, hard to see his American as any more natural than Franklin's. Against his description of flora and fauna must be balanced the equal bulk of description of social customs as, for example, in the chapters devoted to Nantucket. And, indeed, nature's function, in Crèvecoeur, remains chiefly as enabling for culture. Concerned with the sort of historical origins that the origin-obliterating Franklin is not, Crèvecoeur searches out the causes of a society of free assent in the bounty of nature which obviates any Hobbesian or Lockean society of self-interested necessity. Large enough and fertile enough to provide for everyone's needs, the land of America is not so much the cause of American society as what has permitted American society to be something men have freely chosen.

Thus more clearly in Franklin: we have said his world is rhetorical, that his writing, no mere transcription of nature's voice, of a
prior oralness represented in written form, is, rather, the world
itself. Yet, as we may now see, this is not to charge Franklin with
excluding nature, as is generally done, for this would be but to
promote culture to nature via the back door. Accordingly, nature
exists for Franklin only without any positivity, as a merely formal
entity, the structural condition of choice, guaranteeing, by its non-
inclusion in the social, that society may indeed be something chosen.

Consider, for example, Franklin's most notorious comment, his
observations on the Indians at Carlisle, with whom, as member of
a commission, he was negotiating a peace treaty:

> In the Evening, hearing a great Noise among them, the Commis-
> sioners walk'd out to see what was the Matter. We found they had
> made a great Bonfire in the Middle of the Square. They were all
> drunk Men and Women, quarrelling and fighting. Their dark-
> colour'd Bodies, half naked, seen only by the gloomy Light of the
> Bonfire, running after and beating one another with Firebrands,
> accompanied by their horrid Yellings, form'd a Scene the most
> resembling our Ideas of Hell that could well be imagin'd. There
> was no appeasing the Tumult, and we retired to our Lodging. At
> Midnight a Number of them came thundering at our Door, de-
> manding more Rum; of which we took no Notice. The next Day,
> sensible they had misbehav'd in giving us that Disturbance, they
> sent three of their old Counsellors to make their Apology. The
> Orator acknowledg'd the Fault, but laid it upon the Rum; and then
> endeavour'd to excuse the Rum, by saying, "The great Spirit who
> made all things made every thing for some Use, and whatever Use
> he design'd any thing for, that Use it should always be put to; Now,
> when he made Rum, he said, Let this be for Indians to get Drunk
> with. And it must be so." And indeed if it be the design of Provi-
> dence to extirpate these Savages in order to make room for Culti-
> vators of the Earth, it seems not improbable that Rum may be the
> appointed Means. It has already annihilated all the Tribes who
> formerly inhabited the Sea-coast. (Pp. 198–99)

Now Franklin on the Indians needs no defense. His castigation
of the Indian traders, his criticism of governmental policy with

respect to the Indians, are well known. That his point of view is white-centered, of course, goes without saying. But never is that view hypostatized, never elevated beyond the status of the view of white culture. Drunk Indians are not devils, as so many Puritans, for example, considered them. But, given the limitation of the commissioners' perspective ("seen only by the gloomy Light") and restricted to the circumstance of this moment ("In the Evening") and this event ("They were all drunk"), they "form'd a Scene the most resembling our Ideas of Hell." Metaphor is merely metaphor here, doubly qualified in its relation to reality by its artificiality ("Scene") and its inaccuracy ("most"). Metaphor in Franklin is culture's way not of opposing nature nor yet of assimilating it, but of bracketing itself in nonrelation to nature, of asserting nature while drawing nothing from it.

Indeed, for Franklin, the Indians themselves are not natural. Their excuse for their actions, putting it off on the Rum, but repeats what Franklin notes earlier is the Reverend Whitefield's habit of putting off on Christ the obligations for hospitality extended personally to him (pp. 178–79). Accordingly, were Franklin's views of the Indians ever so much more objectionable than they appear here, he allows them the status of equality in nature with the whites, or what amounts to the same thing, the status of a culture whose relationship to his own is not fixed, but, for better or worse, is being worked out, created, by Indians and white men in their interaction.

This is why Franklin's speculation about the "Design of Providence" is cast in the subjunctive. In matters touching on theology Franklin is always provisional. Even the empirical fact of the annihilation of so many Indian tribes by Rum is not permitted to become the projection of a certain destiny. The realm of God, of nature, of Providence, is not excluded from the *Autobiography,* but it exists to force the *Autobiography* back on itself, to make America responsible, as Franklin is responsible, for whatever career it may have.

It is instructive to note the temptations Franklin thus resisted, or rather, though he did not feel them as such, what would become temptations to his more theologically oriented successors, to enlarge the meaning of events in his life. For nature is all around

Franklin, an ally, an enemy, a force to be joined or subdued, and from virtually the beginning of his work. It is to sea that Franklin takes as a boy to escape his family and the sea that, repeatedly, in his voyages, threatens his life. It is the building of a wharf which he cites as his first public project and the ballad of a drowning and a pirate song that he lists as his first two literary productions. Franklin's swimming exploits are rendered in some detail, and at one point, as he tells us, he even considers remaining in England to become a swimming master. Buried here are the makings of a high adventure story in the manner of *Robinson Crusoe* such as would become common fare in American literature, an option for a different sort of life, man pitted against nature, learning from it, mastering it, that Franklin did not take. What he chose to learn, instead, was all directed toward culture. Commenting on a shipwreck prevented in the last minute by the sudden sighting of a light, for example, he thus remarks that his ship's "Deliverance impress'd me strongly with the Utility of Lighthouses, and made me resolve to encourage the building more of them in America, if I should live to return there" (p. 259). If there is lack of vision here, a failure before the moment of death to see nature with all its theological implications, it is, at least, the result not of blindness but of free choice, a disposition toward culture that is all positive. There is no retreat, no turning back in fear, for example, which is nowhere in evidence in Franklin's description of the event, but a commitment made possible by a nature which allows him to choose something outside it. Thus Franklin describes his not, finally, setting up his projected swimming school:

> On one of these Days I was to my surprize sent for by a great Man I knew only by Name, a Sir William Wyndham and I waited upon him. He had heard by some means or other of my Swimming from Chelsey to Blackfryars, and of my teaching Wygate and another young Man to swim in a few Hours. He had two Sons about to set out on their Travels; he wish'd to have them first taught Swimming; and propos'd to gratify me handsomely if I would teach them. They were not yet come to Town and my stay was uncertain, so I could not undertake it. But from this Incident I thought it likely, that if I were to remain in England and open a Swimming School, I might get a good deal of Money. And it

struck me so strongly, that had the Overture been sooner made
me, probably I should not so soon have returned to America.
(Pp. 105–6)

Once again, as in the Indian incident, the Providential hand
might be seen at work, this time at a personal rather than historical level. But Franklin does not see it as such, or rather Providence, introduced, never achieves the force of a fate or destiny.
Franklin's life is his own, and its meanings are not the meanings of
anything anterior to it which it expresses, but itself, the meanings
he creates by living it, writing it.

V. Reference and Ownership

The linguistic side of such a view of nature and culture, the
rhetorical definition of Franklin's career, is something we have
already discussed. Thus we have mentioned Franklin's use of
metaphor, which we may now see never becomes symbolism
because of his great demurral before any God-term that might
sustain a symbolic view of language. Instances similar to the
reference to hell point this up quite specifically. Franklin finds the
breaking of some glasses caused by the rifle salute of his regiment
a portent of the broken commission he is soon to suffer as colonel
of the regiment (p. 238), and he remarks upon his escape from two
prostitutes posing as gentlewomen that "tho we had escap'd a
sunken Rock which we scrap'd upon in the Passage, I thought this
Escape of rather more Importance to me" (p. 84). Here are
Puritan typology and Bunyanesque allegory, except that in both
cases nothing like a God-term is permitted. The "sunken Rock"
metaphor is jammed, not allowed to perform the usual allegorical
mediation of, say, carrying the analogy between physical and
moral danger to the ultimate of spiritual danger. And the glass
analogy is little more than a pun. Indeed, though Franklin's pun-
ning is, in general, ponderous and marked, as if bearing the
weight of a symbolic past, yet, as in his self-conscious cleverness
in speaking to the Quakers of a "fire-engine" instead of a cannon
(p. 190) or in his comment that being a reasonable creature means
being able to find a "Reason for every thing one has a mind to do"

(p. 88), a certain pride of ownership intrudes to block any tele-ological extension. Analogies are limited and cannot be expanded to some infinity. They are made by man, not found in nature, so that it is folly to believe, as the English printer's devils do, that by drinking "strong Beer" one may become strong (p. 100).

As a result, just as Franklin's nonromanticism does not put him in a neoclassical camp, so his nonsymbolism does not put his language in some Port-Royal grammar. Franklin's vaunted clarity of style is as little the function of some transparency of his language, its neutrality in pointing to nature, as it is of any immediacy or replication of nature. A function of rhetoric, as we have seen, Franklin's language is never natural. But a rhetoric which is also owned, it interposes its author as antidote to the tendency of nonsymbolic language to appear to have access to nature. Franklin's metaphors are, as it were, intrinsic, no mere decoration of an otherwise invisible language, but the sign of decorativeness become language's very density. Reason, like nature, is never more than enabling for Franklin, so that rational as his language may be, it remains never more than the property of Franklin.

Consider two passages in which, once again, Franklin distinguishes between speaking and writing, this time, however, extending his earlier interest in freedom of choice to what we might call the particularity which serves to guarantee that freedom. The Reverend Whitefield has been preaching to raise money for an orphans' home to be built in Georgia. Franklin, sympathetic to the project, has yet argued with him that he ought to build in Philadelphia, because better workmen and materials are available there:

> I happened soon after to attend one of his Sermons, in the Course of which I perceived he intended to finish with a Collection, and I silently resolved he should get nothing from me. I had in my Pocket a Handful of Copper Money, three or four silver Dollars and five Pistoles in Gold. As he proceeded I began to soften, and concluded to give the Coppers. Another Stroke of his Oratory made me asham'd of that, and determin'd me to give the Silver; and he finish'd so admirably, that I empty'd my Pocket wholly into the Collector's Dish, Gold and all. At this Sermon there was also one of our Club, who being of my Sentiments respecting the

> Building in Georgia, and suspecting a Collection might be in-
> tended, had by Precaution emptied his Pockets before he came
> from home; towards the Conclusion of the Discourse, however, he
> felt a strong Desire to give, and apply'd to a Neighbour who
> stood near him to borrow some Money for the Purpose. The
> Application was unfortunately to perhaps the only Man in the
> Company who had the firmness not to be affected by the preach-
> er. His Answer was, At any other time, Friend Hopkinson, I
> would lend to thee freely; but not now; for thee seems to be out of
> thy right Senses. (Pp. 177–78)

Now the tyranny of the oral that we discussed in relation to Homer
is Franklin's chief concern. The Reverend Whitefield is a powerful
speaker, his words almost irresistible. It is worth noting, however,
that what must be resisted is not so much the project Whitefield
talks about as Whitefield himself. For although Franklin's initial
refusal to donate money is not quite arbitrary, a matter of thinking
as he pleases, to use Franklin's earlier words, yet, given his primary agreement and the purely practical reasons for his doubts,
what he would assert is surely himself more than his principles.
Reasons, the "right Senses" which Hopkinson seems to be out of,
are "right" rather in the sense of proper, belonging to Hopkinson
and defining him, than in the sense of true. Reason and the
analytic procedures that follow from it, the very particularity that
it allows, are significant because they aid in defining one's separate selfhood, the identity which, though it will consent to other
identities, must yet remain itself. As Franklin continues, describing Whitefield:

> His Writing and Printing from time to time gave great Advan-
> tage to his enemies. Unguarded Expressions and even erroneous
> Opinions delivered in Preaching might have been afterwards
> explain'd, or qualify'd by supposing others that might have ac-
> company'd them; or they might have been deny'd. But *litera
> scripta manet*. Critics attack'd his Writings violently, and with so
> much Appearance of Reason as to diminish the Number of his
> Votaries, and prevent their Encrease. So that I am of Opinion, if
> he had never written any thing he would have left behind him a
> much more numerous and important Sect. And his Reputation

might in that case have been still growing, even after his Death; as there being nothing of his Writing on which to found a censure; and give him a lower Character, his Proselites would be left at liberty to feign for him as great a Variety of Excellencies, as their enthusiastic Admiration might wish him to have possessed. (P. 180)

The great harm particularity inflicts on Whitefield, precisely its benefit for Franklin, is that it confines him. It does not permit his inflation to the generality of a god—"still growing, even after his Death"—but returns him to the circumstantiality of ownership. The "written letter," as Franklin says, always "remains," so that the freedom produced by writing which we discussed earlier may now be seen as guaranteed by the writer's simultaneous responsibility. The letter is a body, never translatable to spirit, and because it is a focal point for argument and criticism, whatever the truth it represents, it may never transcend the conditions of its production and reception. It is the center of that social exchange implied by the correspondence form, the center of disputations which, again, are based not so much on reason conceived as truth, but on reason as an "Appearance," defining the perspective of the disputants. The referentiality of language is questioned, or rather it is wedded forever to its author. Accordingly, we may return to the very beginnings of this chapter and to the issue of authorship we raised there with Lawrence's penetrating misunderstanding.

To quote once more Lawrence's attack on Poor Richard's maxims: "The author of these bits was Poor Richard, and Poor Richard was Benjamin Franklin, writing in Philadelphia well over a hundred years before." Now as we mentioned earlier, Lawrence's projected line of descent is motivated by his attempt to fix Franklin's responsibility much as Franklin would fix Whitefield's. Stopping where he does, however, he so mystifies responsibility as virtually to dissolve it. Refusing to close the circle of his series of identifications, refusing, that is, to identify not only the maxims with Franklin but Franklin with his culture, or at least its language including the maxims in their own turn, he creates the author as God as surely as Whitefield would avoid the responsibility of writing altogether. On the other hand, continued circulation is at least as dangerous. For to merge Franklin indiscriminately into his culture is to create reference itself as a sort of god, the transcendent referent of the so-called spirit-of-the-age. In neither case are authorship and reference bound to each other, but now the one, now the other is exalted. In fact, as Lawrence would have it, Franklin is guilty of doing both simultaneously. Presenting himself in a series of propositions which generalize his personal experience to the community as a whole, he then retreats, putting upon the community what he himself will now no longer be held accountable for. The author is present and absent both, his work a representation of what is no longer there and what, accordingly, we must take on faith. It is the gospel of a hypocritical god, neither our truth nor truth itself, yet masquerading as both.

Let us consider Franklin on the virtues, an especially notable case:

> It was about this time that I conceiv'd the bold and arduous Project of arriving at moral Perfection. I wish'd to live without committing any Fault at any time; I would conquer all that either Natural Inclination, Custom, or Company might lead me into. As I knew, or thought I knew, what was right and wrong, I did not see why I might not *always* do the one and avoid the other. But I soon found I had undertaken a Task more Difficult than I had imagined. While my *Attention* was taken up in guarding against one Fault, I was often surpriz'd by another. . . . I therefore contriv'd the following Method. . . .
>
> I made a little Book in which I allotted a page for each of the Virtues. I rul'd each Page with red Ink, so as to have seven Columns, one for each Day of the Week, marking each Column with a Letter for the Day. I cross'd these Columns with thirteen red Lines, marking the Beginning of each Line with the first Letter of one of the Virtues, on which Line and in its proper Column I might mark by a little black Spot every Fault I found upon Examination to have committed respecting that Virtue upon that Day. (Pp. 148–51)

Now on the face of it, nothing would seem to be more absurd than such a transcendent end coupled to such specific means. Binding the particulars of his method to a universal goal, Franklin elaborates himself to the compass of the world. Lawrence's hypocritical god seems clearly in evidence, and indeed, Franklin's thirteen easy steps to truth have long been taken as a kind of American Bible, the how-to book, or, at least, its ancestor, in which readers who feel their limitations most acutely are promised precisely the most infinite of futures. And yet the hypocrisy that governs the how-to book results from a dialectic of reference and authorship that Franklin's union of these terms precludes.

As most of the how-to books tell us, we are to believe them because they are mere accounts of the practice of successful men. We are to believe not them, that is to say, but the evidence presented in the case histories with which they generally abound. Simultaneously, however—and this is most especially evident in the books whose chief case history is the author's own life—we are to believe the evidence of the particular case at hand because it is related by an author, who, ipso facto, is to be believed. Reference and authorship take advantage of each other, here. They do not so much depend on, as promote, each other, reference grounding authorship but only so that authorship may in turn transcendentalize reference. The terms come together not for the purpose of limitation, but to elevate each other to a kind of truth which is beyond grounding, a truth which is not the connection between the particular and the general but an unbridgeable gap.

Franklin, on the other hand, keeps his limitations always in mind. Limitation is all, or rather, particularity *is* his generality. As we noted early on, Franklin may refer to everything. But everything is what he authors and represents at the same moment. "It was about this time that I conceiv'd the bold and arduous Project of arriving at moral Perfection." The thirteen steps will not be easy, after all, and they will not be because "moral Perfection" is no transcendent, unspecifiable goal, but confined to the total of the particulars involved in achieving it. It is as if Franklin leaves room for the possibility of other moral perfections—groups of thirteen other steps toward other nontranscendent goals to be generated by other authors who, like him, will be listened to or not as any one pleases. As he notes, "In the various Enumerations of the moral Virtues I had met with in my Reading, I found the Catalogue more or less numerous, as different Writers included more or fewer Ideas under the same Name." If Franklin arrives at one set of thirteen it is only "for the sake of Clearness" and only in keeping with what "at that time occur'd to me as necessary or desirable" rather than as immutable (p. 149). Franklin, early in his career, proposed to compose an "Art of Virtue" and issue it as an independent book. But antidogmatist that he was in religion and politics, so he is in morality. The Art of Virtue is inscribed within an autobiographical context. It may never be taken, Lawrence-like, as Scripture. It is to be neither accepted nor rejected, but to be taken like the *Autobiography* itself, *as* itself.

One might almost say that Franklin deconstructs his virtues, except that including them in the *Autobiography* as, in effect, deconstructed from the start, he establishes them in a situation altogether more promising. As Franklin admits:

> something that pretended to be Reason was every now and then suggesting to me, that such extream Nicety as I exacted of my self might be a kind of Foppery in Morals, which if it were known would make me ridiculous; that a perfect Character might be attended with the Inconvenience of being envied and hated; and that a benevolent Man should allow a few Faults in himself, to keep his Friends in Countenance. (P. 156)

Here is doubt, doubt reinterpreted as rationalization, rationalization justified practically, and practicality, finally, ironized. And yet the result is no more the undermining of the project than an exorcism of the doubt that would warrant its undermining. For doubt, like nature and reason in the contexts in which we have already discussed them, is an enablement, not a difficulty. It enlists Franklin's project under the sway of his will, defines it as neither true nor false, but chosen. Franklin does not confess his misgivings. Confession does not emerge in American narrative until Charles Brockden Brown, as we shall see, and even then only as a kind of romantic temptation never really acceded to. And besides, the *Autobiography*, as most scholars of the form have noted, is no confession in the first place. But Franklin does publish his misgivings, which is quite another matter. He is not a representative man. He neither bares nor justifies a soul somehow typical. He is an individual. But, as we have said, he defines his individuality in the context of a community of individuals. He is an author addressing himself to an audience which gives him authority by giving him the right of address. The *Autobiography* is, as we called it, America's *Iliad.* But democratic *Iliad* that it thus is, it is as if told by Achilles, rather than Homer. Its meaning is not in all things nor in everything as invoking all things, but in every thing delimited by its particularity *as* a thing. Its meaning is not in the life of one as embodiment of the life of all, but in the life of every one granted such meaning *by* all.

VI. An Exemplary Life

Admittedly, this is to give to the *Autobiography* a status somewhat different from the status generally accorded it. Denying its typicality, denying its function as model, we would seem to deny that Americanness which establishes it as worthy of attention in the first place. What I would claim, however, is that the *Autobiography* is American in another way. For it is, in a sense, exemplary without being representative. Indeed, the view of it as model proceeds from that fall we described earlier and is a compensatory elevation of exemplariness to the level of representativity. No longer, though readers, participating in the *Autobiography*'s writing, we have projected onto it a reader-writer relationship formalized as anterior to reading and writing. No longer at one with it, we have created it as a proxy unity. We have objectified in the *Autobiography* that very authority which proceeds from its not being an object, and the result has been a schizophrenic appreciation, a Lawrentian aesthetics of deceit that continues to plague our understanding till this day.

As John Bach McMaster, attempting to establish Franklin "as a Man of Letters," first formulated it, the *Autobiography* is no simple political memoir, but a work of art.[18] It is not a record, but a creation. Franklin's achievement, as virtually every critic since has held, was his ability to fictionalize himself so strongly and so memorably. And, indeed, since the New Criticism, this separation between fiction and world has been expounded with increasing vigor. Franklin the man is distinguished from Franklin the character, and even Franklin the character from Franklin the author who tells his story. The book conceals the true Benjamin Franklin in order to portray an artfully typical one. It is the fiction of a Franklinian "persona," and, in a projection of such a persona temporally along the career of the book, its progress is taken to be from an innocent, more nearly "real" Franklin, through the maturer character, to the overly wise author who tells his story. The fun-loving ladies' man describes himself as a sober, industrious citizen; the engaging private person writing to his son elaborates himself more and more dully into the public figure writing after the letters of Vaughan and James.

Now we need not repeat our argument about the epic refusal in the *Autobiography* of any separation of art and life. Nor need we go any further concerning the notion of persona than to note that in its assumption of both an art/life division and a public/private division it is equally untenable. But the idea of development implicit in the further construction that Franklin's life, in the course of the *Autobiography, becomes* art, that private becomes public, seems, from our perspective, so clear an attempt to live off those divisions while simultaneously appearing to repudiate them that it is worth further study. For, in effect, we would have it both ways. Fallen from the *Autobiography,* we project our separation from it onto it. Yet recognizing that the *Autobiography is* us, we deny any separation by giving it a teleological resolution. Difference is acknowledged so that it may end in similarity. The work, after all, we admit, *is* divided, but formalizing that division, we would have it established as unity.

The problem, as we noted early in this chapter, is that a reader's view of his relation *to* a work tends to become the basis of his construction *of* the work. Nor is such a tendency, in all cases, to be deplored, for in epic it is actually solicited. Accordingly, another definition of difference is necessary, difference which is independence not division, and which is embodied in a work not separated from us but whose integrity we have *granted*. Epiclike, the *Autobiography* remains us, but democratically, not because it is our model, but because its author speaks with the authority of one of us. The variousness of its sections may be accepted, even a construction of one section as "private" and another as "public." Yet private and public are related neither dialectically—as the one becoming the other, let us say—nor even diacritically, as paired opposites defining each other *by* their opposition. Rather, they exist at the same level, as names marking difference, perhaps, but without distinction. No development from one to the other is possible, and, indeed, such development as does occur in the *Autobiography* occurs rather within each part equally. Franklin continues to learn in old age as well as in youth. If he develops as a boy, he keeps growing as a mature man. And even as he writes, he would develop in the same way. "That Felicity [of my life], when I reflect on it, has induc'd me sometimes to say, that were it offer'd to my choice, I should have no Objection to a Repetition of the same Life from its Beginning, only asking the Advantage Authors have in a second Edition to correct some Faults of the first" (p. 43). Franklin's revision of himself is an ongoing process, continuing as he writes what occurred in the period he writes about. Development does not begin or end. It occurs in no time which may be formalized as no space. But it is part of a continuous present everywhere equal in the act of its writing.

As we have said, the *Autobiography* is concerned not with the general pattern of things but with everything in itself. It does not subordinate the circumstances of a life to the universals they might be conceived as instances of, but insists that every circumstance counts in its very circumstantiality. To put this in structural terms, the form of the whole of the *Autobiography* is the form, the learning experience, of each section of the *Autobiography*. The part, in the *Autobiography*, is, as it were, not a part of the whole, but is already whole, and the whole is no fixed entity resolving the parts, but infinitely extensible by the addition of as many parts as the author may compose. Trailing back as far as Franklin's researches can take him into his ancestry, the *Autobiography* arrives at no origin to which a part may be more or less near. Ending in an "Etc.," as the outline of the work does (p. 272), it heads toward no telos in the progress toward which a part may be especially critical. Moving from no place to no place, yet always moving, it defines all as new and as equal in the ongoing openness of writing it.

One final time, we may perhaps make things clearer by a comparison with Homer. For the *Iliad* is infinitely extensible too and, indeed, did grow, perhaps considerably, in the course of its retelling. But conceived hierarchically rather than democratically, its growth is profoundly unequal. New elements enter into the work, but as already old, finding their place within a structure that is not them but binds them. Hysteron proteron is the form of the *Iliad*,[19] an early section balanced against a late section, composing a series of concentric figures that enclose all parts within a whole that the part implies but is not. The *Iliad* does begin and does end, avoiding mystified romantic beginnings and endings only by linking the two in a circle which, as we have seen, thus either excludes what is outside it or violates it by assimilating it to itself. The *Autobiography,* however, is open to everything. It neither excludes nor violates, even when what it deals with is something Franklin cannot possibly understand, as, for example, in his memorable meeting with the nunlike lady:

> she had given all her Estate to charitable Uses, reserving only Twelve Pounds a Year to live on, and out of this Sum she still gave a great deal to Charity, living her self on Watergruel only, and using no Fire but to boil it. . . . A Priest visited her, to confess her every Day. I have ask'd her, says my Landlady, how she, as she liv'd, could possibly find so much Employment for a Confessor. O, says she, it is impossible to avoid *vain Thoughts.* I was permitted once to visit her: She was chearful and polite, and convers'd pleasantly. The Room was clean, but had no other Furniture than a Matras, a Table with a Crucifix and Book, a Stool, which she gave me to sit on, and a Picture over the Chimney of St. Veronica, displaying her Handkerchief with the miraculous Figure of Christ's bleeding Face on it, which she explain'd to me with great Seriousness. She look'd pale, but was never

sick, and I give it as another Instance on how small an Income Life and Health may be supported. (P. 103)

Now the awful spirituality of Christianity here, the abnegation of the flesh, the sacrifice of one's life to God, is a mystery simply beyond the apprehension of the enlightened Franklin. And yet no Enlightenment rejection of it, no horror of the lady as irrational, may be found, nor revision of her to make her somehow more presentable in Franklinian terms. Rather, Franklin would make room for everything he meets, noting in detail all he sees and finding in what he notes such matter as he can use. Was Governor Keith bad to him? Had he been guilty of "imposing so grossly on a poor ignorant Boy"? Yet "He was otherwise an ingenious sensible Man, a pretty good Writer" (p. 95). Had his friend Ralph "kept me poor?" Did he owe Franklin "about 27 Pounds; which I was now never likely to receive; a great Sum out of my small Earnings"? Nevertheless, "I lov'd him notwithstanding, for he had many amiable Qualities" (p. 106). There is more than tolerance, here. There is a capaciousness we would not expect to find in the romantic construction of Franklin as leaving out half the world. Neither repressing what is unpleasant nor yet sentimentalizing it in some mellow afterglow of a successful career, Franklin accepts the unpleasant for what it is worth. And everything, in this democratic epic, is worth everything else.

Thus Franklin proposes a new system for cleaning the streets and then concludes:

Some may think these trifling Matters not worth minding or relating. But when they consider, that tho' Dust blown into the Eyes of a single Person or into a single Shop on a windy Day, is but of small Importance, yet the great Number of the Instances in a populous City, and its frequent Repetitions give it Weight and Consequence; perhaps they will not censure very severely those who bestow some of Attention to Affairs of this seemingly low Nature. Human Felicity is produc'd not so much by great Pieces of good Fortune that seldom happen, as by little Advantages that occur every Day. Thus if you teach a poor young Man to shave himself and keep his Razor in order, you may contribute more to the Happiness of his Life than in giving him a 1000 Guineas. The Money may be soon spent, the Regret only remaining of having foolishly consum'd it. But in the other Case he escapes the frequent Vexation of waiting for Barbers, and of their some times, dirty Fingers, offensive Breaths and dull Razors. He shaves when most convenient to him, and enjoys daily the Pleasure of its being done with a good Instrument. With these Sentiments I have hazarded the few preceding Pages, hoping they may afford Hints which some time or other may be useful to a City I love, having lived many Years in it very happily; and perhaps to some of our Towns in America. (Pp. 207–8)

Here is a virtual catalogue of the matters we have been exploring. The street-cleaning proposal is represented as a writing. It is based on the immediacy of experience, of course, derived from "having lived many Years" in Philadelphia, but is "hazarded [in] the few preceding Pages" where, in fact, it appears in correspondence form, in the shape of a letter to a friend. Accordingly, it is no fixed policy, no doctrine of the true which applies in every case, but depends on the circumstances of time and place, as it "may afford Hints which some time or other may be useful." Application to such circumstances remains the business of human activity and is never naturalizable. Happiness is a matter not of "Fortune" but of "Attention," of human effort, what we have referred to as choice, directed at an infinity of particulars. A vision of ceaseless amelioration is elaborated, of development, but to no end, only as amending the particular itself. Continuous amendment of particulars is a fundamental commitment to the generality. It is the "City" Franklin loves, revealing a sense of the particular and the general at one, self and other united, the writer and reader disposed toward each other in an easy integration that American writers will struggle ever after to recapture.

2   Charles Brockden Brown and the Profession of Authorship

At the beginning of his second career as copyist, explaining his new role transcribing governmental reports into his *Literary Magazine and American Register,* Charles Brockden Brown renounces his first career as author: "I should enjoy a larger share of my own respect at the present moment if nothing had ever flowed from my pen, the production of which could be traced to me."[1] A year earlier, Brown had written his last novel and, giving up his life-long resistance, finally joined his brothers' mercantile firm. A year later, he would marry, father two children, and live happily ever after. Brown was becoming a respectable burgher. He was entering the life of his community, and it would seem that, for Brown, such a life required silence. Here is a view of art and the world as mutually exclusive, of writing and living opposed, that embarrasses the common-sensical assumptions we make in describing American literature, crudely reducing them to a position that is untenable. The idea that American literature is valuable because, somehow, it is about America stands revealed, in Brown's leaving literature for America, as a sophistical rapprochement of two orders that cannot meet. The two most usual readings of Brown, despite their ostensible disagreement as romantic versus conservative, are both implicated. Brown as too good or as too weak for America are one and the same. The seer, explorer of the depths repressed by American materialism, like the indifferent craftsman, the writer who began the American novel but who, stuck in its early stages, could not fully use it to engage America, in this respect agree: assuming a division too fundamental to do anything but paper it over, they make a mockery of our valuation of Brown as American in the first place.[2] We must force ourselves to reconsider. We must place under the sign of a question the very oppositions through which we come to Brown, reading them, if we cannot escape them, as the American problematic that his work articulates.

Let us recontextualize the matter. For Brown's earliest idea of writing had been altogether more integrated. America's "first professional man of letters," as he is generally credited with being,[3] the first man to listen seriously to the call for an American fiction and attempt to fashion a life of it, he undertook to make America precisely by making its literature. Writing was to be a social enterprise. Producing respectable fiction, Brown, as he knew, was making America respectable. One of many members of the Friendly Club and Belles Lettres Club, the clubs he found in whatever city he lived in, during whatever period of his life, Brown but shared in the widespread desire to provide for America a literary competence that would match its political heritage. Elihu Hubbard Smith, Charles Adams, James Kent, these were Brown's associates, public men, political men, and men who urged him to write as a practical act of service to the nation.[4] Living and writing were opposed no more for Brown than for Franklin. To give up one was to give up the other. Accordingly, if Brown, unlike Franklin, did give them up, it was not because he conceived of writing any differently, as what must be sacrificed to live, but because he found the life of writing itself a sacrifice. This is how we should read Brown's wish that "nothing had ever flowed from my pen, the production of which could be traced to me." While he lived, Brown, in fact, continued to write, becoming rather anonymous than silent, giving up, in his transcribing and copying, but what had become writing's too heavy responsibility, the burden of its authorship. For authorship, as we have seen, is the owning of writing. It is a sign of the individuality that bears writing through society at large. But thus it makes writing a burden the moment that assuming it becomes an issue. As we pass from Franklin to Brown, we find authorship fallen. It has separated out as a problem, become the object of an intense concern. It is a concern, however, prior to the life-art division, not falling on one side or the other of that division, but creating it.

We may consider Paul Allen, Brown's first biographer, as he wrestles confusedly with the problem:

> How can it be expected that the life [of a literary man] can be embellished by splendid incident, when the very profession of the man allows of no other than what passes while seated in solitude at his writing desk. . . . Incident then so far as it is connected with our present [biographical] purpose, means fairly this, a dispassionate recital of the thoughts which passed in the mind of Charles Brockden Brown. It does not mean, and it cannot mean, that he should have been personally engaged in those marvellous adventures which his pen afterwards describes; for had he *acted in these characters,* he never would have been the *author* of such work. (Italics Allen's)[5]

For Allen, too, there is an opposition between living and writing, society and the artist, figured in the image of "splendid incident," on the one hand, and "solitude," on the other. Indeed, Allen goes further, continuing the opposition into writing itself, where we find a similar division between what is written—the "adventures" of the "characters"—and the man who does the writing, the "author" whose "pen afterwards describes" them. Significantly, however, the opposition is inseparable from the problem of biography itself, which, in Allen's construction, clearly causes it. Focus on the author as separable from his world, and you must, finally, separate him out of his work as well. To attend to the life of the author is to privilege that life beyond the possibility of his writing it. A little history of the decline from epic is encapsulated here. For, to put it in the terms of our previous chapter, to split authorship from reference is to make both unreal. It is to make inauthoritative both the writer and what he has written. Epic autobiography becomes imitative fiction. The self in its world, making its world by authoring itself, becomes the self at a loss, and coming into itself, taking possession of its world, only by copying what has been authored already. Living and writing come apart after all. Fact and fiction—and with them, as we shall see, before and after, exterior and interior—separate. But Brown, struggling against the separation, consistently refuses the commonsense attempt to make do with it and keep on going. Desperately serious about his fiction, he rejects the popular view of fact as generating it. He rejects the reconstruction of fiction as an accessory after fact, as a kind of decorative enhancement of it. But committed to fact as well, he rejects that romanticization which converts fact to a lower form of the supreme fiction. In the anonymity of Brown's final years, as we shall see, there is no yielding to fact *or* fiction, living *or* writing, but an attempt to return them to their condition before separation in the only way remaining for him, by establishing writing on a ground where authorship has yet again ceased to be an issue.

I. Career

We have noted that Brown was America's first professional author. We may now say overtly that his very need to profess marks a crisis in American letters, indeed in American culture itself. The epic unity of Franklin's *Autobiography* has disappeared. Every man is no longer his own writer. The community of men, writing their community by authorizing each other to write themselves, has vanished. Writing has become a specialization. The authority of the author is no longer freely granted but something that must be purchased by a contraction of the sphere of his activity, by the author's admission of a self which does not write and its subjugation to a world beyond his creating. The New World is already old. It is a world commensurate no longer, as Fitzgerald would say, with the author's capacity to wonder, for he must wonder, instead, about a world which is only elsewhere. The American dream, as we may call it, is over almost before it has begun.[6]

In these terms, Brown's extraordinary contribution lies in his refusal to give the dream up. Brown, in a romantic enough way, would not admit any self apart from the writer's ability to regenerate it. And yet, quite pragmatically, democratically, indeed rhetorically, as we called it in relation to Franklin, he insisted that the authority for writing lay with the world of what had become precisely such unregenerate selves. Brown was caught in an impossible situation. On the one hand, he was not content to be the amateur man of letters with which his contemporaries had to make do, the lawyer who also wrote, for that would have been to admit the writer's loss of himself, the reduction of his authority to that over a sort of holiday world. But on the other, in his rejection of transcendence, he would not espouse an authority that extended over the self but by subjugating it, in its own turn, by raising the writer's powers to those of more than self. Brown sought to author America, to author not only a writer's self, either free of, or above, the world, but, as it were, a man-self, a self which was in the world, which with other man-selves *was* the world. Accordingly, Brown sought what in his age had become untenable. His project was to authorize an activity admittedly inauthoritative. It was to realize writing in a writing no longer identical with itself.[7]

As Clara Wieland puts it: "When I lay down the pen the taper of life will expire: my existence will terminate with my tale."[8] Writing madly, producing more pages in less time than appears possible, Clara, and Brown like her, might seem to be in the grip of a romantic compulsion, the terrible necessity to speak the truth that is beyond writing and whose articulation would bring their life of writing to an end. And yet nothing could be further than such an interpretation from what really generates writing in both cases. For Brown's compulsion, Clara's compulsion, indeed the compulsion of almost all Brown's narrators is not to tell a particular story but to keep telling stories forever. They write interminably. They write wildly. But for all that, and most unobsessively, they are constrained, no matter what they say, by no vision. They are bound to no apocalyptic event they are doomed to repeat, for they repeat nothing, telling always new characters and new events with a remarkable, and often criticized, freedom. It is as if their freedom were its own limitation. They fear reflexively, afraid not that something might be left unsaid, but that saying all will yet not suffice. For Brown, as for Franklin, life is work. But Franklin's epic writing-as-living has become, in Clara's formulation, its inverse, not-writing as dying. Writing is all, but doubtful as it has become in the act of its undertaking, it is not enough. Freely granted to have authority, the author *is* authoritative. But once questioned, how can he ever authorize himself? Writing labors to become its own authority, to provide a ground which yet remains writing. Authority is deferred, writing deflected in a self-pursuit that never can be fulfilled.

We shall have to deal differently with Brown. Since his writing points away from itself we cannot, as, in effect, we did with Franklin, merely open it to display. Its meanings are not itself alone, but a context in which it would place itself. And yet it remains true that this context is not something different from writing, either. It is not yet a psyche or world outside writing, reference to which would make its meaning objectively specifiable. We are led to the idea of a "career," to a kind of temporalization of profession, a following of the path of self-pursuit, in which writing becomes its own context. Brown's life is not one work, but a number of works whose meaning is their relation to each other. Even here, however, we must be careful. For although Brown did publish a series of novels whose traditional order, in fact, we will follow in the analysis of this chapter, the series is not so much what Brown wrote as it is the consequence of his writing's malaise. Career, that is, is not the solution of the problem of Brown's meaning, but the problem itself. Writing's context though it is, career is yet not a self-sustaining context. For not admitting any life outside writing, it cannot reconstitute or imitate life, either. The suspicion emerges that it is not itself quite alive. To put this in terms of our traditional methods, Brown's career is not, as a romantic aesthetics would have it, the place of Brown's deepest self-fulfillment. Paul Allen is wrong. "Incident" is not "the thought which passed in the mind" of Brown or even his thoughts as he realized them in formal expression. For Brown's writing is too discontinuous with his living to realize anything but itself. On the other hand, his career is not, as a formalist aesthetics would have it, merely the totality of what he has written, either. For then writing would be so discontinuous with living that expression would be a kind of admission of death. Career in Brown, rather, is the sign of a separation of writing from living just great enough to be a constant problem. It is a context which is extremely useful to us and without which it is difficult to make much sense out of anything Brown wrote. But it is a context Brown presents us with as highly problematical, and we must not undermine its usefulness by taking it as anything very settled.

We will not dismiss as insignificant our difficulties in delimiting Brown's career. The incoherence, the fuzziness, the messiness, as we may say, of its appearance, has proven troublesome to virtually everyone who has attempted to follow it. Here is only a partial inventory: one novel virtually complete but unpublished; another complete but lost; a fragment published; two fragments, each longer than any of the completed novels, unpublished; and sections of many of these scattered throughout each other and others as new work, along with scenarios of works variously said to be in progress or completed, and only some of which have actually been found. Brown presents us with the spectacle of a career in disequilibrium, of an unsettling lack of correlation of projection to completion, composition to publication, achievement to record of it. The case of *Sky-Walk* is, perhaps, paradigmatic. The lost novel we have just mentioned, what many critics regard as Brown's first novel as well, only a fragment of it appeared in the serial which announced its publication. And yet, when the whole of the manuscript was completed and part set in type for publication in book form, Brown turned his attention instead to *Wieland,* composing and publishing it, evidently, inside of six months, content to let the plates of *Sky-Walk* be destroyed. Harry Warfel wonders at the "prodigality in the way Brown cast his manuscripts to the winds."[9] And, indeed, Brown seems to want his manuscripts dispersed as widely as the winds will carry them. For his writing is always spilling across any narrow boundaries. It is writing compromised by specialization, yet resisting compromise, seeking to generalize itself and become integrated into living once again. Where does Brown's career begin? Where does it end? What, even, constitute the particular elements of its advance? At the fringes of it, we can speak at best relatively, probabilistically. Brown's writing shades into his living. His fiction shades into his autobiography. Indeed, the confusing fact is that it is often simply impossible to say which sort of writing a given piece of Brown's is: fiction or documentary, writing as part of his career or the sort of writing not yet so institutionalized professionally, writing such as nonprofessionals do—accounts, reports—negating itself as writing by its presumable transparence to the life on which it depends.

II. Fact and Fiction

Here we may begin even with the ostensibly easy cases, the works usually considered among Brown's social and political writings: *Alcuin,* his first published book and last published work before the "first" novel, *Wieland,* and *An Address to the Government of the United States,* a political pamphlet, the first book of his bourgeois life, written and published just after *Jane Talbot* and *Clara Howard.* These would appear to be works of a clearly nonfictional nature, thus demarcating the fictive career in a firm and coherent way. The pamphlet is a Federalist attack on Jeffersonian policy concerning the Louisiana territory. It calls, in the strongest terms, for United States action to take the territory and prevent France from achieving a stranglehold on the western trade. And yet the pamphlet is cast in the form of a memorandum by a French advisor to Napoleon, translated by an American editor, a literary device perhaps not very important in itself, but of great importance because of the authority with which Brown seems to have invested it. Although Brown evidently meant his device as simply polemical, it was taken up as a hoax, as if a far more profound interpenetration of novel and history existed, a more profound confusion of the novelistic career with the postnovelistic historical career, than has generally been understood. One discourse slides into the other here, and the confusion is even more pronounced in *Alcuin.*

Ostensibly a fictionalized tract on women's rights, a dialogue between Alcuin and one Mrs. Carter which argues for an essentially Godwinian revaluation of the relation between the sexes,

Alcuin would appear to derive its authority from the social conditions of Brown's America, as an attack upon them. But the fiction, which, unlike the pamphlet's fiction, quite clearly *is* but a polemical device in the first part of the work, equally clearly becomes, in the second half, an end in itself. Alcuin, returning to Mrs. Carter's salon after an absence of several days, reports on a visit that, he says, has kept him from her for so long, a journey to a land of free relations between men and women that constitutes a somewhat narrow but, within its range of interest, full-fledged utopia. Brown's point of view becomes obscured. The utopia is elaborated so forcefully, so independently, that it stands on its own, and it is impossible to say if the vision of society it constitutes is something Brown rejects or espouses. Alcuin, who had resisted Mrs. Carter's propositions earlier as too radical, now exchanges roles with her, as she draws back. The polemical force of the book is lost. Its authority no longer derives from its status as cultural critique, but is absorbed into the fiction of the utopia. *Alcuin* is neither novel nor political treatise nor, for that matter, a simple mixture of the two. It is fiction *made* culture, novelistic discourse *as* social. It is typical of the main body of Brown's writing, not something outside it and delimiting it, and in this sense we might say that all of Brown's writing is such limit-denying utopia.

Perhaps this explains why the great utopia Brown was forever composing, as his friends tell us, has never been found, despite various attempts at identification by modern scholars.[10] For utopia is that form of fiction which most manifestly would authorize itself, which, never denying its fictionality, indeed predicating itself upon it, yet insists it would be real. Accordingly, it is everywhere in Brown. Fiction would be fact, and we cannot use either term to define the other against it. Here, again, Brown seems to resist traditional modes of definition, and the best scholarly attempts to insist upon them have produced only controversy, as in the wonderful argument over the so-called Henrietta letters. It is an argument, I would suggest, accordingly, that we may now see as itself a significant insight into Brown, not to be conjured away by too easy a decision in favor of one side or the other.

Brown's habit, David Lee Clark tells us, was to enter into his journals transcriptions of a variety of materials side by side with original lucubrations: news items, works of fiction by other writers, letters to and from friends. Among the last, he classes a series of love epistles to and from one Henrietta G. covering some fifty close-spaced pages in his biography.[11] And yet, although the name of Henrietta is invoked often in letters Brown wrote to friends who are well known, she has never been identified, and the similarity of the series to Brown's later epistolary novels and to Goethe's *Sorrows of Young Werther* has led Eleanor M. Tilton, and others convinced by her, to see the Henrietta cycle as one more early novelistic fragment.[12] Simply enough, one never knows what is real or unreal in Brown, and much as we have learned not to quote the novels of other writers as if they expressed realities concerning the novelist, in Brown we must beware of the "factual" documents as well, for the status of both appears to have been indifferent to him. Sufficient care has not been taken by Brown's biographers in this matter, but identifiable instances remain. To stay within the realm of correspondence, Brown dates a letter he mailed to a friend from Philadelphia as from London and, several times, other letters as from Geneva. In one he refers to his love of literature and of the "beauteous Jacquelette" as equal, though the former is as real as the latter, he also tells us, is wholly a product of his "voluptuous fancy." Even his studies at the law, he writes, are an attempt to "personate" his friend Lauder Allen, himself a character Brown invented, as if his very life were a kind of novel.[13] As Smith wrote to him in consternation:

> you were pleased to have others believe those misfortunes to be real which you knew how so eloquently to describe. The transition is natural, to a mind of sensibility almost unavoidable. You began to fancy that these fictions were real; that you had indeed suffered, enjoyed, known, and seen all that you had so long pretended to have experienced; every subsequent event became tinctured with this conviction and accompanied with this diseased apprehension; the habit was formed; and you wandered in a world of your own creation.[14]

Now it is important to point out that as critical as Smith is being, he is not accusing Brown of mere solipsism. The "world of your own creation" is not delusive or even self-delusive, not so much opposed to "real life" as a problem for it. "You are not charged with intentional misrepresentation of the truth," he says in the same letter, "but with conveying it in such a manner as to make it difficult of comprehension to your friends, or encumbered with such circumstances or deficient in such particularities as to render it unintelligible to them."[15] This is not quite a positivist's sense of the falseness of fiction. Smith acknowledges the propriety of fiction making for certain sensibilities. But he wishes to place Brown's fictions, to contextualize them so that he may know in what way they are to be used. It is with Smith, as with contemporary critics, the status of Brown's fiction that is at issue:

> You "have been the child of passion and inconsistency, the slave of desires that can not be honorably gratified, the slave of hopes no less criminal than fantastic." What, my friend, is the meaning of all this? And what am I to learn from it? Or, rather, what are we—Dunlap and Smith—to learn from it? . . . What do your most intimate friends, my Charles, know of you? What do they wish to know, but that they may be of use to you? Far be from them that teasing curiosity which seeks only its own gratification. If there be any thing you think it your duty to withhold from them, withhold it; they will not blame you. If there be any thing you have not the courage to reveal, conceal it still. They will not commend the cowardice, but they will compassionate, will pardon it. But when you know that these are their feelings, why still do you continue to remind them that there are secrets? that you have science which they must not have? Why will you allude to misfortunes of which they are ignorant, and from which, therefore, they can not relieve you?[16]

Smith, here, in the way of Allen, admits the author's unreachability. He allows that the discourse of an author is not transparent, that it cannot quite make him accessible. Yet as Brown's correspondent, rather than his biographer, concerned with Brown the friend rather than Brown the author, he uses the author's very unreachability as a provocation for friendship. Brown's writing may thus be admitted as difficult to penetrate. The obscurity of its reference may be acknowledged as the sign of his separation from the world. Yet acknowledging its obscurity, precisely, we bring him into the world again. Fiction, here, is not quite fiction. To one who reads it as a correspondence it must be real as well. And, indeed, Brown's fiction asks to be read as just such a delicately balanced correspondence. It is the result not of Brown's division from his audience, but of his refusal to accept his division as authoritative. It is a rhetoric as it were on the verge of externality, appealing to a world almost outside it, but attempting, in its appeal, to place it back inside. It is writing to an audience recalling Franklin's audience, that "Dear Son" which, though it has become but the function of a certain conventional address, Brown believes his address may actually create.

Here we find ourselves, again, at the heart of American writing, that essentially, though now problematically, rhetorical situation out of which it arises, that rhetorical society, as we might call it, that writing exists for, but which at the same time must be created *by* writing. We may see it problematized in the one account Brown ever gave of the origin of any of his works, presented in a letter to Joseph Bringhurst about the early "The Story of Julius," an epistolary novel which, because it too survives in only the most questionable form, as a scenario within a letter, we may take as typical of the status of all of his work.

III. Citation

According to Brown, "Julius" was composed in response to a request by his beloved Henrietta G. The time was 1792, when Brown had published only a series of anonymous letters, "The Rhapsodist," and when, as he states, he still largely doubted his literary powers. Yet having proceeded to read a translation of Rousseau's *La Nouvelle Héloïse* despite Henrietta's refusal to give him the "original," as he calls it, on the grounds that it was immoral, he was enjoined by her to win her forgiveness by a "similar" performance designed to uphold nobler ends:

> She left me at liberty to make either Rousseau or Richardson my model, and to write either in the narrative or epistolary method.

> Nothing could be more arrogant and audacious than for one of
> my youth and inexperience to attempt to tread in the footsteps of
> these illustrious writers, and nothing but the necessity of submit-
> ting to absolute commands could induce me to engage in so
> arduous an undertaking.[17]

Now the truth of this story is, of course, uncertain. Indeed, as
we have indicated, even the existence of the novel is in doubt, for
what follows in Brown's account is but a sketch and the incredible
claim that, though the novel was somewhat longer than the voluminous *Héloïse,* it was composed in thirfy days.[18] Whether the
story is true or not, however—indeed, as we have been claiming,
precisely because we cannot know if it is true—it is a fitting
account of the beginning of a career which, as we have seen,
cannot properly be said ever to have begun. And so what Brown
tells us is that "The Story of Julius" neither quite originated nor
yet always existed. It is instigation, rather than inspiration, that
accounts for it. No longer coterminous with his life, as Franklin's
was, his work is yet the result of no sudden influx of vision, no
romantically inspired impulse, either. Its origin is a muse, but
since the muse is Henrietta, it is an origin he has himself invented.
Brown transcendentalizes his art, yet simultaneously he insists on
the ordinary self—the doubting, inexperienced youth—as creator
of transcendentalizations.

   A related point may be noted. Brown is in some uncertainty as
to what narrative mode he should employ, narrative proper or
epistolary. Something in between these two, in fact, was his choice
for the bulk of his famous novels, and we shall discuss the issue in
greater detail later. But we can say here that the choice, even at
this early stage, would seem to involve the question of how a novel
should be authorized—by the omniscience of the narrator who
knows and who, therefore, may tell, or by a kind of naturalistic
derivation, whereby the event records itself. When the power to
authorize is attributed instead, then, to Henrietta, a created authority, and one whose authority, moreover, is purely over him—
"to forgive me," as Brown phrases it—both transcendence and
naturalism are suspended. An epistolary novel is presented by

Brown in narrative form within an epistle to a friend as authorized by an invented goddess of conversation. Authority circles round and round here. But because authority is thus defined as rhetorical from the very start, the circulation is enabling rather than crippling. Never mysterious, authorship cannot be demystified. Dependent on nothing prior to itself which it does not quite openly construct, its deconstruction is simply redundant. The "problem" of authorship becomes Brown's problematic, and the burden of being an author is neither abolished by some metaphysical hypostatization of it nor turned, with the death of metaphysics, into despair.

This is why, too, in the passage we have quoted, Brown can refer to Rousseau and Richardson as models, even models to which he is inadequate, but without any trace of anxiety about their influence upon him. For the theory of influence, in effect but a kind of personification of the deconstruction proper which it anticipates, assumes a metaphysical, rather than rhetorical, definition of authorship. Originality is equated with priority, with closeness to the first, the original, truth, and accordingly, authorship as an attempt to replace prior authors becomes as futile as authorship which would deny its inescapable reference to them.[19] The originality for which Brown strives, however, is a Franklinian assertion of equality. He would not obliterate the world of other authors in some apocalyptic return to the origin of their authorship, but obliterating the very idea of an origin, he would make all authorship coeval. Brown's reference to other authors is neither pathological nor inescapable. If he is balked before arriving at the "original," something "similar" will do quite well. For Brown is Franklin's reader as writer, writing not because he must, but as he pleases. And because he does please, he is not in competition with other writers, but uses them as Franklin would have his readers make use of him, in a cycle of rhetorical grounding, as example of an independence based upon the independence he, in turn, grants all others. The title, "The Story of Julius," quite pointedly asks us to see it in the tradition of *La Nouvelle Héloïse,* whose full title is *Julie, ou La Nouvelle Héloïse.* And, in an instance celebrated, but wrongly, as evidence of Brown's imitativeness, there is Brown's use of the "curiosity" motif in *Arthur Mervyn,* recalling Godwin's *Caleb Williams.*

Mervyn has been sent by his patron, Welbeck, to deliver a letter into the hands of Mrs. Wentworth's servant without seeing Mrs. Wentworth herself. But Mervyn is not content:

> I arrived at the house and knocked. A female servant appeared. Her mistress was up stairs: she would tell her if I wished to see her, and meanwhile invited me to enter the parlour: I did so; and the girl retired to inform her mistress that one waited for her—I ought to mention that my departure from the directions which I had received was, in some degree, owing to an inquisitive temper: I was eager after knowledge, and was disposed to profit by every opportunity to survey the interior dwellings and converse with their inhabitants. (3.64)

This is not only similar to *Caleb Williams,* but what we might call a citation of it. Godwin has Williams say, for example, in explanation of why he will later open a forbidden chest, "The spring of action which, perhaps more than any other, characterized the whole train of my life, was curiosity. . . . I panted for the unravelling of an adventure, with an anxiety, perhaps almost equal to that of the man whose future happiness or misery depend on its issue."[20] And so Mervyn, about to enter a forbidden room to open a similar forbidden chest, may explain: "The influence of prohibitions and an appearance of disguise in awakening curiosity, are well known" (3.81). What Godwin must labor to psychoanalyze, Brown takes as understood. The priority of another author does not prohibit or even constrain continuing authorship. And, indeed, Brown's first citation of curiosity, added on, as it is, almost as an afterthought, in effect denies the very priority it uses. It is for other authors as for readers, in Brown: on the verge of externality, they are referred to as, yet, internal. All authorship exists at the same level, in a circle of interdependence that guarantees independence. Accordingly, the great struggle in Brown is to establish authorship not as prior, but as democratic. The great tension in his writing is not between himself and other authors considered as godlike, as bearers of a transcendent truth, but in authorship itself, considered as a rhetorically grounded institution, and caught, instead, between internal and external rhetoric, between eccentricity and representativity. It is a tension which, no more than that between fact and fiction, is to be decided in favor of one or the other, nor yet to be resolved in a dialectic end of author and influence resolved, which would obliterate them both. For it is a tension that never even existed in that beginning of authors authorizing each other, in that state of difference with a difference we described in Franklin and which lies as the only true ground of American literature even after its fall.

The problem is everywhere. Whose experience is the writer writing about? On whose truth does his writing depend? Or, as the issue has become formulated most often in Brown studies, how "abnormal" is the peculiar science and psychology which he is forever portraying? Thus against Brown's brother's comments on the "out-of-nature incidents" in his works,[21] we may set Brown's footnotes in *Wieland* "documenting" both spontaneous combustion and ventriloquism (1.19,198). And, more generally, against the criticism that sees Brown's work as an exercise in the horrific, we may place more recent nativist interpretation of Brown as naturalizer, adapting horror stories to the scenery of early America.[22] Most revealing, however, is Brown in his proper voice, addressing the issue in his "Advertisement" to *Wieland:*

> Some readers may think the conduct of the younger Wieland impossible. In support of its possibility the Writer must appeal to Physicians and to men conversant with the latent springs and occasional perversions of the human mind. It will not be objected that the instances of similar delusion are rare, because it is the business of moral painters to exhibit their subject in its most instructive and memorable forms. If history furnishes one parallel fact, it is a sufficient vindication of the Writer; but most readers will probably recollect an authentic case, remarkably similar to that of Wieland. (1.3)

Wieland's delusion is "rare," but therefore it is "most instructive." It is a "perversion," but thus it returns us to the "springs" of the human mind. For mimetic fiction this will become an opposition of the possible and the probable, and mimetic critics such as Henry James will use it to distinguish between romance and realism,[23] to place the work in relation to an anteriority that authorizes it or, at least, authorizes it more or less. But romance conceived of, as we have conceived of it, as deriving from an epic autobiography which denies anteriority, romance as that condition of inauthority in which the work cannot be what it seeks to be—reality itself—is caught in a difficulty which such formulations of division are only an attempt to familiarize. For "an authentic case," though Brown would claim it as "vindication" of the writer, yet remains but "parallel." However well documented the incident with real life occurrences, it does not derive from them. Whose truth the story of a ventriloquist or a sleepwalker or a child murderer presents remains a nagging uncertainty.

We are returned to a problem broached in our chapter on Franklin in our discussion of Gibbon and Jonathan Edwards, the issue of the standing of a writer in his community. For Brown, like Franklin, rejects the representativity that both these writers claim. The mean, the average and uneccentric life of Gibbon will not do, for in the name of authority it sacrifices the writer's individuality. And the typological life of Edwards will not do, for in hypostatizing the writer's individuality, it sacrifices the very rhetoricity which authorizes his writing in the first place. Rather, Franklin's rhetorical authority, his community of independent writers, is Brown's implicit goal, a community, however, whose latent paradox becomes more and more openly developed.

The result is the contradictory claims he makes for virtually all his heroes. Wieland, as we have seen already, is representative *and* eccentric. And, similarly, Clara, who tells his story and has experiences of her own "beyond the rest of mankind" (1.6), yet moralizes that the lesson of her narrative is to exercise an "equanimity or foresight" that is no more than "ordinary" (1.244). Even *Ormond*'s Constantia Dudley, the model lady who so captured Shelley "as a perfect combination of the purely ideal and possibly real,"[24] has been formed, Brown is careful to note, by the educational schemes of a father noted for his "peculiar views" (2.33).[25]

As Arthur Mervyn wonders, attempting to understand his own problematical imagination, "The constitution of my mind is doubtless singular and perverse; yet that opinion, perhaps, is the fruit of my ignorance" (3.76). Brown's work is caught in a break-down of the Franklinian integration, a breakdown he is powerless to arrest, but which, at least at his best, he refuses, spuriously, to resolve—indeed, which he shoulders as the very condition of his writing.

IV. Writing

I should state my preferences openly. It is *Wieland,* Brown's "ear-liest," which is his best, though even his conventional worst, *Clara Howard* and *Jane Talbot,* as we shall see, are not so much a depar-ture from the burden of *Wieland* as works confirming, in their decision to give it up, its immense weight. We may analyze in more detail than we have as yet been able to do.

The usual way of dealing with *Wieland* is to see it in its gothic tradition, as an American version of an English genre. Brown appears as an American "pioneer," as Clark calls him, an "Amer-ican gothic," as a second critic puts it, adapting foreign forms to native materials and thus preparing American literature for a more properly home-grown exploration of the American imagina-tion.[26] Such a view, however, in effect defining Brown's originality as a kind of modified historical priority, is as inappropriate for describing American originality as the notion of metaphysical priority we discussed earlier. Like it, it goes either too far or not far enough, locating the writer in a context which it is the achieve-ment of his origin-obliterating originality precisely to abolish. Thus although Brown admits the existence of other authors, although, because authorship has fallen into effort, he even, as we have seen, may cite them, genre, with its assumption of a context, of an anterior ground for writing far more elaborated than author-ship or even career would admit, must await James Fenimore Cooper for similar citation. On the verge of an external rhetoric, as we have said, Brown does not yet step into it. Accordingly, the audience he addresses is not the readers of a certain kind of novel, but readers of *his* novels, whose independent relationship with him, rather than some larger set of expectations they may have, is what is responsible for his writing:

> The following Work is delivered to the world as the first fruit of a series of performances, which the favorable reception of this will induce the Writer to publish. . . . The memoirs of Carwin, alluded to at the conclusion of the work, will be published or suppressed according to the reception which is given to the present attempt. (1.3)

Here is the work defined as part of a career, a series of works, but those works, in turn, are conceived as a rhetoric virtually constitutive. Nothing anterior to a direct, as it were unmediated dialogue with his readers exists for Brown, for their assent to this work would seem to depend on no prior standards of judgment, no system of received modalities, but simple pleasure or displeasure. I would go so far as to say that *Wieland* is not a gothic novel at all, or, at least, that it is gothic rather after the fact than before it. For its gothicism is a matter of ex post facto critical categorization and wholly without that sense of its own gothicism with which even the very first gothic novel is filled.

Thus, pace partisans of the psychic or expressive nature of the gothic,[27] we may note the beginning of the mode in parody. *The Castle of Otranto* is an extravagance. Underscoring its generic properties by exaggerating them, it assumes a conventionalized world—a semiotic structure, if you will—which it plays against. Simply said, the Richardsonian novel is burlesqued. The world of *The Castle of Otranto* does not even pretend to be the real world, but is already at a remove, bound to refer endlessly to an endless series of signs without termination. The power of the tyrant over his subject is but the power of the Richardsonian gentleman over women, only stripped of any social or cultural justification. The castle of Walpole is but Richardson's house, only reducing the moral pretensions of the father to a mere legality. The incest taboo in all its scandalous irrationality is exposed by the attempt to violate it, revealing the fundamental arbitrariness of the family.[28]

The Castle of Otranto stands as a structural analysis precipitating itself headlong into deconstructive chaos. Assuming as its subject matter not even England, but an England as it were already assumed, it exposes the infinite regress of anteriority, mocking itself from the very start, raising the narrative ante to ever higher and higher levels of absurdity. What Paul de Man has called vertigo sets in,[29] from which the writer opts out, preserving himself but by separating himself from his writing. What strange customs these humans have, he seems, with a kind of aristocratic insouciance, to toss off at his bourgeois audience. Writer and reader come apart. Talking *at* each other, not *to* each other, they stand outside the work, never in it or constituting it, and powerless to do anything about it but watch it explode.

The situation is not fundamentally different even in the bourgeois gothic. Ann Radcliffe and Clara Reeves complicate matters somewhat by appearing to be so much like their readership that the mediation of genre would seem to be precluded. But this is a function of the unconsciousness, the lack of self-knowledge, of the writers, or, worse, the result of a kind of pandering, of generic suppression that, inevitably, will out. Exaggeration is only slightly less extreme than in Walpole and reveals a mystification as vertiginous in its complicated piling of strangeness upon strangeness as *Otranto*'s deconstruction. An essentially vacuous bourgeois structure is contentualized. A dull family life is fulfilled in romance, a secure world made full of breathtaking, but ultimately breath-returning, risk. Radcliffe and Reeves would be one with their audience. But they may become so only by suppressing themselves and by promoting the work as a substitute life, not as life itself.

How different, accordingly, is the self-promoting *Wieland,* which, making no assumptions of an anteriority on which it may depend, does not find itself in either a deconstructive or a self-mystifying bind:

> I feel little reluctance in complying with your request. You know not fully the cause of my sorrows. You are a stranger to the depth of my distresses. Hence your efforts at consolation must necessarily fail. Yet the tale that I am going to tell is not intended

as a claim upon your sympathy. In the midst of my despair, I do not disdain to contribute what little I can to the benefit of mankind. I acknowledge your right to be informed of the events that have lately happened in my family. Make what use of the tale you shall think proper. If it be communicated to the world, it will inculcate the duty of avoiding deceit. It will exemplify the force of early impressions, and show the immeasurable evils that flow from an erroneous or imperfect discipline. (1.5)

This brief introduction is more like Franklin's direct appeal than like the gothic's generic one. As Franklin believes his son may wish to know of the family history, so "I acknowledge your right to be informed." As Franklin hopes his experiences will be of some value, so Clara's story "will inculcate the duty of avoiding deceit." Even as Franklin tells us to read his work or not as we may please, Clara says, "Make what use of the tale you shall think proper." Where *Wieland* does differ from Franklin, however, is in its undeniable intensity, the pressure to justify itself, that contrasts notably with the *Autobiography*'s confidence that writing is itself justify*ing*. Clara's reader, evidently, is not simply entitled to this narrative, but has felt it necessary to demand it. Whatever use to which he wishes to put it is acceptable to her, but she has in mind three or four very specific ones. A certain directedness is evident, a pointing toward an end— something we will discuss soon—and which, we may note here, confirms a breakup of the Franklinian integration of author and audience, as if Clara, still maintaining a sense of herself as in general united to her audience, yet needs to make sure of it by specifying precisely the points on which they unite. Reader and writer are becoming perhaps just a little *too* independent. Difference with a difference, in no danger in Brown of becoming difference as full-fledged division, is yet no longer realized. And, in fact, Clara's justification, not yet *related* to anything outside itself, must yet be *repeated* outside, and just as inauthoritatively.

Here is Brown in his own voice in the "Advertisement." Why does the writer write?

His purpose is neither selfish nor temporary, but aims at the illustration of some important branches of the moral constitution

> of man. Whether this tale will be classed with the ordinary or
> frivolous sources of amusement, or be ranked with the few pro-
> ductions whose usefulness secures to them a lasting reputation,
> the reader must be permitted to decide. (1.3)

These are Clara's sentiments, already quoted, almost precisely.
Justification, once found necessary, must continue. Authorship
and reference, as we have said, have begun to split apart. The
writer both is and is not in his work. And that doubleness, never
to be resolved in some state presumably external to writing, accordingly will generate, internal to the work, separate works, at
once a part of and different from each other throughout the book's
length.

Consider Brown's habit of referring to characters or incidents
introduced for the first time as if they had already been described,
or, even more pervasively, what amounts to the same thing, his
presentation for the first time of events and characters that ought,
in the course of the narrative, to have been described already. As
proof of Clara's integrity Pleyel may note her "treatment of that
specious seducer Dashwood" (1.124), though Dashwood has not
been mentioned and an encounter between Clara and any seducer is a distinct surprise given the portrait of seclusion Brown
has thus far been drawing. Or, we are suddenly told, long after
Clara has detailed her family history, at a point, however, when a
motivation for emigrating to Germany is desired, "My ancestors
were noble Saxons, and possessed large domains in Lusatia"
(1.37). Narrative gaffes like these might seem to be mere sloppiness. Generally, they are attributed to Brown's hasty composition and lack of revision, his failure to keep the whole of his story
in mind at every point in the composition.[30] But such explanations proceed from a formalist aesthetics, from a notion of the
work as object that simply does not govern the American line we
are drawing, or which comes into being in America even later
than a generic aesthetics—in Poe, as we shall see. It is an aesthetics of anteriority which demands literary closure, an end of writing in what is prior to writing, a unitary truth to which writing
may refer but which it is not. Instead, the newness which is every-

where in Franklin, which derives from the authority of every incident being granted by the ever-renewing and object-denying assent of reader to writer, must, in Brown, who is on the verge of separation from his readership, derive from a newness which it is merely like. It is a newness which, too, is the product of reader-writer agreement, but which, though still within the same text, has yet, at least partially, already been written. Even old incidents, that is, are forever renewed, but new incidents must be referred to these renewed old ones. Or, to put this another way, in Franklin the whole work, as we have said, is constituted in each of its incidents, because whole and part are sustained by the very same rhetorical situation. But in Brown the part, not quite so firmly sustained, cannot quite be whole in the Franklinian manner. The whole itself, indeed, contextualized though only, as it were, by itself, imposes a similar contextualization, similarly internal, *on* the part.

An odd symmetry pervades the text of *Wieland,* something less than a structural principle, for the wildness and general irregularity of the text remain, but persistent nevertheless. "The Indians were repulsed on the one side, and Canada was conquered on the other" (1.26). "No scene can be imagined less enticing to a lover of the picturesque than this. The shore is deformed with mud, and incumbered with a forest of reeds. . . . The scenes which environed our dwellings at Mettingen constituted the reverse of this. Schuylkill was here a pure and translucid current, broken into wild and ceaseless music by rocky points, murmuring on a sandy margin, and reflecting on its surface, banks of all varieties of height and degrees of declivity" (1.47). Perhaps passages like these owe something to neoclassical periodizing. But more, I think, is involved. It is a kind of self-contextualization, the invention of a schema not yet generic, not yet prior to writing and imposed on it from without, but projected by writing outside itself. Each new incident or character opens the book to new possibilities, yet is introduced into the book as a repetition of a structure of relationships or activities already present in it. To Clara and Wieland are added Catherine, and with her the idea of marriage, family, children. Yet Catherine and Clara in "sex and age were the same. We lived within sight of each other's abode. Our tempers were remarkably congenial, and the superintendants [sic] of our education not only prescribed to us the same pursuits, but allowed us to cultivate them together" (1.21). Similarly, to the society of Wieland and Clara and Catherine is added "a new member," Pleyel, whose conversation is filled with "novelty" and whose "gaiety," so different from the somber demeanor of the threesome, "was an inexhaustible fund of entertainment" (1.25). And yet Pleyel is but Catherine's brother, in fact someone Wieland and Clara already know, and merely the Allegro to Wieland's Penseroso who enables a reduplication of the pairing already established. Each character here, each part, is surely more than a mere part of the whole, for the whole is collected up in it. Yet the part is not quite itself whole because requiring another part for its existence. As Brown locates Pleyel in relation to Wieland: "His residence was at the same distance below the city as ours was above" (1.25). Here is neither quite difference with a difference nor yet difference as opposition. Rather, it is difference and similarity simultaneously maintained, independence and community as *Wieland*'s problematic.

The situation is perhaps nowhere more clearly evident than in Brown's infamous narratives within narratives, his failure to integrate the events of one life with another, his inability to summarize one character's words in the words of someone else. Whose story is *Wieland* after all: Clara's or Wieland's or Carwin's? And who is supposed to be telling it? Once again, the difficulty is most generally explained as resulting from Brown's hastiness, his forgetting what his story is and who is supposed to be telling it. And yet, Brown's "forgetting" is thus precise. One character's tale exists inside another's, yet, always separate from that other, it would preserve its own and the other's integrity. Independence here, unlike Franklinian independence, is compromised. Independence is, in fact, dependent. As we have said, Franklin's community of individuals is breaking down. But it is not yet broken down, and the result is a characteristic tendency toward completing any separate incident in its own terms precisely because it is felt to be neither complete already as in Franklin, nor yet a fragment of a text to be completed only after all.

Here is Clara explaining why Pleyel urges her brother to return to Germany:

> Pleyel was enamoured of his scheme on account of its intrinsic benefits, but, likewise, for other reasons. His abode at Leipsig made that country appear to him like home. He was connected with this place by many social ties. While there he had not escaped the amorous contagion. But the lady, though her heart was impressed in his favor, was compelled to bestow her hand upon another. Death had removed this impediment, and he was now invited by the lady herself to return. (1.39)

Or, again, she accounts for "the arrival of my mother's brother, Thomas Cambridge":

> Ten years since, he went to Europe, and was a surgeon in the British forces in Germany during the whole of the late war. After its conclusion, some connection that he had formed with an Irish officer, made him retire to Ireland. Intercourse had been punctually maintained by letters with his sister's children, and hopes were given that he would shortly return to his native country, and pass his old age in our society. (1.159)

Or, more absurdly, she describes a fire in which she is almost trapped:

> By neglect of the servant, some unextinguished embers had been placed in a barrel in the cellar of the building. The barrel had caught fire; this was communicated to the beams of the lower floor, and thence to the upper part of the structure. It was first discovered by some persons at a distance, who hastened to the spot and alarmed my uncle and the servants. The flames had already made considerable progress, and my condition was overlooked till my escape was rendered nearly impossible. (1.237)

These are full life stories—of Pleyel, of Thomas Cambridge, of a fire—accounts over and above what motivation in the larger story requires. They are narratives embedded in the larger narrative, yet narratives that must be finished as if they were not.

Of course, I am aware, it might be argued that the difficulty of such stories may be explained away if we do not, as formalists do, try to relate them to the larger narrative in the first place, if we take them purely romantically, purely expressively, as authorized by an instinct prior to form, an originary drive producing form but as expressive iteration, in Emerson's phrase.[31] Even within a formalist framework, we may see at least the narratives within narratives not as a structural problem, but as necessary error, various perspectives from a periphery whose center will emerge only with the completion of the form as a whole. There is some warrant for such an interpretation in the innumerable prolepses of *Wieland*—Clara's prophetic dream of her brother attempting to do her harm, her father's mysterious combustion, the unexplained voices—which seem to point to a final explanation, a superior perspective to be established at last. My point, however, is not that such tendencies toward expressionism or formalism do not exist in Brown, but that, as the result of a rhetorical breakdown, rather than founding, they work not with but against each other. Each iteration, if that is what it is, is yet contained, growing not organically out of the one next to it, but formalized as separate.

Accordingly, perhaps nothing is so remarkable in *Wieland* as its intensely plotted character at the same time that the plot itself remains so incoherent. That is to say, though there is an extraordinary force in everything that happens in *Wieland,* a promise of meaningfulness in every event, yet no event seems to connect very meaningfully with any other. The promise is never kept. At the end of the novel too much remains unexplained. And, indeed, if Carwin's ventriloquism may be said to be the explanation offered, its voice is singularly "biloqual." In fact, in the place of the explanation, the revelation of the end, is really not even Carwin's ambiguous voice, but rather another formalistic fragment, the whole part, as it were, which is the Louisa Conway story, an end which has rightly disturbed virtually every reader of *Wieland.*[32] It is a tale of seduction of no consequence to the novel, a few aimless pages irrelevant to the tales of Wieland and Clara and Carwin, tacked on to the final chapter ostensibly as a kind of minor tidying up or housekeeping, but rather reminding us of characters we have already forgotten than answering any remaining questions we may really have. It is, in other words, one more of those dependent independent narratives forever separating out of *Wieland,* making it a work which, in fact, will not end, but must forever be reworked. It is the sign, even at the "close" of the novel, of the burden of writing that Brown, only now, begins to find too heavy to bear.

V. Writing without an Author

It is time, accordingly, to discuss the rest of Brown's career, and we may begin, in fact, with something remarkable about the Louisa Conway story that intimates its direction. We have said the story is much like all the other stories within stories in *Wieland.* But there is one important difference: Brown offers a somewhat more careful definition of its dependent independence than he gives the rest. As Brown introduces it: "More urgent considerations hindered me from mentioning, in the course of my mournful recital, any particulars respecting the unfortunate father of Louisa Conway" (1.239). A certain relief from the justifying pressure we have been describing is evident here. What Clara is about to proffer for the reader's consideration is not, as the rest of her story was, very "urgent." But even more significant, it is not urgent because it is to be found in an, as it were, unplotted space in the midst of what she has narrated already. More is involved here than simple citation, as, earlier, of *Caleb Williams,* or even in the reference of new events to old ones. Those references were to authorial activity, rather than to what had been authored. Or, if they referred to what had been authored, then they did so either as a sign of Brown's authorial activity or as authorizing such activity as Brown was about to engage in. They were, indeed, references clearly proceeding from Brown the author rather than from the text as object, bespeaking a consciousness beyond Clara's and even undermining her consciousness by keeping her author present before us. The reference here, however, is to the narrative itself—not to writing, but to what has been written. There is a gap in what has been written, and writing is just a filling in of the gap. Contextualization has solidified, and the rhetoricity which sustained even the first events referred to is buried under the events themselves. What is contextualized is not so much an incident in the text, but the text itself. The unplotted space expands. The labor of writing is more and more constricted. Brown would free his whole book of the need for labor, and so he locates it within what is determined beyond his power to write it again. Writing's limits are fixed:

> I now see the infatuation and injustice of my conduct in its true colours. I reflect upon the sensations and reasonings of that period with wonder and humiliation. That I should be insensible to the claims and tears of my friends; that I should overlook the suggestions of duty, and fly from that post in which only I could be instrumental to the benefit of others; that the exercise of the social and beneficent affections, the contemplation of nature and the acquisition of wisdom should not be seen to be means of happiness still within my reach, is, at this time, scarcely credible. (1.235)

And, similarly, the final paragraph of the novel:

> I leave you to moralize on this tale. That virtue should become the victim of treachery is, no doubt, a mournful consideration; but it will not escape your notice, that the evils of which Carwin and Maxwell were the authors, owed their existence to the errors of the sufferers. All efforts would have been ineffectual to subvert the happiness or shorten the existence of the Stuarts, if their own frailty had not seconded these efforts. If the lady had crushed her disastrous passion in the bud, and driven the seducer from her presence, when the tendency of his artifices was seen; if Stuart had not admitted the spirit of absurd revenge, we should not have had to deplore this catastrophe. If Wieland had framed juster notions of moral duty, and of the divine attributes; or if I had been gifted with ordinary equanimity or foresight, the double-tongued deceiver would have been baffled and repelled. (1.244)

These are examples of the sort of neoclassical representativity of which we have spoken. Weeding out, rejecting, discarding, indeed averaging, Clara normalizes her experience. But her experience is, therefore, not hers, for the only "her" that remains is not one which in writing she makes but one which, assimilated to the experience of everyone else, "she" has power passively but to describe.

Clara—and with reason, given the tribulations she has faced—has become tired of endlessly authoring herself. Brown is becoming tired of authoring *him*self. Writing in a difficult rhetorical situation, struggling against the separations of autobiography from fiction, life from writing, independence from community, he simply finds the difficulties too demanding. He searches for a way out. He removes himself from the center of the problem, referring to it, as we have said, without owning his reference, so that it soon comes to seem hardly his problem at all. And yet, thus removing himself, he does not claim to gain anything *but* a certain remove. He does not exalt reference, does not pretend that, in referring, he gains access to a truth which would justify his passivity as wisdom. As we might put it, Brown, normalizing his dilemma, gives it up to the community which has established such norms. But he does not, in turn, mystify the community, does not pretend that the community is anything more than selves that have, indeed, given up, and so he avoids the hypocrisy of asserting the loss of self-determination as the recovery of some truer self in its stead. It is not really "he" who writes. Or rather, since manifestly he does, what he writes is his powerlessness. It is writing as living still. There is for the writer, finally, no other life. And yet, in that case, it is not much of a life, after all. Brown, as a writer, would rather not live than claim a spurious authority for his writing. As we might say, he writes, now, without authorship. But this, for a democrat, is better than authorship without writing. It is, that is, better than the assertion of a self outside the rhetorical give-and-take of democratic writing, and the refusal of such an assertion now governs Brown till the end.

We must be careful in tracing the rest of Brown's career. There is, as it would seem, a development in it toward ever greater realism,[33] a sort of progress within Brown apparently corroborating the progress that, as we mentioned at the start of this chapter, is usually read into American literature in general, from primitive to artistically more and more mature mimesis. The realism proper of *Ormond,* with its Richardsonian concern faithfully to represent the reactions of a representative individual in the grip of various social forces, moves, in *Edgar Huntly,* with its forest scenes and panthers, to the vitalistic naturalism of man in nature, and then, in *Arthur Mervyn,* with its mixed and semidocumentary rendering of the life of a representative individual intertwined with the life of a city in the midst of a plague, to that superrealism of what we might call Dos Passos-like transcription. Formally, the looseness of realism in its simple mimetic stage yields to the tightness of mimesis given a point and, finally, to the looseness of mimesis as the point itself. It is, in its way, breathtaking. How much Brown encompasses of what will come after him is extraordinary and has hardly ever been explored. But it has not, I would suggest, because the whole mimetic mode is one Brown does not value. It is one he sees as inauthoritative or, rather, authorized by a rhetorical surrender, a refusal to struggle to authorize the subject as well as the means of his reference. It is a refusal, indeed, to authorize the means as creating its subject, a refusal which he announces forthrightly rather than attempt to conceal it.

Thus, in *Ormond,* the narrator, Sophia Courtland, declares:

> You are anxious to obtain some knowledge of the history of Constantia Dudley. I am well acquainted with your motives, and allow that they justify your curiosity. I am willing, to the utmost of my power, to comply with your request, and will now dedicate what leisure I have to the composition of her story.
>
> My narrative will have little of that merit which flows from unity of design. You are desirous of hearing an authentic, and not a fictitious tale. It will, therefore, be my duty to relate events in no artificial or elaborate order, and without that harmonious congruity and luminous amplification, which might justly be displayed in a tale flowing merely from invention. It will be little more than a biographical sketch, in which the facts are distributed and amplified, not as a poetical taste would prescribe, but as the materials afforded me, sometimes abundant and sometimes scanty, would permit. (2.3)

Writing has become no more and no less than an imitation. More abundant where the incidents described are more abundant, scantier when the incidents are few, it exerts no force of its own, has no independent reality. Clara's intense sense of writing as burdensome is gone. The tale is told at Sophia's "leisure," and its irregularity is not even the result of her struggle to organize her report in accordance with the event, but because her report is nearly transparent to the event. And yet this "leisure," so far from Franklin's, does not belong to Sophia, but is what is left her when everything else is exhausted. It is not the condition of some thoughtfulness in which she reengages what she has seen. It is not some deliberation, a "second edition" of life in which what she reports will be enacted more consciously. But it is a sign of the inactivity which is all that remains. Sophia, as her name signifies—the "wisdom" of the story of Constantia, as we might say—*is* Constantia, but robbed of all identity. "I am well acquainted. . . ." "I am willing. . . ." "My narrative will have. . . ." And then, "It will therefore be my duty. . . ." "It will be little more than a biographical sketch. . . ." The "I" struggles reflexively with itself. It runs to stay in the same place, bending all its activity to become as inactive as it may. Autobiography becomes biography. "I am willing" yields to "It will." "I" becomes "it." As an "it" arising in the loss of "I," however, it is not a ground on which the "I" might establish itself on a firm footing, but a receding ground where all power to establish has been surrendered once and for all.

And so in *Edgar Huntly,* the "I" continues:

> I sit down, my friend, to comply with thy request. At length does the impetuosity of my fears, the transports of my wonder, permit me to recollect my promise and perform it. At length am I somewhat delivered from suspense and from tremors. At length the drama is brought to an imperfect close, and the series of events that absorbed my faculties, that hurried away my attention, has terminated in repose. (4.3)

What is the connection between the Huntly who narrates and the Huntly who is in the tale? What is the connection between Huntly now and Huntly then? Calm where the other is excited, "in repose" where the faculties of the other were "absorbed," Huntly now is not superior to Huntly then. He is not more tightly in control—one, say, who has learned from the conclusion of his experiences and understands them in their fullness—but one who reiterates them in dispassion. He is the present which a tale of the past has not so much produced as allowed to endure, the last remnant of an authorship disappeared into a tale concluding neither in a knowledge of anything new, nor, without anyone to author it again, in something that may be *re*newed. The old opposition between expressionism and formalism is not forsaken, but mooted, the tension frozen. On the one hand, as has been often noted, *Edgar Huntly* would seem to be the most organic of Brown's novels. In its forest setting, in the free reign it gives to dreams, realizing them even in the external events outside its characters' dreaming,[34] it is the most seemingly "natural," an expression of life rather than a construction after it. *Edgar Huntly* has fewer digressions than any of Brown's other narratives, fewer dependent independent stories. On one occasion, for the first time in Brown, I believe, we even get, in place of a story within a story, so-called free indirect discourse, in which the two narratives become merged (4.48). The tale moves inexorably forward. Plotting never interrupts plot, always furthers it. And yet, on the other hand, as Brown freely acknowledges, naturalness, organicity of this sort, is no more than a matter of a sort of naturalized craft, of precisely that adaptation of genre to event that is generally claimed for Brown but which, to him, only gives nature art's derivative status. The much quoted preface to *Edgar Huntly* announces the substitution of "Indian hostility and the perils of the western wilderness" for "Gothic castles and chimeras." These are materials which the author "has been ambitious of depicting in vivid and faithful colours." They are what "for a native of America to overlook . . . would admit of no apology." Nature is a gothic novel, reality the construction of art, and the writer, no longer its author, yields to a convention he has agreed to beyond any ability further to shape. It is true that his "success" still "must be estimated by the liberal and candid reader" (4.3). But it will be estimated according to standards thus already determined apart from any direct relation reader and writer may wish to build. Indeed, in *Arthur Mervyn,* it will be estimated by no one at all.

Arthur Mervyn presents certain textual difficulties. Part 1 was written and published before *Edgar Huntly,* part 2 after, and the first nine chapters of part 1 are among Brown's earliest productions.[35] Still, the various parts taken as a whole are notably a next stage, and taken sequentially constitute a movement toward a next stage, of Brown's career:

> I was resident in this city during the year 1793. Many motives contributed to detain me, though departure was easy and commodious, and my friends were generally solicitous for me to go. It is not my purpose to enumerate these motives, or to dwell on my present concerns and transactions, but merely to compose a narrative of some incidents with which my situation made me acquainted (3.5)

This is a "confession," the form that *Clara Howard* and *Jane Talbot* will take, and presumably the prelude to a revelation of soul. But it is a confession in which nothing is confessed, or rather which, while claiming to reveal the truth, simultaneously admits that the truth is a narration to which the narrator is largely irrelevant. Not the speaker's "motives," after all, not his "concerns and transactions" will be presented, but only his purpose "to compose a narrative." Telling remains the only being, writing the only living. But as writing no longer requires an author, it is difficult to establish what its real authority is. As William Spengemann has noted, the movement of *Arthur Mervyn* from Dr. Stevens' narrative, to Mervyn's own, to Mervyn writing a letter which is itself the text of *Arthur Mervyn* and so without any narrative frame, appears to be a movement toward life presenting itself.[36] And yet, if life is thus presentation, presenting no longer quite lives as it once did. We have, in Arthur's closing letter, not Franklin's letter to his son, not a correspondence simultaneously real and fictional. Nor do we have Clara's letter to her uncle, a fictive letter yet attached to, by attempting to recreate, the reality of Brown's prefatory letter to his audience. Rather it is a letter self-contained, neither authored nor even, for that matter, read—transcribed, as we have called it, but by the copyist Brown has become and to be no more than perused by the observers who now replace his once constitutive readership.

What I believe has happened is the fullest yielding of writing to what has been written. The gap opened up at the end of *Wieland* will be recalled. Narratives are no longer dependently independent of each other. They no longer must struggle to assert themselves on their own. They no longer need affirm, within the context of their continuation of the world authored in the novel before them, that the world is a function of their independent authorization as well. They find their place only too comfortably within prior narratives now taken as authorized already. Writing is not obliterated. Indeed, it takes over all. But it is placed beyond the writer whose activity it first was.

Toward the beginning of part 2 of *Arthur Mervyn* the story of Mrs. Villars and her three prostitute children is thus introduced: "There lived in a remote quarter of the city a woman, by name Villars, who passed for the widow of an English officer" (3.220–21). This sounds like the prelude to one of those independent dependent stories we discussed in *Wieland,* a story instigated by a demand of the book as a whole, yet constructed as if it were complete in itself. But the story of Mrs. Villars is not such a story. It does not, in fact, depend on the tale as a whole, nor yet, despite its elaborateness, does it insist on itself *as* whole. Neither disrupting the plot of *Arthur Mervyn* nor really contributing to it, the story, with all others like it, rather *is* the plot. There is, as it were, room for part 2 of *Arthur Mervyn* within part 1, whose reality is now seen as so capacious that it may include virtually everything inside itself. Of course, in a sense, the Villars story exists as a clarification of part 1. It is an elaboration of Welbeck's character: "A man like Welbeck . . . was the slave of depraved appetites. . . . Some accident introduced him to the knowledge of this family, and the youngest daughter found him a proper subject on which to exercise her artifices." It is an explanation of some earlier puzzles: "It was to the frequent demands made upon his purse, by this woman, that part of the embarrassments in which Mervyn found him involved, are to be ascribed," and "His silence, with regard to Clemenza's asylum, will not create surprise, when it is told that she was placed with Mrs. Villars" (3.221). But clarification or explanation is rather the excuse for this story than its cause. We might even say the story is of equal weight with what it explains, so that part 1 comes to seem to reside within part 2 as much as part 2 within part 1. We approach Franklinian particularity again, the existence of all parts as equal. But if equal they really are, their equality is based not on Franklinian rhetoric but on, as it were, the separation of rhetoric from the "rhetors," on the equidistance, we might say, of all parts from the reader and writer, who, having once supported everything, no longer can support anything. It is difference with a difference, it is true—it is equality—but not because audience and author make all equal, but because, no longer making any difference, all might as well be equal.

There is a remarkable scene, some pages later, which demonstrates the situation most fully. It is the scene in which one Mrs. Althorpe, a woman of good character known to Dr. Stevens, gives evidence of the generally bad repute in which Arthur is held, a long scene whose exquisite comic character, so rare in Brown, may offer some excuse for quoting at great length:

> I remember calling at their house one evening in the winter before last. It was intensely cold; and my father, who rode with me, having business with Sawney Mervyn, we stopped a minute at his gate; and, while the two old men were engaged in conversation, I begged leave to warm myself by the kitchen fire. Here, in the chimney-corner, seated on a block, I found Arthur busily engaged in *knitting stockings!* I thought this a whimsical employment for a young active man. I told him so, for I wanted to put him to the blush; but he smiled in my face, and answered, without the least discomposure, just as whimsical a business for a young active woman. Pray, did you never knit a stocking?
>
> Yes; but that was from necessity. Were I of a different sex, or did I possess the strength of a man, I should rather work in my field or study my book.
>
> Rejoice that you are a woman, then, and are at liberty to

pursue that which costs least labor and demands most skill. You see, though a man, I use your privilege, and prefer knitting yarn to threshing my brain with a book or the barn-floor with a flail.

I wonder, said I contemptuously, you do not put on the petticoat as well as handle the needle.

Do not wonder, he replied: it is because I hate a petticoat incumbrance as much as I love warm feet. Look there (offering the stocking to my inspection) is it not well done?

I did not touch it, but sneeringly said, excellent! I wonder you do not apprentice yourself to a taylor.

He looked at me with an air of ridiculous simplicity and said, how prone the woman is to *wonder.* You call the work excellent, and yet *wonder* that I do not make myself a slave to improve my skill! Did you learn needle-work from seven years' squatting on a taylor's board? Had you come to me, I would have taught you in a day.

I was taught at school.

And paid your instructor?

To be sure.

'Twas liberty and money thrown away. Send your sister, if you have one, to me, and I will teach her without either rod or wages. Will you?

You have an old and a violent antipathy, I believe, to any thing like a school.

True, it was early and violent. Had not you?

No. I went to school with pleasure; for I thought to read and write were accomplishments of some value.

Indeed? Then I misunderstood you just now. I thought you said, that, had you the strength of a man, you should prefer the plough and the book to the needle. Whence, supposing you a female, I inferred that you had a woman's love for the needle and a fool's hatred of books.

My father calling me from without, I now made a motion to go. Stay, continued he with great earnestness, throwing aside his knitting apparatus, and beginning in great haste to pull off his stockings. Draw these stockings over your shoes. They will save your feet from the snow while walking to your horse.

Half angry, and half laughing, I declined the offer. He had drawn them off, however, and holding them in his hand, be persuaded, said he; only lift your feet, and I will slip them on in a trice.

Finding me positive in my refusal, he dropped the stockings; and, without more ado, caught me up in his arms, rushed out of the room, and, running barefoot throught the snow, set me fairly on my horse. All was done in a moment, and before I had time to reflect on his intentions. He then seized my hand, and, kissing it with great fervor, exclaimed, a thousand thanks to you for not accepting my stockings. You have thereby saved yourself and me the time and toil of drawing on and drawing off. Since you have taught me to wonder, let me practice the lesson in wondering at your folly, in wearing worsted shoes and silk stockings at a season like this. Take my counsel, and turn your silk to worsted and your worsted to leather. Then may you hope for warm feet and dry. What! Leave the gate without a blessing on your counsellor?

I spurred my horse into a gallop, glad to escape from so strange a being. I could give you many instances of behaviour equally singular, and which betrayed a mixture of shrewdness and folly, of kindness and impudence, which justified, perhaps, the common notion that his intellects were unsound. Nothing was more remarkable than his impenetrability to ridicule and censure. You might revile him for hours, and he would listen to you with invincible composure. To awaken anger or shame in him was impossible. He would answer, but in such a way as to show him totally unaware of your true meaning. He would afterwards talk to you with all the smiling affability and freedom of an old friend. Every one despised him for his idleness and folly, no less conspicuous in his words than his actions; but no one feared him, and few were angry with him, till after the detection of his commerce with *Betty*, and his inhuman treatment of his father. (3.234–36)

Here, for perhaps the only time in Brown, is a scene that would seem to stand on its own merits in the perfect repose of being itself. Plotting has disappeared. The plot, not interrupted, becomes no longer an overarching shape, but the very event, the undoubted deed. Subtle discrimination replaces the tension of independent dependence, a nuanced attention to detail the pulls of conflicting interpretation. Nothing in the scene is to be thrown out, neither yielding romantically to some greater truth that will reconstruct it, nor yielding neoclassically to some lesser truth that will reduce it. Everything is what it is and is savored as such. The contradictory poles of Mervyn's character are resolved in no ultimate explanation of him, but constitute his character themselves. The scene is so perfectly mimetic as to go beyond mimesis. Here we behold not the author's version of the world, but the world itself.

Yet how, we must ask, is such a scene possible in Brown? How has he become capable of comedy? How has it come to pass that people now talk in tones recognizable as theirs rather than in the single tone of Charles Brockden Brown? And, indeed, we must answer, because Charles Brockden Brown—*as* Charles Brockden Brown—has given himself up. Continuing the submerging process we have noted, author and audience are surrendered to the work, are dramatized in it, in a dialogue, a little play where a speaker and a listener communicate with each other directly. This communication does not appear to be written or read. The trick of realism, precisely, is to make us forget about reading and writing. For a moment Brown makes us forget. Perhaps he forgets himself. His comic acceptance, he supposes, is critical insight. His powerlessness, he imagines, is power, after all. The first professional American writer becomes an English writer. And yet he remains an American writer, and the proof is how derivatively English his last "realistic" works are.

Clara Howard, significantly, is not introduced by the author. The justification for presenting the story that we have seen given in Brown's other works by one of the characters as a duplication of Brown's own justification, here wholly supplants Brown's justification, appearing both in the place of the author's advertisement and in the story proper as a repetition of itself. In *Jane Talbot,* both introductions are lacking. The unauthored work proceeds apace. Still, authorship has not been forgotten, and its presence as the uninvoked standard of his writing remains in the near universal judgment that *Clara Howard* and *Jane Talbot* are tediously conventional.[37] Their "realistic" pretense of transparency to life is revealed as transparency to other fiction. Their claim to imitate living is granted, but the writing which living still remains is no longer quite true. Brown compares unfavorably with the Richardson he could once so fearlessly cite without danger of imitation at all. As we have said, only when writing is, finally, owned, only when it is authored in however problematical a rhetorical situation, will the question of imitation be forestalled. And, indeed, in his final unpublished works, the fragmentary *The History of Carsol* and *The History of the Carrils and Ormes,* Brown shoulders the burden of authorship once again. He owns his writing. Only now, shielding ownership from that professionalism in the intensity of which it broke down, he refuses, as it were, to broadcast it. As we shall see in Melville, who develops it with characteristic energy, the issue of nonpublication for a nonreadership will return to trouble American literature. Meanwhile, however, we may note something more immediate, Brown's recapitulation in *Carsol* and *Ormes* of his early interest in utopia. The indiscriminate blend of fiction and fact in these works, indeed, even led Brown's first modern scholars to date them as early.[38] They are, however, late work, skeptically utopian, if not exactly abandoning what Warner Berthoff, arguing for their late date, calls Godwinian dreams of cultural reformation, yet, as we might say, holding them in abeyance. Berthoff, still bound to a mimetic theory of development, does not get it quite right. As he puts it, the work "indicates that the good society is not to be created by some philosophically superior theory or plan of government but by an animating cultural unity, shared, diffused, instinctual, without which no constitution or government can hold together."[39] I would say rather that cultural unity in America, as Franklin makes clear, depends, however, not on instinct but on an authorship universally granted. And because, after Franklin, authorship of this sort no longer is possible, it may exist only underground or, more interestingly, in myth. It may exist, that is, as we may now proceed to discuss it in Cooper, only as it emerges from the retreat of an authorship that would yet publish itself once more.

3   Cooper's Myth

At a particularly awkward juncture of a plot nowhere smooth, Cooper, in *The Prairie,* finds that "in order to preserve an even pace between the incidents of the tale, it becomes necessary to revert to such events as occurred during the ward of Ellen Wade." It is a sort of flashback, though of no one in particular—of the narrative consciousness, we should like to call it, were it not that unconsciousness seems more appropriate a description of a writer so bound even to the flaws in his narrative as to conceive of them with the inevitability of "it becomes necessary." Cooper is explaining why the camp to which Ishmael and Esther return is empty, beginning with Ellen's preparation for defense against its imminent attack:

> It was a fearful moment for Ellen. Looking around at the juvenile and frightened flock that pressed upon the skirts of her garments, she endeavored to recall to her confused faculties some one of the many tales of female heroism with which the history of the western frontier abounded. In one a stockade had been successfully defended by a single man, supported by three or four women, for days, against the assaults of a hundred enemies. In another, the women alone had been able to protect the children, and the less valuable effects of their absent husbands; and a third was not wanting, in which a solitary female had destroyed her sleeping captors and given liberty not only to herself, but to a brood of

helpless young. This was the case most nearly assimilated to the situation in which Ellen now found herself; and, with flushing cheeks and kindling eyes, the girl began to consider, and to prepare her slender means of defence. (Chap. 14)[1]

This is an only too typical passage in Cooper. Instead of the rendering of an experience in its particularity, we get a kind of meditation on the particular's relation to other experiences no more fully rendered. Instead of the event itself, we get an abstraction away from the event, displacing the expected fast-paced adventure into a network that constitutes the adventure story in general. We might almost, in the modern mode, be tempted to say that Cooper's work is especially self-reflexive. Cooper is concerned to place not Ellen, but himself. He is portraying not her constraints, but his own in attempting to portray her. And yet an evident lack of reflection—that unconsciousness, we have said, in which the story's necessity is framed—rather collapses the frame into the portrait, in effect denying Cooper any position from which to reflect at all. "Cooper" wavers between being a subject and an object here. Or, to stay closer to the terms of the Ellen passage, he seems too thoroughly unconcerned with the very difference between himself and Ellen that makes us want to say his description of her is a displacement in the first place. Representing Ellen's life, he does not notice that the language he uses is appropriate, rather, only to his life. Writing a fiction, he yet writes as if autobiographically, unaware that the autobiography of a writer is marked as sufficiently unique—a matter of the profession of writing—to render it, in our eyes at least, as but a specialized sort of life.

Let us say that there is a difference between our eyes and Cooper's, a distance between us and him. Or rather, to accept the difference, taking it too as what we see when we look at Cooper, let us say there is a distance within Cooper, putting him under the sign of a question, dividing him, so that it must seem as if he were separate from himself as well. Is Cooper conscious or unconscious, and why does the issue of consciousness even come up? Is Cooper's life his own, or does he live vicariously, describing the lives of others or even describing his own life become, now an other? Selfhood is compromised, finding itself no longer guaranteed, but divided, by other selves. Community is no longer a community of individuals. For individuals communicate across a gap that may be bridged but at the very risk of individuality. "This was the case most nearly assimilated to the situation in which Ellen now found herself": "assimila*ted*," not assimil*able*, as if such effort as is required to make one life available to another need hardly be noted. And yet that the effort *is* noted, that it remains, and attached to the life that is being made available, suggests the almost proprietary interest of one self in another that is required for availability to be established. "A third [tale] was not wanting": tales, that is, are everywhere, and an appropriate one, more or less, will always be found. And yet Cooper's formalization of life as a tale which may be appropriated in the first place is his acceptance of the division between lives even in his act of overcoming it.

The well-known tale of the beginning of Cooper's career will be recalled, and it will be recalled, too, that it is almost too well known, known even unattached to Cooper, as the tale of the beginning of almost any author's career.[2] Reading, one evening, an English novel to his wife, he complained, "I believe I could write a better myself." And so he tried, and encouraged by his wife to finish and then publish it, he was launched. Here is our dilemma redoubled. Is this the story of Cooper the artist, or is it the story of the artist in general? And even if it is Cooper's story, then is not Cooper installed as Cooper by his act of appropriating to himself—as one who could write more perfectly, a "better" version as he calls it—a writing he acknowledges is properly beyond the self? Tales are no longer, in the Franklinian mode, exemplary. They no longer, that is, sustain each other's individuality. And if they are not yet—as we shall see they become in the more rigorously formalistic mode of an Edgar Allan Poe— quite in opposition to each other, still a certain tension between them is evident, stabilized in a mediate category, the store of "tales . . . of the western frontier" in which they are conceptualized. Tales circulate, still freely enough. But they circulate within bounds to which they must always refer. They are bounds generated in the continued problematization of authorship, in authorship as it becomes a problem, an issue to be thought, nor any longer, as in Brown, to be unthought, resulting in a kind of writing neither quite individual nor quite communal and whose limits we must take it as our task, now, to map.

I. "Our National Novelist"

As everyone knows, Cooper was America's first truly national artist. Far more than Brown, he was recognized as the literary voice of his new country. Writing in an even more intensely nationalistic period than Brown, or at least in a period when the nationalism that had already spilled over into letters was reaching its high-water mark, he became the first professional novelist in America actually to make a financial go of his work. His early popularity was immense, and even after he had suffered some serious reverses, after he had fallen from popular favor, he was recognized as the one really "American" American writer. "Our national novelist" was what Melville, most people's current choice for the title, called him, "the most thoroughly national," in Francis Parkman's words, a man whose "Americanism . . . would move us to forgive him all his faults, were they twice as many," said William Gilmore Simms. He was "a Leaves of Grass man," said Walt Whitman, a particularly interesting remark, for it suggests an identification of writer and reader even some fifty years after the period in which we have said it was breaking down.[3] And yet, is there not something more than a little odd in this unanimity about Cooper's speaking for us? Melville, the ardent democrat, finds himself in the quasi-Federalist sympathizer; Parkman, the Indian reviler, in the popularizer of the noble savage; Simms, the Southern separatist, in the Northern Union man; Whitman, the carpenter and journalist, in the writer for whom the lowness of tradesmen and positive baseness of journalists was a constant theme. The insistence of Cooper's nation on his Americanness, its single-mindedness in maintaining that this is what Cooper ought to be praised for—to this day when many otherwise do not praise him at all—renders the judgment problematical. And, indeed, it was Cooper's vaunted Americanness that was itself the cause of his public's finding fault with him, as he, and they, seemed to take him rather too seriously as American, as "national."

Let us, before undertaking a wider investigation of the works proper, before, especially, dealing with the novels by which he is most remembered, briefly analyze the crucial turn in Cooper's reputation. The disfavor into which he fell is extraordinary considering his early celebrity and is therefore a kind of crux. Most usually, it is explained as the result of an ill-advised five-year sojourn abroad he made at the height of his fame, a belated grand tour he took along with his family and extended beyond any ordinary term. His nation felt abandoned. He lost his feel for America. He cut himself off from his sources and thus lost much of his power.[4] This is a popular Americanist argument. In reference to writers of the nineteenth century alone roughly the same case has been made against Washington Irving before Cooper and against Hawthorne and Henry James after.[5] It is an argument which reads literature against the background of history, which sees the literature of America as American because it proceeds from the history of America. From the perspective of an Americanism more integrated than the traditional one, however, such an argument does not go to the heart of the matter. For if expatriation is the trouble, it is rather an internal expatriation, an alienation of the writer from his country that takes place as it were within writing, perhaps corroborated by, but never dependent on, some physical remove. In the case of Cooper, indeed, he never ceased to speak as American even, and most especially, when he was abroad. If his distance from his community is particularly easy to point to in his later novels, it is yet present even in his most applauded early work, becoming perhaps more manifest only because his years abroad focused attention on his being our chief American novelist, because they made him rather more, than less, American.

In 1826, then, Cooper traveled to Europe. Already famous on both sides of the Atlantic, he sailed from New York not just to see the world, but to confront it, to present to the Old World, in his formidable person, the New World of letters it had too lightly assumed was too young yet, or perhaps ever, to amount to anything it would have to reckon with. The send-off he was given was a veritable commission, and armed as an unofficial ambassador with letters of introduction to all the literary lights of Europe, armed more officially with a nonpaying commission as a consul in France, he seems to have been almost too true to what he conceived were his responsibilities. Tirelessly he defended his country against slights, real and imagined. "I would strenuously urge on every American who really loves the institutions of his country, never to make any concessions to mere politeness, on these topics, when actually required to say anything in England," he says in *Gleanings in England*.[6] And in Paris, as his friend S. F. B. Morse notes, "he is courted by the greatest and most aristocratic, yet . . . he never compromises the dignity of an American citizen, which he contends is the highest distinction a man can have in Europe."[7] When he persisted, however, arguing against even so manifestly irrelevant a French claim as that democracy was more expensive than monarchy, he ran into trouble with the very American paid to be America's American abroad, the real ambassador to France, who diplomatically had held his peace in response to the French claim, choosing silence over a pointless argument. A scandal ensued, as newspapers in the States played the incident up, the ostensible beginning of Cooper's troubles, but in terms that suggest a more fundamental difficulty. For Cooper was attacked, ironically enough, on the score of a want of proper patriotism, and he counterattacked in the same terms. Gone abroad to defend America, he was accused, as he saw it, by those who had stayed at home but to truckle to Europe. And so, faced with his first really bad American review of a novel, *The Bravo*—whose burden was, in fact, a critique of Europe—he assumed it was a surreptitious translation of a politically motivated French review. It was as if Cooper felt so fully the American that he could not accept any criticism of him as itself American. To his contemporaries, it seemed as if he were trying to play the hero, to deny to his comrades in nationalist arms any power of their own and engross the field of the battle for America to himself.

This engrossing, of course, has its positive side. It is a kind of glory not unappreciated, especially today. Bryant, in his "discourse" at the Cooper Memorial, the great celebration held to honor Cooper after his death, tells, admiringly, this story, again the kind of story likely to be told about any author in general, but to which Cooper lends himself so well: "A gentleman who had returned from Europe just before the death of Cooper, was asked what he found the people of the Continent doing. 'They are all reading Cooper,' he answered." And, similarly, Longfellow remarked that in some countries of Europe, where American letters were hardly known, Cooper was "almost the sole representative of our literature."[8] Yet the potential hostility of these stories, the competitiveness they imply, ought not to go uninvestigated. I take Longfellow's word—"representative"—to be the key term, here, reading "sole representative" as an oxymoron which highlights the problematical "difference with a difference" that American writers cling to even as it breaks down. For although, from Franklin through Brown to Cooper, a steady disruption of America's community of individuals is evident, a more and more intensive effort to repair it may be traced as well.

As we have seen, Franklin's writing was his living. If his book was American, it was not because it somehow spoke for America, but because its author, himself an American, was authorized by his fellow Americans to write it. It was exemplary, as we have said. It did not represent Americans, but guaranteed them. It was the life of one of them whose telling in turn authorized their own. In Brown, already, exemplariness is no longer so certain. It must be maintained in the teeth of becoming mere eccentricity. Brown's books, no more than Franklin's, speak for America. But the activity of their author, threatening to be of only professional concern, is extended—at least while he still remains an author—at the price of a certain intensity, a pressure on his readers to join him, which formerly did not have to be exerted. In Cooper, accordingly, exemplariness becomes "representativity." The individual and his community are brought together by making such pressure the very principle of identity. Cooper, becoming more than one with his community, would replace his community with himself. He remains an individual, the author of a series of novels, but his individuality consists in his more than anyone else *being* everyone else. Cooper would wage a lifelong battle with his readers. Needing them, but only so that he might speak for them, attacking them, but thereby undermining his very authority for attack, he would struggle to extend his own rights over the public's rights in a writing that kept holding him back.[9] A division opens up in the heart of writing. Writing is in competition with itself. The self, once public, is public still, but at war with the public and so with itself.

We have said that Cooper was "our national novelist." But it should come as no surprise, now, to note that his other, equally current epithet, and one he always hated, was "the American Walter Scott." First and foremost, he is simultaneously secondary and derivative. Even his Americanness is defined in terms of its opposite, someone else's Englishness. These are couplings new to the democratic writing we have been tracing, but they are to be expected. The self, no longer authorized by other selves, would take their place. The dream of the equality of writers, of the obliteration of origins such that every writer is equal to every other, is under increasing strain. The writer is not even equal to himself.

II. Genre

Let us approach the problem squarely. In what, precisely, does Cooper's acclaimed Americanness consist? If we acknowledge, with everyone else, that he is our representative, where does his representativity lie, in what characteristic, what body, even, is it located? The ambiguity of Melville's phrase, "our national novelist," is apposite. Is this merely a metonym? Is it the writings that Melville is praising, using the name of their author as shorthand notation, or is it Cooper, the author himself? For a confusion between the man and his writing is everywhere in his praise, suggesting they both are and are not divided. Cooper's Americanness is difficult to localize. It floats remarkably unmoored to any of the usual anchors. On the one hand, his writing is not expressively American, is not the style or temperament of a man American as if, somehow, by spirit. All the obvious things we might point to are easily dispensed with. His neoclassicism is too English, his picturesqueness too international to take very seriously, and his style proper is notoriously awkward and muddy, too simply incompetent to be national, international, or anything but dismissable. On the other hand, neither is Cooper's Americanness to be found in the secure and formal concerns of American subject matter. His novels of social observation are conceded by all to be his worst,[10] and more generally, whether writing with social observation especially in mind or not, he was peculiarly slack about detail. Vagueness and generality, rather, cutting him off from direct dependence on the realities of America, from America conceived of as a reality expressed within or referred to as outside his writing, mark his writing as American in what we might call a purely discursive manner. Cooper's Americanness, that is, is a function of writing, though writing hard pressed, still a making of America rather than an expressing or reporting of it. But it is a making of it in a field that has opened up between the poles of expression and reference and from which Cooper could not quite escape.

To put this in other terms, we may describe Cooper's nationality more closely as an extraordinary categorical power. It is a power operating at the level of what in literature is called genre, of form for better, of formulae for worse. Cooper was, in fact, America's great genre giver. Author of the first American sea story, the first American historical romance, the first western, he established the conventions which American novelists after him could not help but follow. But more, with his light ladies and dark ladies, his America and England, his land and sea, white man and red man, culture and nature, he established conventions he would himself be doomed, over thirty-two long and sometimes dreary novels, to repeat. The generic quality of Cooper's writing is thus not, like Brown's so-called gothic, merely the function of belated critical analysis, to be established only after the fact. It is the result not of comparing one group of novels with another group, one novel with another novel, but of comparison become constitutive of any particular novel taken individually as well. For in genre, every particular of writing would claim the status of writing in the abstract, every word placed before the reader claim the generality of all the words that might be placed before him. A pattern of standing in opens up, spreading out against all that Cooper produced. It is the projection of the writer's representative relation to his community onto the field in which he is representative and, indeed, creating the field as a separate entity. Writing achieves a certain density. It draws a circle about itself. Writing is no longer, as it was in Franklin, one with living. Even more than in Brown, it is a profession. And yet this profession, as but writing professionalized, is even yet not dependent on some history prior to it. For genre's authority is not in its lying outside writing, but in its being able to be written, lying as it does only beyond the writing of the moment.

Let us consider, as a beginning, Cooper's first novel, *Precaution*. It is not much discussed in Cooper criticism. A domestic romance in the manner of *Persuasion,* perhaps, or some lesser production, it is usually dismissed as too imitative, too conventional—in effect too un-Cooper-like—to read as part of his more serious oeuvre.[11] Conventionality, as we have seen, however, should not be dismissed in Cooper, and I should say *Precaution*'s failure to be Cooper-like is the result as much of its not being, in a sense, conventional enough—of its generic quality not penetrating sufficiently to its core—as of its being conventional at all. In effect, *Precaution* gives us our ammunition against it. Despite its really remarkable fluidity for a first novel, the smoothness and sureness with which its elaborate complications are handled, its manifest attempt to match some model of the English novel in general prevents us from reading it as a writing really continuous with Cooper. And yet it refuses to make matching a thoroughly pervasive matter either, indeed hides the matching in almost every particular of its construction. The setting is English, the plot turns on the structure of the English aristocracy, every single character is English, and the author, speaking of "our" things as the things of England, even pretends that he and his reader are English. The book might as well be English. But although it is not, that Americanness which, had Cooper frankly owned his attempt to reach England, would have displayed itself, is never even hinted at. In effect, *Precaution* prevents us from reading it as what we might call authentically imitative. It suggests the inadequacy of writing after a model. But it is inadequate, too, because it does not take the further step of declaring that modeling is its especial mark, that this novelist makes modeling his particular pride. Accordingly, in the genuinely Cooper-like novels that follow *Precaution,* the ones that first established his reputation, competition is asserted openly and as constitutive.

Already in *The Spy,* Cooper's second book, we have a kind of coming clean, the sordid business of professional jealousy openly avowed and so converted into the honesty of writing in a declined rhetorical situation. *The Spy* is "A Tale of the Neutral Ground," clearly Scott's "neutral ground," which in turn is itself the object of competition, like the border territory of his next novel, *The Pioneers,* and the seacoast of the next, *The Pilot,* betwixt and between, "Afloat and Ashore," as the title of a late novel has it, and so on throughout his career. As he tells us of *The Pilot,* whose title itself challenges Scott's *The Pirate,* he would show Scott up. It is "A Tale of the Sea" that he writes, a subtitled kind of tale like every one of Cooper's novels but *The Monikins,* at the least like *The Pioneers* "A Descriptive Tale," but always competitive, always generic, and defining even seeming description as categorical.[12] To quote at greater length:

> It would have been hypercritical to object to the Pirate, that it was not strictly nautical, or true in its details; but, when the reverse was urged as a proof of what, considering the character of other portions of the work, would have been most extraordinary attainments, it was a sort of provocation to dispute the seamanship of the Pirate, a quality to which the book has certainly very little just pretension. The result of this conversation was a sudden determination to produce a work which, if it had no other merit, might present truer pictures of the ocean and ships than any that are to be found in the Pirate. (Preface)

Reality is a function of competition. It does not found writing, but is what writing, grown competitive, must pretend to in order to

authorize itself. Cooper may well have been, at least among novelists, something of a nautical expert. But as Robert Grossman,
perhaps his most responsive general reader, has noted, no non-
seaman could possibly understand the bulk of what Cooper, in his
sea-speak, was talking about.[13] His descriptions do not let us see
anything; they beat us into submission. Not verisimilitude but
power is their net effect. Competition, displacement—of other
writers, of the reader, of himself—is everywhere.

Mark Twain's wonderful remark that Cooper "saw through a
glass eye darkly," is very much to the point.[14] As Twain charged,
Cooper did not observe. He wrote "romances," as they are usually called, and this absence of realism results in our disbelief.
"Cooper does not convince," as Twain put it. It is important to
note, however, that Cooper seems actually to court such noncon-
viction. His lack of realism is almost, we should say, deliberate, at
any rate so thoroughly a part of what Cooper is that calling it a
lack is to give away the game in advance. It is to measure Cooper
from a perspective that simply has no standing. It matters very
little that Cooper, in what are generally regarded his most important novels, was writing about what he seems, historically speaking, to know. In some of his least he was, too. Rather, his
importance lies in his refusal to give what he knows—indeed,
especially what he knows—weight, his refusal to derive himself
from it. Cooper always argued that his works, whatever their
appearance, were not based on his life. But this is not to say that
he meant they were unreal. It is only that reality is not yet sufficiently alienated for him to know, that his life has not precipitated
out of his writing. He never "endeavored to delineate myself in
any character of any book I ever wrote."[15] For a "real" Cooper, an
unwritten Cooper, is not Cooper at all. Or rather, it is a failed
Cooper, the writer thrust outside his writing and in danger of
losing himself.

Quite simply, Cooper would not base his authority on anything
he might merely portray. He would not found the writer's identity
on what he identifies. For such an ungeneric conception of identity, admittedly uniting the world and the self, yet thereby allows
that the self's world might be something other than what it writes.
Thus Cooper could not so easily put off his borrowed glasses. He

could not stop modeling himself on England. In effect, as Twain implies, he could not really become himself. His lesson, however, is that, in the condition of writing as he found it, a self become itself in disregard of modeling would not be an American self at all. And his problem is, rather, to assert *his* power of modeling against his community's in a situation where the community has asserted that all models are its own. This is a situation in which the writer is always in danger of losing himself, in which to describe himself is to alienate himself in a language he can never quite possess. But it is a situation unlike description outside of modeling, in which the self described would be alienated beyond even the struggle to possess it. Such a self would be beyond the writer's ability to do anything about it but copy it. It would be an imposed self, always determined in advance, tyrannical—in plain, undemocratic. And, in fact, this is precisely the lesson of such overt essays on democracy as *A Letter to His Countryman* or, more especially, *The American Democrat* proper. These, presumably, are genuine descriptions of "reality." They are writing in a purely referential sense, unlike even Brown's *Alcuin* or his utopia, outside our more literary concerns. Most of the critical evaluation of them has, in fact, come from Cooper scholars like Robert Spiller and Dorothy Waples, more interested in Cooper the political and social analyst than Cooper the novelist.[16] And yet the descriptiveness we find in them is severely compromised by Cooper, lest it endanger the very democracy that, presumably, he would describe.

It is tempting to compare *The American Democrat* with Tocqueville's *Democracy in America.*[17] Written only three years after Tocqueville, like it an ostensibly analytic work on the American political system, certainly no defense, though generally favorable, it confirmed public opinion of Cooper's incorrigible Europeanness. It sealed his community's opinion of his hostility to it, of which we have spoken, though, as we are likely to see it today, its tone is rather more like Tocqueville's objectivity than hostility. Still, with Cooper, unlike Tocqueville, we cannot find any secure harbor from the problematic of authorship in the presumably "objective." However sympathetic the Frenchman, however distant the

American, they do not meet in some impassive middle distance. It does not even matter how many opinions the two men shared, that they both, for example, detested the press, both feared the mass. Cooper was, no matter what he said, an insider, and though he might thrust himself outside, he remained inside to the end. The result was more than greater subjectivity on Cooper's part. Subjectivity, with objectivity, is a possibility arising only in the assumption of descriptiveness that Cooper challenges. And so Cooper's hostility to America in these works is not to be contrasted to his earlier identification with it, but is spread out within his identification, which remains inescapable. America is no external reality to be described more or less objectively, but is recaptured as writing after all.

We may note, for example, the judiciousness of *The American Democrat,* so evidently foregrounded as, in effect, to modalize itself. Cooper would be accurate, unbiased, or, at least, he would not let his bias interfere with his descriptiveness. But judiciousness, taking the form of a striking balance—between praise and criticism, attack and defense—is more than mere accuracy but, as we have called it, virtually generic. Everywhere there is an effort at distinction, at "just discrimination" or "rigid analysis"[18] or the like, a breaking down, that is, of the whole into its parts, but only to put the parts back together in a manner that threatens to obliterate them again. America, Cooper maintains in an effort at precision typical of the book, is not the people who live in it, but the several states who adopted the Constitution and who, in turn, have peoples of their own. And yet neither are these peoples quite themselves, for they are but that portion of the populace granted voting rights by the governments of the states, which in turn are not quite sovereign either, having submitted in law and in fact precisely to America as a unified political entity.[19] Cooper goes down the ladder only to go up it again. Distinctions firmly made are made only to dissolve. The individual, who is no longer his community, must struggle eternally with the community he would become. This is the situation of Cooper's own representativity. And, in fact, the notable absence in this context precisely of any portrait of such a representative is a sign of Cooper's dilemma.

This is one of the most startling features of *The American Democrat*. For on the face of it, as an analysis of the American system and not at all of its inhabitants, its title, like *Democracy in America*, should equally have referred to the system. And yet the title, quite otherwise, exposes an America*n*, Cooper himself, who thus seems bent on concealing and revealing himself simultaneously. Who or what is "The American Democrat"? Is it the book or its author? Rather, the author has begun to separate out of the book, which, if it is a system, is rather a systematization *of* the author. I would say the title is the beginning of the emergence of description out of a writing essentially nondescriptive. It is an as yet obtrusive hiding of his authorship that will produce, however, when Cooper has hidden it more completely, no longer Cooper after all, but Ned Effingham of *Homeward Bound* and *Home as Found* or Corny Littlepage of the rent-strike novels. These are not representative democrats, but democrats represented—that is, Cooper othered as an object *to* be represented—thus destroying the very democracy they are meant to describe. The writer is removed from any active role in creating democracy. He does not make his world *in* writing, for writing, now, is but the reporting of a world as it were already made, a world constituted as something of which the writer *as* writer is no longer a part. Writing, we might say, is what we called, in our discussion of Franklin, naturalized. It would authorize itself as proceeding from what the writer does not write. As Cooper's writing reminds us, however, it proceeds still from the writer who is in danger of being displaced by nature, and whose battle with naturalization we may, accordingly, describe more fully.

III. The "Nature" of America

Let us look more closely at Ned Effingham, as Cooper sums him up in a passage in *Homeward Bound:*

> Edward Effingham was a singularly just-minded man, and having succeeded at an early age to his estate, he had lived many years in that intellectual retirement which, by withdrawing him

from the strifes of the world, had left a cultivated sagacity to act freely on a natural disposition. At the period when the entire republic was, in substance, exhibiting the disgraceful picture of a nation torn by adverse factions, that had their origin in interests alien to its own; when most were either Englishmen or Frenchmen, he had remained what nature, the laws, and reason intended him to be, an American. Enjoying the *otium cum dignitate* on his hereditary estate, and in his hereditary abode, Edward Effingham, with little pretensions to greatness, and with many claims to goodness, had hit the line of truth which so many of the "godlikes" of the republic, under the influence of their passions, and stimulated by the transient and fluctuating interests of the day, entirely overlooked, or which, if seeing, they recklessly disregarded. (Chap. 5)

Here is the representative of America presented overtly as a "nature," the democrat as democratic almost, we might say, by aristocratic right. For Effingham's Americanness is guaranteed by "the laws" and "reason" as one. It is carried in his "hereditary estate," where heredity, no doubt still to be understood largely as a matter of rank and social position, has yet begun, even in 1838, to slip over a kind of Darwinian line. In Effingham culture has in effect become natural, democracy become hereditary. And they have precisely because of a certain sacrifice in Effingham, a sacrifice, indeed, *of* Effingham, who, in fact, does not really exist except as what remains after any trait that might be particular to him is removed. An American by virtue of his steadiness and calm, his Americanness is what is left when "faction," "interest," "passion"—all that goes into making any individual American—disappear. In the condition of representativity, that is, it is some general "other" that is made responsible for the self. And this other is no self itself, either, for only as an other can it resist the necessity of appealing to yet an other again. The individual, democrat though he be, is authorized no longer in his individuality, but in terms of a generality to which he must always refer. Expression is no longer of him, but of a him problematized. "He" is to be no longer taken unquestioningly, but forced into appealing to what lies outside him. Representativity becomes representation, and Twain is not after all wrong in faulting Cooper for what he sees as mimetic inadequacy. It is only that Twain follows the logic of Cooper's position—follows it as if it were a logic—further along than Cooper, still committed to the self, wished to go. It is that he reads Cooper in the light of his own greater alienation as a writer, his greater difficulty in imagining that community of individuals, as we have called it, in which Cooper for all his wavering still took his stand. In Twain, to write is to go into exile.[20] It is to speak the self in a language that denies the self. But exile is something to which Cooper has not quite yet been banished, or from which, if he has, he is always in the process of a certain return.

To put this another way, if Cooper is in the position of Ned Effingham—the position, as we have said, of a general man robbed of all his particularity—yet still living his writing, he makes such generality particularly his. Describing his position, he makes it *his* position—his position because *he* describes it. Cooper is no Franklin, nor even Brown, writing rhetorically, authorized to write *as* an American rather than because America is what he writes about. But he is no Tocqueville either, a European outside America and authorized to write by his total alienation from what he writes about, given a kind of scientific prestige under the name description. Instead, outside America and inside it, descriptive *and* rhetorical, Cooper is fallen into a kind of rhetoric of description. As we have said, his language is naturalized. Yet even nature, though it figures prominently in Cooper, figures as his "theme," not his object—as something writing is about which is admittedly not coterminous with writing, but which is yet not something autonomous and merely to be uncovered *by* writing either. Nature, in Cooper, is not meaningful in itself. But as a theme, it is meaningful by virtue of its disposition within a field of themes. It is meaningful not *as* nature, but in its relation to culture, a relation as it were preceding nature and culture, instrumentalizing them—if not, as in Franklin, entirely denying them any positivity, yet allowing them just such positivity as the author who "relates" them may yet claim for an instrument of his own.

As the Leatherstocking, appearing as Natty Bumppo in *The Pioneers,* after the massive bird kill, responds to Judge Temple's program of legislation designed "to put an end to this work of destruction": "Put an ind, Judge, to your clearings. An't the woods His work as well as the pigeons?" (Chap. 22). Neither nature nor culture exists independently here. For it is not nature that civilization opposes but itself, which it divides into civilization proper, as what is allowed by law, and nature, which is rather civilization acting outside its law. Nature and culture, that is, come into being together, in relation from the start. They are not objects in themselves, but the product of a kind of objectification of a world no longer at one with itself. This world has its representative—Natty Bumppo—who, though he has saved the Judge's daughter from a panther and a forest fire, must yet be punished for having killed a deer out of season. But thus his representativity, also, is instrumental, born out of society's confrontation with its divisions, the too ready acceptance or too facile resolution of which, by contrast, characterizes nearly all the other so-called American writers of Cooper's era.

To take two of the most popular "national" novelists also much read in Cooper's day, William Gilmore Simms and John Pendleton Kennedy: their "theme" would appear to be nature too. Their stories, like Cooper's, are about man in the wilderness, and with Cooper, if not so profusely, they were celebrated as helping to give America a distinctive literature. Yet their America is not, after all, theirs. For if it is not exactly nature's, it belongs to a nature and culture compounded as parts of a nature which, describe it as they will, they may not possess. Kennedy and Simms are regionalists, something Cooper could not be even when he attempts to be particular about locale. For the regionalist describes but a particular part of what he knows is whole already, and accordingly he may seize indifferently on the characteristics of his region—call them natural or cultural characteristics—in the full faith that they are equally sources of power. The work of the regionalist is always convincing. But that is because he has turned over to what is not him all possibility of being convincing or, where he would be convincing himself, because he would resolve his dependence on his region in a kind of naturalization that becomes almost theological.

For example, as an instance of the first case, there is Kennedy's best-known work, *Horse-Shoe Robinson,* for all its charm—and bulk—a distinctly minor effort.[21] It is a novel of the Revolutionary War set in Tory country in South Carolina, a perfect "neutral" ground, as Cooper called his similarly disputed territory in New York State in *The Spy.* The neutral qualities are never exploited, however, for competition over the area is rather stabilized by description of the area as, in effect, a kind of home for competition. The grand portraits of the landscape on which the story takes place do not simply set the scene for conflict but contain conflict in scene: this field is where history took shape. A double containment occurs. Historical division is contained by culture, the stability of whose present fixes history, turning it into a matter of but antiquarian interest. And cultural division is contained by nature, in whose massy otherness culture, however conflicted, finds its outermost limit. The consequences are most evident in the figure of Horse-Shoe Robinson himself. A figure not unlike Cooper's own Leatherstocking, a wise but primitive irregular in the army, he is a border figure potentially pivotal in the nature-culture opposition. And yet, nothing is made of him. He is no representative figure, not even a fallen or represented representative. For no conflict exists which might generate representativity. Kennedy too fully accepts his division from his writing, and the result is that even the division within his writing is presented not as *his* division, but as a reflection of an order outside him. The novel is skillfully done. Fact and fiction are delightfully interwoven, the daring adventures of the characters threaded around documented historical events. But Kennedy is so careful not to upset history with adventure that he subordinates adventure, and even document, *to* event. Writing may be reporting or it may be a kind of decoration. But in either case, it is secondary to a world over which it is powerless. Horse-Shoe is a quaint regional character that Kennedy has copied. Or, if he is the author's still, a part of Kennedy's writing after all, he is a made-up hero we need not take seriously.

More dangerous is the case of Simms. Simms *was* a serious writer, and he claimed much for writing, most notably in his famous preface to *The Yemassee,* a novel about the Indian uprising of 1715, where he gives the American romance epic status.[22] Yet by "epic" Simms does not mean the rhetorical writing we have been tracing, but fiction as a universal fact. In a certain sense nature is acculturated, rather than culture naturalized, for the venue of the uprising does not contain it, as in Kennedy, but is made significant *by* it. And yet culture, thus enlarged, is not culture at all, for the job of the romancer is to use culture as an instance of humanity conceived in a kind of acultural eternality. To take the best scene in *The Yemassee,* a vivid depiction of an Indian mother hatcheting her son to death to protect him from shame[23]: we are unsettled, but in a peculiarly redemptive way. Nature and culture struggle within her, the love of a mother and the pride of a squaw. But the struggle, real enough at its start, is ritualized and so settled, even ennobled, after all, despite its horror. The white man does not confront himself in his depiction of the Indian, but uses the distance the Indian gives him from himself to avoid himself. His causal role in the incident—his agency in producing the shame and his function as Christian counterfoil in the demonstration of pride—is transformed by a portrait of savage, but surely human, heroism. We are not Indians, for we would not act so barbarously. But if the Indian is nevertheless heroic, are we not, in our advanced state of civilization, even more so? A conflict otherwise intractable is externalized so that it may be resolved. Once resolved, however, it is reinternalized and presented as if nothing were lost in the transaction. The white man is only more confirmed in his own humanity, which is even extended.

Once again, the writer's alienation from his writing is the trouble. For though Simms admits that culture and nature exist only in relation to each other, yet having lost possession of the writing in which the relation is rendered, he avoids a Kennedy-like secondariness only by letting what he writes possess him. The writer transcendentalizes himself. Exiled from his work, he returns to it exalted. Not even a potentially representative figure may emerge here, because the writer places himself beyond the possibility of representation in both senses of the word. Simms, in effect, claims a visionary knowledge, an authorship unconditioned by any transaction between writer and reader. His various views, about Indians or blacks or women, are no longer what we might expect of a Southerner of the early nineteenth century, but something worse, the same views transcendentalized, masquerading as a worldview, to which no Southerner of the early nineteenth century—nor anyone else—has any claim.

> "There is one riptyle the less—"Pathfinder muttered to himself—"I've seen that vagabond afore, and know him to be a marciless devil. Well, well; the man acted according to his gifts, and he has been rewarded according to his gifts. One more of the knaves, and that will sarve the turn for to-night. When daylight appears, we may have hotter work." (*The Pathfinder,* Chap. 24)

There is this much truth in Natty's pronouncement, that it truly represents the opinion of the white man, with whom Cooper sides, about Indians. Yet in Cooper's very condescension toward his representative, in his satiric treatment of him as limited backwoodsman, the white man is invited to be skeptical of white opinions. Cooper is hardly less prejudiced a man than Simms. At his best, however, his prejudice bears quite overtly the sign of its author. He is not completely open, like Franklin. His opinions are not authorized, as Franklin's were, as among the peculiar notions that all of us, in a democracy, are allowed. As we have seen, Cooper's representativity is the loss of the possibility of such freedom of opinion, and indeed, it is the simultaneous naturalization of a multiplicity of opinion that actually creates what we call prejudice. And yet it is largely *as* prejudice—that is, retaining their peculiarity—that Cooper's ideas are naturalized. This is why, despite Natty's remarks, Cooper really is remarkable for his time concerning the Indians. It is not that he understood them or liked them any better than most of his contemporaries. It is certainly not that he used them, in the manner of Simms, to uncover something eternal about humanity. But he situates them in a field of differences, as a thematic that always retains its thematicity.

Indian ways are "gifts," as he calls them.[24] A measure of the innate is allowed. Such gifts as these are received passively, for they have been given by a kind of supranature or God himself. But as gifts, they remain, finally, acquired and not fully innate. Culture is not quite promoted to nature. As George Dekker has noted, "race," as Cooper sees it, "does not matter in the eye of God and would not matter in the eye of man either if racial lines were not identical with cultural lines."[25] This is a nice description of Cooper's equivocal position. And, indeed, it is only, as in *Precaution,* Cooper's failure to foreground this equivocation—to own it, as we may call it—that produces problems. A certain corrosive progress of alienation takes hold, what we called, in discussing Twain's reaction to Cooper, a logic, or rather what seems to be a logic to the author who is removed from his writing. No longer divided *in* his writing, he is divided *from* it. He becomes, like Kennedy, divided from his own divisions. Even so, however, he does not quite report them, but formalizes them. And against this formalization, appearing to him now with the force of a certain necessity, he struggles to maintain his own, after all.

IV. Authorship and Ethics

We have seen the problem before in connection with the technical issue of ending. The necessity of stopping is not merely a publishing necessity, the requirement of the printer reflecting marketplace conditions. For such a requirement may constrain an author in different ways according to his more urgent demands. Franklin, as we have seen, though a more commercial man than Cooper, did not, in fact, end his work. Identical with his writing, he could not stop it until he stopped. Closer to Cooper, Brockden Brown found ways of undermining an end. Forever on the verge of a separation from his writing, he ended with another beginning or with an ending that concluded but a small portion of his book, and so with what was no ending at all. In Cooper, however, the half formalization of writing is a halfway appealing relief from the burden of writing, and so he rather defers than abolishes the end, conceiving of his novels as novels, indeed, though continuing in a larger group. The Leatherstocking Saga is the famous example, to which we shall return later. But the rent-strike trilogy and the European trilogy are also notable, as is Cooper's early projection of *Lionel Lincoln* as one of thirteen "legends of the Thirteen Republics."[26] As Cooper worries the issue in his preface to *Home as Found,* the sequel to *Homeward Bound* originally meant as part of the same book until the material, as he tells us, took its own way away from him:

> Those who have done us the favor to read "Homeward Bound" will at once perceive that the incidents of this book commence at the point where those of the work just mentioned ceased. We are fully aware of the disadvantage of dividing the interest of a tale in this manner; but in the present instance, the separation has been produced by circumstances over which the writer had very little control. As any one who may happen to take up this volume will very soon discover that there is other matter which it is necessary to know, it may be as well to tell all such persons, in commencement, therefore, that their reading will be bootless, unless they have leisure to turn to the pages of "Homeward Bound" for their cue.

The communication of writer and reader is not direct. Some prior agreement, a relation already formalized in the past, intervenes between them. The writer and the reader are not quite denied. They remain the foundation of the work. But as the work is made already—or, at least, as it exists in relation to what is made already, a prior work to which it refers—so are the readers already made, defined as those who have read the prior work, and so is the writer, who can but finish what he began before. A kind of artistic fatalism dominates Cooper's remarks now. The most basic conditions of his art are "circumstances over which the writer had very little control," and it is "bootless," really, to protest against the situation. Either become that prior writer and prior reader, or give up writing and reading altogether. Cooper does not argue to persuade his audience. But that is not because he is convinced that persuasion is impossible. Rather he knows that his audience has been persuaded, one way or another, only in advance. To put it another way, the truth is not yet natural. It is not yet what is. It remains what has been asserted. And yet Cooper seems very little troubled that it was he, after all, who had been doing so much of the asserting, who, accepting his audience's leave, had taken upon himself the burden of making truth. We have, here, the beginning of a certain irresponsibility not much studied in literature, but which is at the heart of what the American writer must confront. Wrestling with it is the ethical consequence of democratic writing, and the ending of *Home as Found* is thus an attempt to battle out of the surrender that the preface had so inconsiderately made.

Having discovered that the Paul Powis she is to marry is really Oliver Effingham, Eve engages him in this remarkable bit of dialogue. The question is what to call Jack Effingham, Eve's cousin, now also found to be Oliver's father. Perhaps "cousin Jack might prove too familiar and disrespectful a term," Eve wonders. And Oliver replies:

> "So much stronger does your claim to him appear than mine, that I think, when that blessed day shall arrive, Eve, it will convert him into my cousin Jack, instead of your father. But call him as you may, why do you still insist on calling me Powis?"
>
> "That name will ever be precious in my eyes! You abridge me of my rights, in denying me a change of name. Half the young ladies of the country marry for the novelty of being called Mrs. Somebody else, instead of the Misses they were, while I am condemned to remain Eve Effingham for life."
>
> "If you object to the appelation, I can continue to call myself Powis. This has been done so long now as almost to legalize the act."
>
> "Indeed, no—you are an Effingham, and as an Effingham ought you to be known. What a happy lot is mine! Spared even the pain of parting with my old friends, at the great occurrence of my life, and finding my married home the same as the home of my childhood!" (Chap. 27)

A series of options opens up, of identities to be chosen, names to be assigned. Shall it be cousin Jack or father Jack, Eve Powis or

Eve Effingham? The choice is difficult, the claims of each legiti-mate. Culture and nature are weighed equal in the balance, for usage establishes as strong a right as consanguinity in the first case, legality as strong as birth in the second. Culture admitted, however, is as rapidly denied. Eve's assumption that Effingham she must, after all, be called now retrospectively implies that there never really was any choice, that the options presented were merely fanciful. A new order is established, a comic resolution provided for the divisions of a book that throughout its length is not quite comic enough to sustain it.

We might say that Eve is a kind of author of her own end, of the close which will define the tensions of her career. But she denies her authorship, signifying herself in a name which, she declares, is not the one she makes but the one she has had from the start. The novel's difficulties are solved, the work is "ended," indeed. And yet, at the level of the work's writing—as far, that is, as Cooper is concerned—is the egregiousness of this end, what most critics see as a too evident heavy-handedness, not the saving sign of Cooper's resistance? It is difficult to judge. As we noted at the beginning of this chapter, a certain dissolution of Cooper into his characters, of his consciousness into unconsciousness, makes it impossible—though also imperative—to distinguish. The the-matization we have discussed is a blind. Letting Eve struggle, Cooper projects his own burden onto a character in his book. But does he thereby shoulder or bury his burden? What kind of work does this work do? Does Cooper present his difficulty plainly for our consideration, or does he represent it, thereby distancing himself from it as mere imitator, copying the truth? The issue is not one of ambiguity or, even, one of ambivalence, the subjective equivalent of ambiguity. Such terms assume the writer's distance from his writing, his exile from his work, in advance, rather than consider it as the problem itself. To put the matter in other terms, the marriage of the young couple, or the friendship of the two cultures, or the meeting of the hostile races so typical in Cooper may be merely conventional, a requirement of the genre. But since it is as foremost practitioner of the generic—as represen-tative novelist, we have said—that Cooper defines himself, he is at once responsible and not responsible, intending his endings though not quite meaning them after all. Whose end is the end of a Cooper novel? Is the proper frame of interpretation the book at all, or is it the series, or perhaps writing in general? If the question has become familiar in contemporary criticism, we must nevertheless not fail to see it in the newness of its emergence. For it is a question not about reading as it must necessarily be, but about reading as it came to be, at least in America, in the context of a particular rhetorical dilemma and which, therefore qualified, consistently bore for American writers and readers the mark of an ethical rather than existential difficulty.

To continue our discussion of writing and reading in what we may now openly call ethical terms, then, we have described genre as writing in effect prior to itself. As we may now redefine it ethically, it is writing not wholly owned. It is something made, something that is still not natural, but for which no wholly responsible maker can be found. It is not writing to which an idea of authorship has yet to be attached. Authorship here, no more illusory than necessary, exists, rather, only in a difficult rhetorical context. Accordingly, no longer independent *in* writing, like Franklin, nor yet independent *of* writing, like a completely descriptive writer, the author struggles to repossess himself. Cooper seems always hypocritical, to be uncharitable. Or, more sympathetically, we simply cannot know how much he knows about what he writes. Cooper has always seemed a not especially acute intelligence whose writing yet defines the dilemmas of his nation more fully and more sharply than anyone else in his age. Spiller and those in his tradition who have carefully attempted to work out Cooper's political and social positions against the complex positions of others of his period have thus surely, precisely in their discrimination, misrepresented his significance for America.[27] But D. H. Lawrence and Leslie Fiedler and the other myth critics of America, who see Cooper as giving voice to broad notions ingrained in the American psyche,[28] have equally avoided the problem of Cooper's complicity in their sense of that ingrainedness, his naturalization of what is otherwise strictly a matter of assent. Let us, therefore, look at last at what he himself acknowledged he would be remembered for, the Leatherstocking series, his "myth," indeed, though we will need to define myth more narrowly than do Lawrence or Fiedler and in light of the developments we have traced thus far.

V. Myth

I shall want to concentrate on *The Prairie* for most of this discussion. It is Cooper's middle book in the series, a position we might expect to be privileged in a representative writer, as Brown's first book was privileged by its position before his own decline toward representativity and Franklin's book, at one with his life, is privileged everywhere. Still, we cannot expect to escape from the dilemma that representativity poses, its generation of an only half realized formalism. As with *Home as Found, The Prairie* both is and is not an independent piece, requiring us to have read already a series of pieces, and yet requiring us as well to apply lightly the limitations that any knowledge of having read them might impose. Brown's tendency toward what a formalist criticism sees as contradiction, forgetting, sloppiness, will be recalled. As we explained, it is rather a function of the independent dependent status of events in his writing. Similarly, an even more problematical allusiveness in Cooper is a function of an even greater dependence meeting a therefore greater resistance.

"Be careful to have my mark painted on them," *The Prairie's* "Trapper" tells Middleton of the skins he is to trade when he gets back to the settlements, "a letter N with a hound's ear, and the lock of a rifle" (chap. 33). The Trapper, then, is the "Natty" of *The Pioneers*. And yet his not having any name, or rather his having the natural name of his calling rather than the arbitrarily given one of Christian culture, is made much of in the novel. Cooper would seem to want it both ways. Leatherstocking is to unite culture and nature, a point well known and to which we shall return later. But we may note here that this union can, then, take place only as the consequence of a writing severely compromised, in a context precisely fuzzy, which the author both will and will not define. To whom does "a letter N with a hound's ear, and the lock of a rifle" really refer? To the hero of this book, of the three Leatherstocking

books so far, of the three so far and the two written later? And
what of the Leatherstocking who appears but as a voice in the falls
in *Home as Found?* Since a formalist view breaks down in the face of
Cooper's allusiveness, one might attempt some maximalist view
and say that Leatherstocking is, simply, what everything Cooper
writes, taken together, makes him. But the difficulty is too basic
for such a solution, either. The ill-definedness at the level of the
book is reimposed at the level of the series. This Leatherstocking
is not continuously developed. He does not come into being as a
full-blown conception. He is discovered as much as he is invented,
as Leon Howard points out in relation to *The Pioneers.*[29] He both
is and is not Cooper's, who seems in part to be making his own
ideas as he goes along, but also to be exploring an idea already, if
obscurely, in place. The series is a series in a very peculiar sense.
It is five books clearly depending on each other and yet a proper
pentalogy only after the fact. And, indeed, critics have even
argued over the order in which we should read the books, the
order of their writing or the order of Leatherstocking's aging.[30]
We must not suppose that a definitive answer to these problems
can be given. But we have explained why they should open up in
the first place. They are the result of Cooper's representative
position, the growing assumption of the burden of which provides
the order we shall choose in the main, rather, to follow.

Let us touch but lightly on the two novels really outside
Cooper's problematic, *The Pathfinder* and *The Deerslayer,* in which
Cooper affects a Simms-like resolution. Both books have had
their vogue, *The Deerslayer* in particular, whose famous description
of Leatherstocking's initiation into battle is often cited as demon-
strating Cooper's grasp of the contradictory foundation of peace in
war, of wisdom in the experience of folly.[31] And yet such a
description, more forced than the resolution of *Home as Found,* is
worse than merely egregious as well. For the experience, as presented in *The Deerslayer,* is not an experience but a kind of magical
sublation of it. It is a cosmic mime, translating the experience of
killing into a kind of expiatory ritual redeeming killing:

> Such was the commencement of a career in forest exploits that
> afterward rendered this man, in his way, and under the limits of

his habits and opportunities, as renowned as many a hero whose name has adorned the pages of works more celebrated than legends simple as ours can ever become. (Chap. 7)

Heroism is assumed here. It is a status which we have granted Leatherstocking already no matter what he is shown doing. The event is effectually framed. It is not part of a narrative conceived of as a series of particular events, but generalized out of its particularity, typifying the narrative as a whole and enlisted, though at the beginning of the hero's career, under his career as it becomes established only at its end. Throughout *The Deerslayer,* accordingly, all is always complete. Life is elevated, a life larger than life. An Indian gives his war whoop, and it is "the yell that has become historical for its appalling influence" (chap. 7). The possibility of building a raft is considered, and it is with "the celebrated American axe" (chap. 8). In such a situation, Leatherstocking's passage from boyhood to manhood, from peace to war, from innocence to experience is properly a rite of passage. Ethical concerns are turned into existential ones. A heroism ostensibly democratic becomes heroism in Simms's sense or the Homeric sense we discussed in relation to Franklin. Leatherstocking, representing culture's divisions, represents them not *as* those of culture but as those of culture become a kind of nature or demigod, rather exalting itself than owning itself. It is not surprising that critics have wondered how, nearly fifteen years after the last of the first three Leatherstocking novels, a no longer popular Cooper, a Cooper increasingly disaffected with America, could have found the popular Leatherstocking in himself once more.[32] It is, however, precisely because Leatherstocking is no longer inside Cooper but removed, as distant from him as is his public, or rather because Cooper may take Leatherstocking inside himself only by affecting a kind of self-transcendence, giving himself up to his public and ceasing to be Cooper at all. Accordingly, we may turn instead to the series' beginning, *The Pioneers,* a book in which Cooper has not yet quite found the self he will give up, but in which he has already gone some distance in that direction.

Now *The Pioneers,* despite its obvious personal associations, no

more than any of his other works draws its authority from a
Cooper conceived in some strictly biographical sense. As fictionalized biography, *The Pioneers* would be only somewhat more interesting than *Horse-Shoe Robinson,* and its author, if interesting at all,
interesting no longer as our celebrated national novelist but as the
son of the founder of Cooperstown. Rather, Cooper's manifest
appeal to biography in *The Pioneers,* his reliance on the life of his
father for his portrait of Judge Temple, on Cooperstown for Tem-
pleton, should be read as it enters into a dialogue with a more
discursive conception of representation and which, alone, as we
have seen, is authentically Cooper's. "Thou art an exception,
Leather-stocking," says Judge Temple in response to Natty's
anger at his picture of the vicious life of hunters, "for thou hast a
temperance unusual in thy class, and a hardihood exceeding thy
years" (chap. 18). And, indeed, throughout the novel, concerning
Indians, concerning half-breeds, concerning land agents, concerning frontier maidens, Cooper is correcting general opinion
about pioneering with what as an eyewitness he knows, correcting
fiction with life conceived of as divided against fiction in the
manner of Kennedy. And yet, this having been said, it must be
said too that precisely from the perspective of our national novelist, writing what is neither quite fiction nor quite life, Cooper has
begun to take the division up into his writing. If he "takes" one
side of the division, that is, he takes the other side, too, as setting
up the possibility of his side. As the judge admits, the exception of
individuality to the class exists. But it exists, therefore, in terms of
the class, and it remains only for Cooper to own that—for him—it
does, for his development to go as far as his representative situation will allow.

The problem, let us say, is only the old one of point of view,
though the very fact that point of view should arise as a problem is
what is at issue here. For if, indeed, it is as national novel that we
read *The Pioneers,* then our temptation to objectify it as the life of
the son of the founder of Cooperstown is no more than Cooper's
temptation to read his own life as an object. Or better, Cooper's
temptation is to objectify his life variably in a variety of "themes,"
as we have called them, in life conceived of as material to be

written about, a temptation, indeed, which will increasingly exert on Cooper a force not so easily deflected.

Here, for example, is Cooper's rendering of a discussion of maple sugar making:

> Marmaduke had dismounted, and was viewing the works and the trees very closely, and not without frequent expressions of dissatisfaction at the careless manner in which the manufacture was conducted.
>
> "You have much experience in these things, Kirby," he said; "what course do you pursue in making your sugar? I see that you have but two kettles."
>
> "Two is as good as two thousand, Judge. . . . First, I choose, and then I tap my trees; say along about the last of February, or in these mountains maybe not afore the middle of March; but any way, just as the sap begins to cleverly run—"
>
> "Well, in this choice," interrupted Marmaduke, "are you governed by any outward signs that prove the quality of the tree?"
>
> "Why, there's judgment in all things," said Kirby, stirring the liquor in his kettles briskly. "There's something in knowing when and how much to stir the pot. It's a thing that must be learnt. . . . I never put my axe into a stunty tree, or one that hasn't a good, fresh-looking bark; for trees have disorders, like creaters; and where's the policy of taking a tree that's sickly, any more than you'd choose a foundered horse to ride post, or an overheated ox to do your logging."
>
> "All this is true. But what are your signs of illness? how do you distinguish a tree that is well from one that is diseased?"
>
> "How does the doctor tell who has fever, and who colds?" interrupted Richard. "By examining the skin, and feeling the pulse, to be sure." (Chap. 20)

Now the opposition being represented is Cooper's old opposition of nature to culture. Experience is set against method, the particular against the general. The judge, in keeping with his judicial position, wants to know the laws of making maple sugar, while Kirby, a simple sugar maker, wants only to continue doing his work. Cooper is not especially either man's partisan. Nothing is really at stake, for the judge after all is not about to make maple sugar himself; nor is Kirby about to become a jurist. Accordingly, each position is allowed a degree of its own positivity. Since no decision need be made, since no person who might have to decide between the two is really envisaged, each is really independent of what, in a conceptual scheme, would be its opposite number. At the level of maple sugar making, that is, in relation to life thematized at this far a remove from the life of our national novelist, our national novelist may stay removed and, even, call it objectivity. Yet at levels of thematization closer to home, "objectivity" comes to look perilously like repression, as for example in this rather typical instance of Cooper's "picturesque":

> "This is indeed a subject for the pencil!" exclaimed Elizabeth. "Observe the countenance of that wood-chopper, while he exults in presenting a larger fish than common to my cousin Sheriff; and see, Louisa, how handsome and considerate my dear father looks, by the light of that fire, where he stands viewing the havoc of the game. He seems melancholy, as if he actually thought that a day of retribution was to follow this hour of abundance and prodigality! Would they not make a picture, Louisa?" (Chap. 24)

What is repressed, of course, is Elizabeth's own role in composing the picture, the recognition that such pictures, harmonizing culture and nature, are composed only by a culture blinding itself to the destruction of nature which its harmonizing is causing. And, indeed, while Louisa, Elizabeth's companion, responds to Elizabeth's "composition" by asserting that she is "ignorant of all such [artistic] accomplishments," we should rather respond as Natty does to Judge Temple after the bird kill, that accomplishments such as these are themselves a kind of ignorance. Quite simply, Cooper's picturesque is an irresponsibility. Nor ought it to be redefined as responsible by placing it in some picturesque tradition, as is common in those Cooper studies that look to similar contemporary behavior, particularly in the fine arts.[33] For Cooper himself works hard to free himself from that tradition.

Already in the next book in the series, *The Last of the Mohicans,* a different, tough-minded look at destruction replaces the merely

melancholy spectacle of overfishing. Cooper's rendering of the
massacre at Fort William Henry is often cited, in fact, as a sort of
realism that, romance writer though he was, appears often
enough in his work to make it more than merely romance.[34] And
yet it is not realism that makes Cooper's rendering so vivid, but a
kind of realization of the picturesque itself. Looking back at the
scene, he does put aside that "congenial atmosphere which com-
monly adorned the view." With nothing "veiling its harshness,
and softening its asperities," nature stands out in bold relief. Yet
"harsh and unmingled" though the elements of nature now
appear, it is not nature which makes itself appear harsh. "The
whole landscape, which, seen by a favoring light, and in a genial
temperature, had been found lovely, appeared now like some
pictured allegory of life, in which objects were arranged in their
harshest but truest colors, and without the relief of any shadow-
ing." The elements stand side by side, confronting each other:
"nothing was left to be conjectured by the eye, or fashioned by the
fancy" (chap. 18). There is no room, that is, for a picturesque, for a
merely speculative or, as Cooper now calls him, a fanciful observer in between. Yet it is important to note, too, that the space of
the observer is not so much abolished as laid onto what he ob-
serves. Elizabeth's "picture" remains, intensified, become a "pictured allegory," and it is, in fact, in this picture alone that the
elements stand side by side. If the "eye" and the "fancy" have
nothing left to do, it is only because they have already done—
because they are now doing—a deeper than fanciful work. In
Cooper, it is never that a writing opposed to reality opens transparently onto a reality that stands naked as a thing exposed.
Rather reality, becoming writing, is taken up in a series of divisions which, so far from being imitative, so far from depending
upon the divisions of nature prior to writing, depend upon the
writer himself.[35]

It is not surprising that *The Last of the Mohicans* is so much more
heavily modalized than *The Pioneers*. In place of the friendship of
Natty Bumppo for Indian John we have the friendship of the last
of one dying breed for the last of another. And even within the
breed, among the Indians as Cooper describes them, if there

exists an even "greater diversity, or, if we may so express it, greater antithesis of character" than perhaps among any other men, yet antitheses are thus "so far the predominating traits of these remarkable people, as to be characteristic" (Introduction). Division is not between the individual and the type, but at the level of the type itself. *The Pioneers'* exceptions to the class have become the class.

In such a situation, there can no longer be any suspicion that fiction is a fictionalization of reality. The biographical "reality" of *The Pioneers* has been genericized as a reality in "history," termed fiction's "sister muse" (chap 18). The mildly decorative adventures of hunting and contending with forest fires have been intensified as the wild adventures of Indian chasing and contending with forest warfare. We might even say that in *Mohicans* reality and fiction are generically combined, that, as Fiedler—whose favorite of the pentalogy *Mohicans* is—might put it, Cooper has created a kind of legend or folktale, loosely speaking a myth, that abolishes the opposition of reality to fiction. We must also say, however, that this generic combination is not the end but the start of our investigation of Cooper, that to take the end of such an opposition as the end of the opposition in Cooper that really matters is a serious mistake. For just precisely where the problem of fiction and reality disappears, genre emerges, reminding us of the more important problem of whom we can attribute the disappearance to, Cooper *or* "the folk." To speak plainly, Fiedler is a populist. But Cooper is a democrat, however much his democracy is compromised, which means that the folk is his problem, not his answer, that, indeed, he will resist the very idea of "the folk" as a naturalization of culture that would be the immediate consequence of surrendering his writing to myth.

There is a remarkable scene in *Mohicans* that we may perhaps be forgiven for taking as an allegory of the problem. It is the scene in which Natty, in order to rescue Alice from the cave in which the Hurons are holding her, disguises himself as a bear (chap. 25). Now Duncan, ordinary white man that he is, and accepting, accordingly, the white man's ordinary distinction between fact and fiction, takes the bear figure for a real bear, until Natty's unmask-

ing, when he learns the bear is fiction. Magua, more knowledgeable about real bears, knows the bear is really a man in disguise.
Yet tied to bears by more than what the white man would call
knowledge, indeed with a totem beaver as his ancestor, he assumes it is an Indian shaman enacting a bear, a sort of real
fictional bear. Significantly, both men are wrong. Natty, in the
position closest to Cooper, is in the position of knowing that, if the
bear is not simply a fiction, yet neither is it a real fiction, only a
fictional real fiction. For Natty, as a white man, cannot be a red
man. Or, rather, what he can be is the white man who lives like a
red man, an untenable condition, Cooper's own, of appropriating
as his a language which is forever someone else's. As Mahtoree,
the adversary Indian of *The Prairie,* puts it:

> Mahtoree has but one tongue, the grey-head has many. They
> may be all straight, and none of them forked. A Sioux is no more
> than a Sioux, but a Pale-face is everything! He can talk to the
> Pawnee, and the Konza, and the Omahaw, and he can talk to his
> own people. (Chap. 26)

Here, for a moment, pressed against the wall, confronted with the
false position in which his hero, presumable exemplar of a man
always at one with himself, seems again and again to find himself,
Cooper evidently discovers the only way out of falseness: the
speaking of many tongues, "all straight." It is a conception of
language without generality, language not formalized, not extended as a system, but as particular as the particular situation in
which it is employed, hence by definition "straight." It is a conception of language that answers Mahtoree's continued charge
that Natty "has said one thing when he meant another," that he
has "looked before him with his eyes, and behind him with his
mind." For in it there is no opposition between saying and meaning, between the eyes and the mind, only different languages
appropriate to different senses and different organs. These languages, subject to no master language, no "one tongue" against
whose interest, Sioux-like, they must all be measured, stand in
agreeable independence. And, accordingly, even when such inde-

pendence dissolves, when Cooper's moment of insight passes, he will not resort to the single unified language of the folk, but struggling for what he is not quite aware of, he will struggle against such a language, replacing the oppositions it resolves with the greater opposition of his own authorship. "Teton, I am your prisoner," Natty responds to Mahtoree's accusation. "Though my words are white, they will not complain. Act your will." Turning no-answer into a kind of stoic Indian silence, claiming for his "white" impotence, that is, the red man's power, Natty thus continues the impersonation he has just been berated for, making it, even, his strength. "Practyse all your cunning," as he says to Duncan, toward the conclusion of the bear episode. "You must give 'em your jargon, major." For "If I open my lips to speak . . . my English, which is the genuine tongue of a white-skin, will tell the varlets that an enemy is among them." As he makes into his own a language that looms before him as somebody else's, the "practyse," not the forgetting, of all his "cunning" will now be Cooper's most constant effort.

VI. *The Prairie*

At some little distance in front of the whole, marched the individual, who, by his position and air, appeared to be the leader of the band. He was a tall, sun-burnt man, past the middle age, of a dull countenance and listless manner. His frame appeared loose and flexible; but it was vast, and in reality of prodigious power. It was only at moments, however, as some slight impediment opposed itself to his loitering progress, that his person, which, in its ordinary gait seemed so lounging and nerveless, displayed any of those energies which lay latent in his system, like the slumbering and unwieldy, but terrible, strength of the elephant. The inferior lineaments of his countenance were coarse, extended, and vacant; while the superior, or those nobler parts which are thought to affect the intellectual being, were low, receding, and mean. (Chap. 1)

Here, at the beginning of *The Prairie,* what Cooper calls "some little distance" has achieved a powerful density. In the passage it is evident not only in Ishmael's separation from the group he is leading, but in a kind of separation within the language describing Ishmael, as description proceeds almost wholly by classification. This is a quality typical of the book. It is an intensification of that generic force we have noted in *Mohicans*. And it is evident architectonically, as well, in *The Prairie*'s insistently static character, the way in which plot is hardly more than a progress through levels of culture schematically arranged.[36] It is as if the "folk" culture of *Mohicans* has been formalized in *The Prairie*, the legends of the folk objectified at a distance whose measure Cooper is always taking. It remains, of course, a powerful distance, as we have said. It is capable of rendering not only gross but ever finer details, not only the landscape but the body, and not only the body but the face. Accordingly, it is the sign of Cooper's maturity, of his having come into the fullness of his identity as a writer. But thus the inherently problematical status of this identity is faced as it was not quite in *Mohicans*. Let us agree to call the story of *Mohicans* a "myth," after all. But let us remember that "myth" is what we call the stories that others believe and that we—though we understand how, in their place, we might—do not. In this sense Cooper is always writing myths. For he is the other. And he only might believe what he himself writes.

Thus in the most particularizing of the classificatory lines describing Ishmael, in Cooper's rendering of the "coarse, extended" "inferior lineaments" and the "low, receding" "superior parts," we hear more than an echo of the language of that absurd naturalist, Dr. Obed Bat. It is the same Dr. Bat whom Cooper so ridicules for his classifications. And yet here he is using what he ridicules without the trace of a sense of himself as being ridiculous. A sort of unconscious parody takes over that cannot be eliminated. The self and the other do not join. Cooper's rendering of the voice of the other is not, say, "dialogical," as partisans of the folk might wish.[37] This is no revolutionary moment in a progress toward the unity of self and other. For in parody the space between self and other is never bridged. The other remains other, and the self remains superior to it, though bound to other itself as it speaks its superiority. The most we can say is that Cooper's unconsciousness of this parody, never resolving his distance from his community, internalizes it. And this internalization raises with the greatest force the ethical issue at the heart of representativity which we outlined earlier.

The incident of Ellen Wade defending her fortress with the legends of the West will be recalled. And, indeed, throughout *The Prairie,* is Cooper criticizing or affirming the legends of the West? Does he, and to what extent, attack or establish the language of his culture? The sheer allusiveness of *The Prairie* is an intractable problem. The Indians speak, and it is in Homeric similes. Cooper himself describes the prairie, and it is with words that might be borrowed from any handy encyclopedia. In this context even the traditional epigrams from Shakespeare and the Bible which grace the beginning of each chapter appear to be more than merely traditional. Here is Natty speaking to Dr. Bat: "Nay, you're a dealer in ailings and cures: what is life, and what is death? Why does the eagle live so long, and why is the time of the butterfly so short?" (chap. 17) This is straight out of the Book of Job. Natty, asserting a sort of old-fashioned humility against the arrogance of science, asserts it in the conventional language of old-fashioned humility. And yet as Natty continues, convention is problematized. "Tell me a simpler thing: why is this hound so uneasy, while you who have passed your days in looking into books can see no reason to be disturbed?" The hound, Hector, has smelled an Indian hiding nearby, and we are brought up short. The dignity of the Bible's stately periods is interrupted by the snuffing of an animal. But there is no sign that Cooper is himself brought up short. Or rather, if he too is surprised, his surprise is as rapidly buried. Borrowing the authority of his culture, Cooper would then forget that that authority exists only because he has himself lent it its authority. Reminding us that the power of culture is carried only in the self's speaking of it, he yet claims for himself our assent as if by nature.

The complex of difficulties, as we might expect, comes together in the figure of Natty. The hero of the Leatherstocking series, Cooper's central figure, his myth, he yet remains impossibly difficult to grasp. It is not, of course, that we cannot, as it were, locate

Natty properly. Certainly his place at the meeting point of culture and nature, of self and other, individual and community is clear. And yet there is a way in which Natty does not quite fill his place, a way in which, if we know with almost too much certainty his position in the economy of Cooper's writing, he occupies that position by virtue of a certain faith Cooper asks of us but never quite justifies in the telling. In a certain sense, Natty is not really written. He is dramatized—as in the scene of his first appearance, where he looms as a gigantic illusion against the distortions of the sunlight (chap. 1). He is invoked—as at the end of *The Prairie,* where his grave serves as a memorial of what for a white man was once possible (chap. 34). But as he is rendered in himself, he is too comic, too ineffectual, too unsettlingly an odd duck like the Obed Bat with whom he is constantly having the conversations that are the ideological crux of the book. He is portrayed as a garrulous old man, a portrayal resulting inevitably from Cooper's internal parody, what happens when a cultural convention like Nestor, the wise man of the *Iliad,* is translated into a discourse too democratic to venerate what culture has established as wisdom.[38] In short, Natty is what we might expect of a representative democrat, for his place is itself out of place. He is like Middleton, the official representative of America, who yet may assume his representative function only when—as Cooper did—he leaves America, or at least that part of America in which he properly belongs. Or he is like Paul Hover, representative bee hunter, who must venture beyond the territory where bee hunting is generally practiced in order to become "the" bee hunter. Perhaps he is even like Inez, that flower of the Old World, who stands for the Old World only in the wastes of the New. He is "A prodigy! a lusus naturae! a monster that nature has delighted to form!" (chap. 17). These are Obed Bat's words about a disguised Indian whom he mistakes for a buffalo, and Natty ridicules him for "the distinctions of class and genera" which he so confounds. But we may suspect a certain defensiveness in Natty's ridicule, for a white man disguised as an Indian is the real "lusus naturae," and a representative individual is an exposure of class and genera as conceptualizations confounding themselves.

> Look around you, men; what will the Yankee choppers say when
> they have cut their path from the eastern to the western waters,
> and find that a hand, which can lay the 'arth bare at a blow, has
> been here and swept the country, in very mockery of their wick-
> edness. They will turn on their tracks like a fox that doubles, and
> then the rank smell of their own footsteps will show them the
> madness of their waste. (Chap. 7)

In this one moment of consciousness, in this supreme instance of
self-awareness, Natty speaks a language which is indeed the language of representativity. Culture others itself as nature, confronts nature as culture othered. For there is no nature and no
culture in the passage but as culture creates them. The law of
nature is the choice of culture turned into law. The force of necessity is the power of freedom which has given itself up. Such a
consciousness, like a "rank smell," is everywhere and nowhere.
"Doubling back" on itself, it cancels itself out. It is unsustainable,
since the individuality which alone would guarantee culture's
freedom to choose has already been surrendered. The language of
representativity, unlike the language of individuality, is a language of "madness," as Natty says, and Cooper is just not quite
mad enough to continue writing as representative individual for
long. Not quite denying himself, he yet gives himself up too.
Natty gives himself up. "Therefore forget anything you may have
heard from me, which is nevertheless true" (chap. 33), as Natty
says in almost the last words of his life. As we shall see, Poe, just
barely sane, will begin at this point. Asserting a self which has
precisely been denied, he asks us to *remember* everything we have
heard from him, which is nevertheless *false*.

4   Poe and Plagiarism

Poe's myth is *Eureka,* a work almost no one likes, though a suspicion, difficult to resist in Poe, that he wrote it—perpetrated it, even—precisely to test the extent of our sympathies may, in a sort of perverse Poesque way, perhaps serve to redeem it in part. "To the few who love me" he says that he writes it. "And whom I love,"[1] he adds, rather too much as an afterthought to give much hope that many more lovers than loved exist. It was wise of Poe to provide himself with an alternate reader, Alexander von Humboldt, his dedicatee, for whom he writes it as well. A man who did not even know Poe nor whom Poe knew, perhaps he could read it avoiding the issue of love altogether, though, of course, this hardly helps anyone who finds Poe's urgency unseemly enough to wish to resist.

What does Poe want of us? How would he like *Eureka* to be read? An apologia in the form of a cosmology, a "prose poem," as the subtitle calls it, but in the language of a treatise on astronomy, it makes very few concessions even to the most well-disposed of Poe's readers. It would perhaps be well for the reader just not to dispose himself toward it at all—in Franklin's words, let us say, to please not to read it. But a certain simple pleasing—the "love" Poe asks for, though he does not deserve it—is, in fact, asserted in *Eureka* with the force, even, of a demand. To the lovers and the loved only is "this Book of Truths" being made available. And

"Truth," by his own account just what he will not provide, as he says in "The Poetic Principle," is what here, however, Poe would claim, finally, to deliver. Here at last, Poe seems to be saying, he will tell it straight. Here at last, if only we will overcome our resistance to him, all the difficulties between us will be ironed out. Everywhere *Eureka* is filled with the sense of past error now set right. Now an explanation has been formulated. The mystery of his life, the path of his and our sufferings will be finally revealed. "I design to speak of the *Physical, Metaphysical and Mathematical— of the Material and Spiritual Universe:—of its Essence, its Origin, its Creation, its Present Condition and its Destiny*" (16.185). Picture the man laboring over this design.[2] The love of his life dead, his own health bad, as poverty-stricken as ever and, now, because of his poverty and a certain sense of deadness to the world, exiled to a tiny cottage away from literary Manhattan in the wilderness of Fordham, he will make one last effort before his end. He will write the work "to be judged after I am dead" (16.183). It will explain his life, clarify all those misunderstandings that caused him so much trouble. And yet the work, when all is said and done, turns out to be this *Eureka,* this impossible mélange of physics, superstition, and poetry that we will not like (*will not,* as Poe would have italicized it, a point we shall come to later). It is a work of neither wisdom earned nor bitterness justified, but a cracked pot, explaining nothing anyone might want to know. "What terms shall I find sufficiently simple in their sublimity—sufficiently sublime in their simplicity—for the mere enunciation of my theme?" (16.185) Evidently this is revelation, both personal and philosophical, a theme of Miltonic sublimity. Yet it is spoken in the crazy accents of, say, the narrator of "The Tell-Tale Heart." Poe drops the mask to reveal a mask. Not for *no reason* was he exiled. Just as we prepare ourselves to welcome him home, he reminds us of how uncompanionable a person he really is. Just as we get ready to give his writing its due, we find that what we are reading is an absurdity. Poe, there can be no doubt, was desperately serious about *Eureka.* But, as so often in his career, to speak his heart was to become a brick. *Eureka* is Poe's "myth," indeed—the discourse of the other, as we said in reference to Cooper. Only Poe's self is othered at a distance far greater than Cooper's. The man who might love him best he takes to be a scientist he knows the least. The poet defending his life of poetry turns astronomer in the very act of defense.

It is not really enough that this astronomer then proceeds to reconceive himself as a poet. It is not enough that he turns astronomy itself into poetry. "I offer this Book of Truths, not in its character of Truth-Teller, but for the Beauty that abounds in its Truth; constituting it true" (16.183). Poe, evidently, would recuperate himself. He would turn the self that has been othered back into himself in a romantic act of idealization. The poet, become a scientist, would redefine science dialectically as more highly poetic. And yet Poe's statement is not really as much like Keats as it sounds. Truth and Beauty could not, in the faculty psychology which Poe held, so easily be united. As the sentence twists and turns, the insufficiency of the one only provokes the insufficiency of the other. The redoubling qualifications, the jerky turnings and returnings, do not even come close to Keats's ravishing stillness. We are perhaps distracted, pushed, before we quite grasp it, from one inauthority to another, but inauthority thus remains. *Eureka's* Truth and *Eureka's* Beauty seem to cancel each other out rather than unite. Or, if they do unite, they do so but on the basis of a sort of mutual reduction rather than idealization, a common inadequacy rather than dialectical transcendence. As we might almost say, Poe makes his very inauthority authoritative. Unable to overcome his insufficiency, he would be only too faithful to it. And, indeed, *Eureka,* Poe's rendering of himself in a language which is inauthoritative, just may be the real Poe after all. For Poe the author authors what is not quite his. "He" appears but in a language he cannot quite believe. Let us say that Poe is too democratic to believe that a self unauthorized by his community may be expressed, that, as in Brown and Cooper, his appeal to an audience that will not quite grant him the right of appeal threatens to establish his language as what cannot be his expression at all. Yet, too, pressed harder on the score of democracy, too alienated to unconceive his alienation or even, in the manner of Cooper, to contain it by writing as his audience's representative, he would make of what he does not believe a kind of ideal itself. Poe's language is, as we called the Trapper's, a "madness." But it is madder yet, and infectious madness, too.

Bitten, like Legrand with his gold beetle, by the Poe bug—feigning to feign madness, as it were—I have an obsession, a reading of a Poe poem, that, though I know it is not true, I cannot shake. Why is it that "Annabel Lee" haunts me so? In its rhymes I find no delight. For its repetitions I have no desire. I think it is the "bell." Yes, it is the bell-like sound of its name. "Annabel Lee":

> It was many and many a year ago,
>   In a kingdom by the sea
> That a maiden there lived whom you may know
>   by the name of Annabel Lee;
> and this maiden she lived with no other thought
>   Than to love and be loved by me.

(7.117)

In its way, this is as difficult to take as *Eureka.* It is the poetic equivalent of that cracked metaphysical pot, doggerel pretending to be poetry. Still, though we ought not exalt Poe's doggerel in the manner of the French symbolists who theorized that, slipping its connection with words, his verse was really aspiring after pure musicality,[3] we should not dismiss it as merely doggerel either. What haunts is the hesitation between music *and* words. "Lived"/ "loved." Is the connection aesthetic or moral? "A maiden there lived" and "this maiden she lived"; she lived "to love" and she lived to "be loved." Swelling and subsiding, "Annabel Lee" moves, like *Eureka,* to the throb of what Poe calls the "Heart Divine."[4] Yet, as we asked of *Eureka,* is this heart divine Beauty or Truth?

To put this in more direct terms, we may want to believe Poe when he says of Annabel Lee that she is a maiden "whom you may know." We may wish to rise above ourselves, to free ourselves from the falseness of everyday knowing and come to know that true self beyond. Still we cannot help suspecting that Poe is being more than a little arch, that Annabel Lee represents no truth after all, but is to be known only as a fairy tale, a story of kingdoms by the sea, "many and many a year ago." As in *Eureka,* Poe speaks of love—of love enjoyed, love lost, love mourned. No one would deny Poe his right to such a subject. The death of his mother when he was a baby, the death of his first love when he was a young man, the death of his wife, the third death of his nearest and dearest, when he was only in his thirties, gave him experience enough. We would learn what he thinks and how he feels about such a matter. Yet, again, "he" is not to be found. The "experience" is nowhere in evidence. Poe does not write biographically. Nor, quite, if he would universalize his biography, does his universalization carry any force not more than checked by the poem's utter conventionality.

Wordsworth's Lucy poems, and in particular "A Slumber Did My Spirit Seal," may serve as a useful comparison:

> A slumber did my spirit seal;
>   I had no human fears:
> She seemed a thing that could not feel
>   The touch of earthly years.
>
> No motion has she now, no force;
>   She neither hears nor sees;
> Rolled round in earth's diurnal course,
>   With rocks, and stones, and trees.[5]

Like Annabel Lee in her kingdom by the sea, the "she" who, Wordsworth imagines, does not feel the "touch of earthly years" seems protected in a world of perfect love. Like the Annabel Lee who suffers "chilling and killing," she, too, ceases all motion. And again, like Annabel Lee still, whose "eyes" are the "stars . . . [that] rise" and whose "dreams" bring the "moon . . . beams," she transcends chilling and killing when, "Rolled round . . . With rocks, and stones, and trees," she is reconceived as nature. We move from unity through loss, to unity again. It is a pattern perhaps a little too familiar and one whose familiarity, as it manifests itself in Poe, makes us question whether he really means what he says. Yet Wordsworth, making familiarity, as it were, his theme, means what he says with a vengeance. He has committed himself to his poem so fully that it overwhelms him. It threatens him, now, even as he sings it, so that his very absence, our inability to find him, unlike our difficulty in finding Poe, bespeaks him all the more. The lack of specification of the "She" of the first stanza is the generalization of her which he has wrought in the second read back onto her in the first. The "I" who is already not quite "human" at the start is just precisely "I" under the influence of his dissolution into the pantheistic vision he has imagined at the end. Whether the second stanza is a completion or an ironic reversal of the first stanza, as different readers have maintained, need not concern us here.[6] In either case, the effect is of a disclosure or discovery that "Annabel Lee" cannot produce. Fulfilled or surprised, the poet is revealed.

We might say that "Annabel Lee" is too much just what it is to reveal anything. Or if it too may be said to have a theme, then recalling our definition of theme in Cooper as the objectification of the writer into his work, as the alienating of the subject into objectivity, let us say that alienation has gone so far as to leave no subject who might be revealed anymore. Nothing is discovered in "Annabel Lee," because there is nothing *to* discover. Do we pass from love to its loss? Yet our love "was the reason" it was lost. Is our loss then restored? Well, but nothing "can ever dissever" our souls in any case. The poet is not absent in "Annabel Lee." His conflicts have not been abolished. Conflict, indeed, is everywhere in the poem. But reiterated rather than resolved, repeated not taken up, it is the poem itself. "I was a child and she was a child": this is nonsense logic, the logic of "And one . . . and one . . . and one" as Elizabeth Sewell calls nonsense.[7] It is logic assuming an insufficiency it would repair. It is the whole of parts whose explanation it would be. Yet insufficient itself, an explanation in need of explanation, it places itself side by side with its parts in a version of Franklin's "whole part" turned inside out. Or, to put it in more personal terms, the Poe whom we seek, like the purloined letter, is just there where he is. It is only that "there" is a permanent place, and if we would bring it "here," we must bring its thereness here as well.

I have, as I said, a reading of "Annabel Lee" to which I am
committed, although I do not believe it. For the maiden who
"there lived" I do happen to know. Annabel Lee: she is Annabelle
written long. And who is Annabelle but—after the repetitions are
canceled—Anbel. And what is Anbel but—with some nonce letters added for euphony, to make it ring, so to speak—"A,B," the
letters of the alphabet and—most wonderful—the initials of my
maiden wife, I mean the maiden initials of my wife. "Chilling and
killing," indeed. Pity this poor reader, alienated himself in the
very act of his reading, pursuing his meaning and finding it but in
the form of meaning in general. What can be his when even so
original—at least eccentric—an interpretation as this is but a
rehearsal of interpretation as anyone might perform it? What can
be his when what lies nearest to him is discovered, like the mockery of an epitaph on a tomb, in the arbitrary letters of the alphabet? Still he would continue to believe in himself. Does not Poe
continue to believe in *him*self? There must be no mistake about
what has really been discovered. It is not that language is inadequate to the self nor yet, more fashionably, that the self is an
illusion of language. It is rather that, in Poe, the inadequacy of
language has become the very perfection of selfhood, a proposition that reflects the development of democratic authorship, as we
have been following it, to its most problematical point.

I. The American Poe

Let us put this in the rhetorical terms with which, by now, we have
become familiar. On what basis does Poe appeal to his audience?
Separated from himself as he is, what "he," even, makes a claim
upon us? After all, Poe appears so frivolous, so, frankly, absurd.
As Henry James put it, "an enthusiasm for Poe is the mark of a
decidedly primitive stage of reflection." Or, in the words of James
Russell Lowell, though Poe may be three-fifths genius, he is two-
fifths fudge.[8] Still, the genius must be admitted as well. Poe has
been to generations undeniably compelling, and accordingly, to
read Poe is to face an impossible problem. On the one hand, we
would forgive Poe his absurdity. We would not, by calling him

absurd, in effect not really read him in the first place. And yet, on the other, to fail to see him as absurd is to give our sensibilities up, relinquishing any "we" that might read him at all. How is Poe to be taken? As he seemed to those Northern publishers he was forever railing against, he appears to be too much the Southerner. Or, as he was to those Southerners forever railing against him, he seems not quite a gentleman.[9] Still, Poe remains one of us. Though we are rather happier with him abroad than at home— "in Northlight," as a student of his reception in Scandinavia puts it, or in Russia, or in Hungary, or to wherever the critics so enjoy relegating him—he is yet "our cousin," as Allen Tate calls him in a famous essay.[10] He is a relative for whom allowances must be made. And it is only because Poe seems to stretch the allowances beyond any reasonable bound that difficulties arise.

In the terms of our book so far, we should say that there is, in Poe, a crisis in the relation of the writer to his readers. Poe would not seem to be able to depend quite as much on his audience for authorization as did Franklin or Brown or Cooper. If we read Poe, it is not really, in Franklin's words, as we "please." And yet, though we may even not please, Poe no more than the others would either give up all claim to authority or claim as his authority something other than us instead. Rather he turns our not pleasing itself to use. He seems to find in it a kind of pleasure nevertheless. Poe, as we might put it, is not absurd *and* compelling, but compelling in his very absurdity. He is not part fudge and part genius. But assimilating his reader's doubts about him into his writing, he writes fudge as his genius precisely. To continue our argument to this point, unlike Franklin or Brown or even Cooper, Poe can no longer rely on that disposition to read him in which the American author finds his strength. The unity of producing and receiving which we discussed in relation to Benjamin Franklin has broken down hopelessly. Poe's readers are not disposed to him, and he cannot really do anything about it. Accordingly, embracing his reader's very indisposition, Poe makes it its own antidote. He writes what his work declares everywhere is foolishness. But foolishness is thus no more than indisposition positivized, indisposition established as a kind of authorization despite itself. Poe, as it were, makes our lack of interest in him its own transcendence. He sweeps us away on the strength of our very denial of him. Catching us up in his imaginings (though we dismiss them out of hand as ridiculous), captivating us with his terrors and his wonders (though we are not primitive enough quite to be terrified or to wonder), Poe turns us back against ourselves. As we might put it, that solicitation in which American literature is born has become a demand and the demand grown tyrannical. It is only that, in Poe, tyranny is but solicitation maintained in the condition of its refusal and so rhetorical all the more. With its suggestion of a kind of internal opposition, "our cousin," in its way, is as precise a description of Poe's relationship to America as "our national novelist" is of Cooper's. The problem of Poe *is* a problem. It is an American problem because it is a problem of his claim upon his readership even when it would not read. And, indeed, though it has grown so problematical that it has led many readers to attempt to find its solution by reference to what is outside writing and reading altogether, it can be approached in this way no more than the problems of Brown and Cooper.

By way of example, let us consider some of these attempts in more detail, beginning with the biographical explanations so common in Poe studies. We may for the moment try to suspend our dogmatism in the matter. Though an autobiographically based tradition of literature, as we have been claiming the American tradition is, is different from a biographically based one, we might hope to be more fortunate in the case of the biography of a writer whose life is so interesting. Here is a man, after all, with a fascinating life, a life lived out at a particular time and place. Still, as we have seen, America conceived of as a time and place is a shaky ground for American writing. And, indeed, that endless fascination which Poe's life has exerted from his time to ours only shifts the difficulty of coming to terms with the fascination of his writing a little further down the line. What we have called, in relation to Brockden Brown, the irresponsibility of the cult of the artist is promoted even more egregiously in Poe's case. The biographer finds he is not quite sympathetic to the writer's writing. Unwilling to read it, he attempts to read "him." And yet, finding "him" always escaping into yet other levels of writing he will be equally unwilling to read, he soon comes to give him up as well. In its very fascination, Poe's biography would seem so peculiarly Poe's own that it is difficult to sympathize with it at all. It is the biography of a writer whose writing is taken increasingly as representational and comes, finally, to exist as a representation of a life so pathological that it vanishes altogether as what might be represented for us. Poe was a drunk, as his contemporaries insisted on seeing him. Or he was a dope addict, as, somewhat later, to account for his writing's seemingly hallucinatory qualities, it was proposed.[11] Even at the more sophisticated level of a dawning psychology, he never resolved his Oedipus complex, as Marie Bonaparte, with Freud's own approval, maintained.[12] Or, as in Joseph Wood Krutch's hilarious reduction to absurdity of Bonaparte, Poe was impotent.[13] This is a judgment wholly without evidence, a biography whose "facts," to be entertained, would require a knowledge so objective that, under normal conditions, it might as well be given up from the start. But, then, to conceive of a writer biographically is precisely to give him up. It is to avoid rather than confront him. It is to conceive, in fact, not of him but of an object, indeed—to conceive not of the writer, but of what hides behind his writing and so, ultimately, of what cannot really be conceived at all. Poe cannot be reached. His history is a case history too particular to grasp.

It will not help to generalize this case and so to make it conceivable once again. This is the phenomenological method. But phenomenology, though it has always insisted on the necessity of "bracketing" biography, as it calls it, rather mystifies biography instead. Indeed, phenomenological approaches to Poe, perhaps the most compelling body of Poe criticism we have, yet in their creation of a certain Poe mystique compel only too deeply.[14] Here the progress is the opposite of that which occurs in biographical study. Poe's biography is frankly rejected for Poe's writing. "Poe" is taken to be not the facts of his life but the consciousness which his writing expresses. And yet this writing, unmoored to the life of anyone who does write, is increasingly enlarged until it passes beyond the possibility of writing and reading just the same. Writing is conceived of as the expression of a subject rather than the representation of an object. It is held to exhibit a consciousness which may, presumably, be grasped by anyone at all. And yet this consciousness, as just exactly what does not belong to anyone, is all the more difficult to grasp. One need only look at Daniel Hoffman's extraordinary *Poe Poe Poe Poe Poe Poe Poe*.[15] Analysis or exorcism—for much of the book it is difficult to say which—it is a reading of the Poe inside him which he can neither quite accept nor dismiss. Yet in the end, construing his refusal to accept Poe as a repression, accepting him into himself, he cures himself and effectively dismisses Poe all the same. With Poe, he joins the larger world of the transcendent oedipal subject, and the letdown of his book's resolution, the discrepancy between his confrontation with Poe while he still reads him and his identification with him when he finishes can lead only to a kind of deconstruction of identity in which the discrepancy takes center stage.

We are well on our way here to what Louis Renza calls the purloining of Poe from America to foreign shores.[16] The contemporaneous rejection of Poe as un-American yields to a generalization of him as universal and finally to a denial of universality as a fiction. No wonder, rejecting Poe, Americans have rejected also the "French Face of Poe," as one critic has called it.[17] For some sense of what is still Poe's Americanness, a sense that he writes no more as everyman than as no man, insists that acceptance as well as rejection is an evasion. It is a sense that being un-American is American too, and that if Poe turns away from America, even as the writers we have examined thus far turn toward it, it is in the exercise of a self formed in his relation to other Americans that he turns.

As Baudelaire put it in what we are, I think, justified in taking as his most complete comment on Poe, "Hypocrite lecteur,—mon semblable,—mon frère!"[18] Baudelaire begins just about right. Poe's alter ego, his substitute in the French-speaking world where, in fact, his translations are often preferred to their original, he makes Poe's writing his own, taking Poe in and projecting him out onto his readers, who will, presumably, write him in their turn. The writer, for all of his pretensions, is no more than the reader.

The reader, for all of *his* pretensions, is no more than the writer. I am like you. You are like me. You *are* me. Only here, refusing to confront the difficulty of such a situation squarely, Baudelaire escapes the burden of shouldering this "you are me," preferring the suicide, as it were, of "therefore we are nothing." Baudelaire gives us a kind of negative phenomenological rendering of Poe. And, accordingly, though the line from Baudelaire to Valéry is straight and has been well traced, its extension to Derrida, we might add, is only a step.[19] The poet finds his language no longer "his." Avoiding contending with such a difficulty, however, he transcendentalizes himself as nonbeing. What, in the language of Poe's era, we might call the Kantian antinomies or, in today's language, as we would term it, a play between idealism and deconstruction takes over. The poet has ceased to exist. His "presence" as a simple self is denied. Since, however, he would present himself all the same, he declares existence an absence which his poetry expresses instead. Symbolism is born. Existence, as a negativity, strictly speaking cannot be written. But since the poet would write, he must write a kind of incomprehensible poetry as music. He is, as the symbolist tradition would make him, a sort of gnostic priest. Nothingness, as incommunicable, is a mystery; poetry, as the cult of noncommunication, is mystery's religion; language, the celebration of poetry, is a kind of transubstantiation in which words, essentially meaningless, discover that meaning meaninglessness of "pure" poetry in which they abide. Writer and reader, negatively glorified, simultaneously disappear. They exist, but as an emptiness into which also they dissolve. How can we not reject Baudelaire's version of Poe? Nor in so doing are we merely being, as Baudelaire charged, defensive. Or rather, defensiveness is a kind of acceptance after all in which the priest or keeper of the cult is reconceived as a writer only:

> It was hard by the dim lake of Auber
>   In the misty mid region of Weir—
> It was down by the dank tarn of Auber,
>   In the ghoul-haunted woodland of Weir.
>   (7.102)

> While I nodded, nearly napping, suddenly there came a tapping,
> As of someone gently rapping, rapping at my chamber door.
>
> (7.94)

> Keeping time, time, time,
>   In a sort of Runic rhyme,
> To the tintinnabulation that so musically wells
>   From the bells, bells, bells, bells,
>   Bells, bells, bells.
>
> (7.119)

This has always seemed, to the ears of English speakers, trans-mogrification rather than transubstantiation, not poetry at all in Baudelaire's sense, in fact, but poetasting.[20] Admittedly, there is music here. There are catchy rhythms, striking sounds. But the rhymes and rhythms do not rarify the poetry but solidify it. They do not free Poe from his words but return him to them only more strongly. If they do not communicate, it is not by virtue of their being too fine for thought, but because they are thought itself become too thick to think. Poe's verse hardens rather than musicalizes. It exploits rather than symbolizes. And what it exploits is writing in the condition of an alienation not to be symbolized away, but to be itself written. In rhetorical terms, language, which is shared, has become formalized as an object therefore unsharable. Yet this unsharability is shared all the more. Poe's nothingness is a familiar nothingness, as we might call it, nor can its familiarity be escaped, as Baudelaire would wish.

Let us say that Poe did not discover nothingness at all. Or, at least, if he set himself up as discoverer, yet, as in his mock journals of discovery, he was exploring a popular mode. He might pretend to poetry as an aristocratic calling, but aristocracy was never more than a claim to private ownership of a poetry that, even as he claimed it, he acknowledged as a common property. He might fancy himself Israfel, singing to the heavens alone, but even at the start he would submit himself, poems and stories alike, to a newspaper competition whose winning constituted the only heaven he ever hoped for. Poe's lifelong ambition of conducting a popular periodical is perhaps the clearest example. For he might project for it, as he tells us in the "Prospectus of *The Penn Magazine,*" a "criticism self-sustained; guiding itself only by the purest rules of Art," yet as he himself announced, its larger aim was "chiefly . . . to *please.*"[21] More is involved here than a certain mere practicality on Poe's part. It is not that, say, in deference to the necessity of selling his work, Poe takes an intrinsically ideal art and makes it pleasing by, all extrinsically, popularizing it. Rather, art's ideality is itself to give pleasure, as he tells us in "The Poetic Principle." It is what makes it art. A poem is no more and no less than its "effect," and if it fails "in effect"—say, if it goes on too long— "then the poem is, in effect, and in fact, no longer such" (14.266). Poe more than addresses his audience. Like Cooper he would *be* his audience. And if, unlike Cooper, he would go beyond his audience too, he conceives even of this "beyond" in what are manifestly his audience's terms.

"Hypocrite lecteur . . . mon frère." Baudelaire does not really address an audience at all. He addresses a coterie and not really a coterie either. The poet *maudit* speaks but to a few readers *maudits.* He knows a secret, and if others perhaps know it too, yet they know it, still, only *as* a secret. Poe's "as you may know," however, as we discussed it in "Annabel Lee," is a secret addressed to everybody and is not, therefore, really a secret at all. His mysteries are, we should say, the most public of mysteries. How does Maelzel's chess player, a Barnum-like hoax of a robot, really work (14.6–37)? The expert cryptographer publishes a regular newspaper column on cryptography (14.114–49). The decipherer of autographs chooses for deciphering the signatures of writers "of celebrity rather than that of true worth" (15.179). Even "The Mystery of Marie Rogêt" is really only the sensational mystery of Mary Rogers. "It is impossible to say how first the idea entered my brain," says the narrator of "The Tell-Tale Heart" (5.88). "I cannot, for my soul, remember . . . where, I first became acquainted with the Lady Ligeia," says the narrator of "Ligeia" (2.248). "I was sick, sick unto death with that long agony," begins the narrator of "The Pit and the Pendulum" (5.67). Mysteries are everywhere in Poe. How did the idea come to him? Who is

Ligeia? What, exactly, is "that long agony"? Significantly, however, although these mysteries are placed at the beginning, they are introduced as in medias res. They take their place within a running dialogue, an interchange already in progress. To know them is not, like the Ancient Mariner, to generate the stories, but to be part of the stories themselves. Let us say, if we will, that in Poe writing is, indeed, mystery's cult. Yet even cult is finally a profession, even that profession which, as we saw in Brockden Brown, is but a certain rhetorical distribution, an authority for writing not itself unwritable but, as part of an ongoing story, given *in* writing, precisely.

As Poe has Dupin explain his own authority in "The Purloined Letter," it is the result not of special knowledge, of "spurious profundity," but of "identification," which he describes as not a function of knowing anything after all, but as a certain talent for replication:

> I knew . . . [a boy] about eight years of age, whose success at guessing in the game of "even and odd" attracted universal admiration. This game is simple, and is played with marbles. One player holds in his hand a number of these toys, and demands of another whether that number is even or odd. If the guess is right, the guesser wins one; if wrong, he loses one. The boy to whom I allude won all the marbles of the school. Of course he had some principle of guessing; and this lay in mere observation and admeasurement of the astuteness of his opponents. For example, an arrant simpleton is his opponent, and, holding up his closed hand, asks, "are they even or odd?" Our schoolboy replies, "odd," and loses; but upon the second trial he wins, for he then says to himself, "the simpleton had them even upon the first trial, and his amount of cunning is just sufficient to make him have them odd upon the second; I will therefore guess odd;"—he guesses odd, and wins. Now, with a simpleton a degree above the first, he would have reasoned thus: "This fellow finds that in the first instance I guessed odd, and, in the second, he will propose to himself, upon the first impulse, a simple variation from even to odd, as did the first simpleton; but then a second thought will suggest that this is too simple a variation, and finally he will decide upon putting it even as before. I will therefore guess even;"—he guesses even, and wins. (6.40–41)

Poe's aristocratic fantasy that everyone, compared with him, is a "simpleton" of some "degree" or other is evident here. His dream of winning "all the marbles" is clear. The fact remains, however, that winning the marbles is no mystery but a boy's trick. It is a knack for playing a game, and by the analogy for which the game of marbles is intended, the poet himself—something Dupin insists both he and the Minister D. are—is but a master game player too.

Significantly, the game depends upon no principles external to its players. The players, in fact, are oriented not toward some goal whose achievement would constitute winning, but toward each other alone. Indeed, even in relation to each other their goal is not so much mastery over, as a more successful being of, each other. Winning the game is not the transferring of the other's marbles to oneself, but the taking possession of them by oneself becoming the other. Knowledge is but knowledge of what the other knows. And yet, since what the other knows is only what you know, and so on in a never ending cycle, the self, in becoming the other, still remains itself. The self, as we should say, is the other *as* itself. Nor can it resolve its condition either by self-aggrandizement, obliterating the other, or by self-abasement, in which, rather, the other is aggrandized at the self's expense. To put this in a franker way, Poe is a plagiarist, and this in a sense so bound up with what he is as not to be separated out of him.

II. Hoax, Burlesque, Plagiarism

Now the issue of Poe's plagiarism is, of course, well known.[22] From the beginning of his career, when he leaves his reader a manuscript to be found in a bottle, to his death, when, perversely, he leaves his career itself to his enemy, Rufus Griswold, by appointing him literary executor, a general aura of misappropriation hovers around him. Poe stole from others, as his first critics liked to point out. Others stole from him, as he liked to point out about them even more. Nor, even, if we find the charge of stealing greatly exaggerated, can we quite get rid of the charge, which seems too much a part of Poe's canonical position to discard so unproblematically. With those scholars of Poe bent on defending him against imputations of immorality, we may attempt so to individualize works as to make plagiarism impossible. With those theoreticians bent on attacking such concern for morals in the first place, we may so generalize plagiarism that it becomes, in effect, what all writing is and so vanishes. Yet in either case we cannot deny that if we thus address the problem of plagiarism, it is *as* a problem that we address it. For as we may now see, in the light of our discussion of the previous section, whether the self does in fact steal from the other or only seems to, the issue of stealing must arise because the oppositional pair of self and other has been conceived of *as* in opposition. There is a crisis in the relation of readers and writers. Reading and writing, properly one, have been separated. As we have said, "pleasing to" has failed. The author is authorized to write no longer as one acceptable to his reader. And yet, unable to authorize himself by reference to anything else, Poe thus, as it were, makes a virtue of unacceptability, becoming his reader's impersonator. Maintaining the democracy of authorship in the conditions of a writing moving to deny authorship as democratic, he makes stealing the very basis of his writing. Accordingly, as it will not do to deny Poe's stealing, no more will it do to promote it, Prometheus-like, as a kind of high poetic calling. The problem of stealing is just what Poe's work keeps always in the fore.

We are in a theater, here, different from that of romantic—say, Coleridgean—plagiarism, from the plagiarism of a symbolism more positive than that of the French, where stealing is rather concealed or, if admitted, redeemed.[23] For in romantic plagiarism, authority, located beyond the relation of selves and others, justifies the self's taking from the other by invoking a higher cause. Selves and others are not really acknowledged as determining their own ends, but exist only that they might be refined away in an end rather determining them in advance. As in Coleridge, the poet, who is variously conceived as independent of the poets he feeds off or, more usually, as combining, pantheistically, with them in poetry in general, is said to be inspired rather than a thief. If we find he depends on others we will find, too, his creativity which elevates him above others. Or, even better, as in Livingston Lowes's *Road to Xanadu,* if we more than find, if we pursue his sources, yet we pursue what we may comfortably assume is but the ultimate source, both of him and of those he steals from, something Lowes, with others, calls "imagination."[24] In Poe, however, pursuit of sources is never comforting. As in Burton Pollin's *Discoveries in Poe,*[25] rather, it yields either the literary equivalent of case histories, names and works that in some respect or other are similar to but shed no light on Poe's work or, considered from a different perspective, a kind of deconstructive repetition of Poe's own procedures in the detective tales, where he pursues sources himself. For Poe's plagiarism lies not in his stealing from others, but in his conceptualization of others as those who are to be stolen from. Franklinian coexistence with others has yielded to Brown's citation, Brown's citation to Cooper's competition, Cooper's competition to outright theft. Poe's "imagination" lies not before or beyond the other, but at its level.

He writes what we have always seen as "burlesques," rather than satires: "The System of Dr. Tarr and Professor Fether," "The Literary Life of Thingum Bob, Esq.," "Why the Little Frenchman Wears His Hand in a Sling." He writes what we call not "parodies," but "hoaxes": "Hans Pfaall," "Von Kempelen and His Discovery," "The Balloon Hoax," so-called, itself. As we seem to sense, Poe does not ridicule his audience's faith so much as he plays upon it, takes advantage of it. He does not, as in satire or parody, expose its assumptions, but exaggerates them, taking the assumptions themselves as his medium, in a sense as exposed already, so that he is not superior to them but in fact their master. Thus he Tarrs and Fethers himself with his own brush. He fills his balloon, as it were, with a hot air as much his own as anyone else's. He steals not, indeed, *from* others, but others themselves, thus exposing himself too to theft for having credited otherness in the first place.

This is the explanation for that sort of inverted plagiarism constituted by Poe's false erudition, his claim to base himself on nonexistent sources, his quotation of passages that cannot be found. It is the reason, too, for his habit of burlesquing himself, the presence in his oeuvre of a "King Pest," which treats absurdly the plague banquet that so terrifies in "The Masque of the Red

Death," or of a "Loss of Breath," which seems to laugh at the idea of suffocation so luridly depicted in "Premature Burial." An opposition of self and other has opened up, and Poe, refusing to resolve it extrarhetorically, by recourse to a self or other transcending its dialectic, allows the other to enter the self itself. Poe makes fun of himself, takes the self he has just made fun of seriously, and, in general, just plain repeats himself in different contexts and modes so often that neither self-authorization nor self-undermining seems to be the issue but self-othering, which is prior to both. As David Halliburton notes, "Once Poe has done a thing it is likely that he will do it again, wholly or in part." But it is not, as Halliburton goes on to argue, that "a kind of purification or heightening" is at work "testifying to Poe's persistent quest for the ideal."[26] This is phenomenology speaking, not Poe, in whom, rather, which version of his work might be considered "higher" is peculiarly difficult to determine.

Thus consider, for example, "Thou Art the Man," perhaps Poe's earliest detective story. It is a semicomic tale in which the ventriloquist narrator, having read the rather obvious clues unnoticed by his ignorant fellow townspeople, wrests a confession out of a murderer by having the rigor-mortised victim, whom he doubles over in a box, seem to spring alive and ejaculate the accusation of the title. This would appear to be a study, a sort of groping toward Poe's more "mature" work in the vein, "The Murders of the Rue Morgue" or "The Mystery of Marie Rogêt." The materiality of "Thou Art the Man" is, in the later stories, essentialized. The clues become more subtle. The body "speaks" only metaphorically, what a gifted interpreter can reason from its condition. Even the comic stupidity of the townspeople is transformed, becoming, in the person of the narrator, that more widespread blindness of ordinary men compared with the insightful genius of a C. Auguste Dupin. Yet if "Rue Morgue" thus seems an idealization of "Thou Art the Man," in such a pair of tales as "Ligeia" and "The Man That Was Used Up" the order of the material and the ideal is precisely reversed. "I cannot just now remember when or where I first made the acquaintance of that truly fine looking fellow, Brevet Brigadier General John A. B. C.

Smith" (3.259). Here, in a wonderful send-up of "Ligeia's" famous "I cannot, for my soul, remember how, when, or even precisely where, I first became acquainted with the lady Ligeia" (2.248), it is idealism that appears as immaturity, and that materialism which in the other pair had seemed to be transcended appears rather as a mature wisdom reminding us of the absurdity of transcendence.

Again, we may take a somewhat more complicated example, "The Scythe of Time," the story of Psyche Zenobia, who, in pursuit of an affecting experience to thrill her readers, details her feelings before, during, and after her head is cut off by the hands of a bell-tower clock. It is an absurd rendering of what will later become "The Pit and the Pendulum." Yet as part of a larger article, an example of "How to Write a Blackwood Article,"[27] as it is also called, its very absurdity thus becomes a set of procedures which Poe, in "The Pit," would accordingly seem to have followed. Beginnings and endings become difficult to sort out. Do Poe's stories progress toward some generalized story to which, perhaps, *Eureka* comes nearest? Or are even such seemingly ideal stories but materializations of more general instructions in a sense more ideal in the very technicality of their specifications? Poe gives us "The Raven," and he gives us "The Philosophy of Composition," an explanation of how "The Raven" was composed. But "The Philosophy of Composition" stands not only as an explanation of a prior work it would elucidate, but, in the absolutism of its prescriptions, prior to any future work for which it lays out the terms of composition as a whole.

It is not surprising that, though the classification is his, Poe does not tell us which of the stories he calls "grotesques and arabesques" are which.[28] A scale opens up, a measure of writing marked by the contingent at one end and the essential at the other. We tend to regard the grotesques as founded in a certain provisionality, exploding by exaggerating that materiality which the arabesques, in their freedom from historical or corporeal specificity, would spiritualize. And yet, as in, say, "Hop Frog," the story of an outrageous joke by which a dwarf jester avenges the wrongs inflicted upon him by his jokester king, exaggeration would seem to be Poe's very spirit itself. Arabesque, we should say, does not transcendentalize grotesque, but performs it. Poe, asserting the scale, does so only to overwhelm it in a sort of rhetoric of assertion. For to return to our sense of Poe's work as hoax rather than parody, his aim is not a foundation for belief, but belief itself. He would authorize himself not on the grounds of an idea, an actuality prior to his reader's faith, but on the grounds of faith alone— as we might say, that faithless faith which demands grounds in the first place. Accordingly, he would command not even representation. He would command not one mode or other more or less adequate to actuality, but that mutual assent which representation, as a demand for adequation, rather denies.

As he says of "The Murders in the Rue Morgue," "where is the ingenuity of unravelling a web which you (the author) have woven for the express purpose of unravelling?"[29] There is no truth according to which the writer, by explaining it, might truly become himself as well. Rather, othering himself so that he might exist as explainer, he declares the invasion of himself by otherness the only truth he might hope to know. Again, as he puts it in his "Marginalia," "It is the curse of a certain order of mind that it can never rest satisfied with the consciousness of its ability to do a thing. Still less is it content with doing it. It must both know and show how it was done."[30] There is a fall here of which we have spoken in regard to Franklin and Brockden Brown. It is a movement from doing to consciousness of doing, from writing as living to writing as representation of a living separate from it. But representation, no sooner than it emerges as consciousness, is returned to doing as "showing." If the self is no longer in its writing, but divided from it, yet Poe will take pride in writing that division all the more. He does not evade but performs himself. Or better, he embraces a selfhood to which evasion, he insists, is a particular return.

Poe, we should say, is a little like the narrator of "The Fall of the House of Usher," another "arabesque," as it is generally classified, perhaps Poe's best, which we should like mightily to distinguish from the "Mad Trist of Sir Launcelot Canning," the "grotesque" tale-within-a-tale inside it, and surely, as all critics agree, one of his worst. For the narrator, though he has fallen into distinguishing too—the "lofty and spiritual ideality" of the one from the "uncouth . . . prolixity" of the other (3.292)—finds that settling the representational status of things will not settle their authority after all. Indeed, at the level of his narration, the two tales, despite his distinctions, seem to authorize each other equally. Ethelred breaks down the hermit's door, and Madeline breaks open her coffin; the dragon shrieks, and Madeline screams; the brass shield falls to the floor, and the metal gates of the mausoleum open. An idle romance designed to "pass away this terrible night" draws forth a terrible story that will not "pass away." But the idle romance will not pass away either. As agent of the story of Usher proper, an "utterance" in which "there had been found the potency of a spell" (3.296), it is validated and validating simultaneously. It is an "extremeness . . . of folly." But thus it is realized precisely *as* folly, a true fiction, as it were, whose truth and fictiveness are categories called into being but by the demand for representation which lack of faith creates. In Usher's term, "The Fall" is a story told by one whom—in a surprising turnabout, considering the ostensible assignment of madness and rationality in the tale—he calls "madman" (3.296). As we explained in relation to Cooper, madness is the speaking of otherness as one's own. For as both a friend and a stranger, an "intimate associate," as he terms himself, of one whom, yet, he "really knew little" (3.275), the narrator tells a tale whose significance is just the irrelevance of knowledge, a tale as true and as false, rather, as his relation to Usher is true and false.

We should not be overly proud of our acuity in noting how obtuse the narrator seems to be. We must not think to escape the consequences of our relation to him quite so easily. The narrator sees, it is true, too little. His hearing is weak, his taste dull or, at any rate, his hearing is too weak, his taste too dull to detect the subterranean events which all go on below the threshold of his awareness. "I know not how it was" (3.273), he fails at explaining; "it was a mystery all insoluble" (3.274); "I still wondered" (3.277); "I could not, even with effort, connect" (3.279). The narrator's madness, that is, is certainly not romantic madness. It blocks rather than conveys to knowledge. It cuts short the possibility of vision. Yet we cannot dismiss him as "unreliable" for all that, at least not in the sense that we maintain some transcendent standard of reliability to which we may hold him. For if the narrator is not quite sensitive enough, yet neither has he taken leave of his senses. Rather he has become sensible of his senses themselves, possessing precisely his dispossession as the only standard he needs. "There can be no doubt that the consciousness of the rapid increase of my superstition . . . served mainly to accelerate the increase itself" (3.276). This is spoken about the incident of the tarn. Changing his perspective in order to modify the mournful effect of the house upon him, the narrator finds only a duplication of house and effect in the lake. He has created out of his senses, that is, an object. He gives his senses over to the house—to the house of Usher, the building and the man, whose senses have, in fact, been augmented to an extreme degree. He separates himself from himself. He is quite literally a third person, neither Usher nor Madeline, whose story "The Fall of the House of Usher" is. Yet he takes possession of what he is separate from by narrating it. Speaking this third person as a first person, in the first-person narrative in which "The Fall of the House of Usher" is rendered, he thus owns third-personness *as* his. Nor is this third-personness to be resolved away as we, perhaps, wish it would, in favor of some higher perspective which might constitute a truer authority, for the perspective of third-personness is the only authority he allows. As he says of Usher's belief in the sentience of inanimate objects, a sort of pseudoscientific redaction of his own experience at the tarn, "Such opinions need no comment, and I will make none" (3.287). He will never resolve his dispossession, only possess it, explaining it but with itself, the tale whose only explanation *is* the tale, though that this still seems not sufficient an explanation after all is something we must investigate in somewhat more detail.

III. The Work

"Such opinions need no comment, and I will make none." This is a formulation more intense than Cooper's "Forget everything you have heard which is nevertheless true" and almost as intense as Archibald MacLeish's classic statement in the same vein that a work "should not mean / But be."[31] The irresponsibility of Cooper's writing would seem to achieve new heights in Poe, surpassed only by the irresponsibility of writing as formalism more fully conceives of it and which MacLeish's statement describes. Indeed, formalism, as a kind of begging of the dialectic of grounds and trust that we have just been discussing, formalism as a construction of writing—as the narrator constructs "the house of Usher"—as an object responsible only to itself, is one of Poe's proudest inventions. As Poe insists again and again, the aim of a poem is itself. Its truth is its own fullest elaboration. Its meaning is its "unity." And yet, as Poe also knew—and this is why, rather than MacLeish's "being," he offers "no comment," taking a sort of poetic fifth amendment in relation to what he means—the democratic poetics he could not help but believe demands that a poem, as we should say, rather should not be but mean or, even, should not mean but be told. That is, to put in the foreground what has been in the background of our consideration all along, it is just the absence of a second person, the demurral of any assenting readership to whom a story might be told with confidence, that produces first third-personness. Poe's stories are never quite as independent as he pretends. Written by a writer addressing a reader who, for all his reluctance, cannot absolve himself of the responsibility of reading, they simply will not explain themselves in terms for which writing and reading are not required. Objects, as he might ever so insistently claim they are, they are a reminder that it is the writer and the reader who have created them as objects in the first place. Thus Poe's address just will not let the reader alone. "Let me call myself, for the present, William Wilson" (3.299). "You, who so well know the nature of my soul, will not suppose, however, that I gave utterance to a threat" (6.167). "Why will you say that I am mad?" (5.88). Of course, he can call himself whatever he pleases. No one does know his soul after all. No one has said he is mad. The narrator seems, here, almost to be talking to himself. He is the persona of a work whose meaning is its own.[32] He speaks a truth nobody else seems to see. But, after all, the persona is the writer nevertheless, and the writer would speak to himself only if madness were an alienation more total than it is. The writer writes to those who would rather have no connection with him. What he writes must seem to "mean" not its writing but its being, what "is" rather than what is told. Yet therefore, precisely—and showing us this is, despite himself, Poe's merit—it exhibits the problem of meaning, meaning as it becomes a problem, as a function of just that telling which formalism, in its more advanced state, refuses to acknowledge.

Let us, accordingly, describe writing in such a formalist situation. Let us define, since it has now come to that, the formal object writing has become, and in a manner parallel to the way in which we have defined Cooper's genre. It is the author's othered relation to his audience projected onto the field of their relations and creating it as a field. It is a field which would appear to leave no room *for* the author and audience, a "work" already written, from which the author and his audience, writing and reading, would seem to have been totally abolished. But as Poe's work reminds us, it is a field of author and audience nevertheless, who have not been abolished but who have surrendered their authority to it instead, and which therefore declares their surrender at every turn. What Poe's work "is" is his audience, only alienated from him. It is his work's object or, as we might say, the object's object and formalized within the work, in fact, as its very center.

> A skilful literary artist has constructed a tale. If wise, he has not fashioned his thoughts to accommodate his incidents; but having conceived, with deliberate care, a certain unique or single *effect* to be wrought out, he then invents such incidents—he then combines such events as may best aid him in establishing this preconceived effect. If his very initial sentence tend not to the outbringing of this effect, then he has failed in his first step. In the whole composition there should be no word written, of which the tendency, direct or indirect, is not to the one pre-established design. And by such means, with such care and skill, a picture is at length painted which leaves in the mind of him who contemplates it with a kindred art, a sense of the fullest satisfaction. (II.108)

Here is perhaps the first modern pronouncement on the work of art qua art, an unabashedly technical assessment of the work, proposing as criteria for its judgment wholly aesthetic rather than moral or philosophical criteria. Continuing the rigorous distinction of "The Poetic Principle" between truth and beauty, Poe here, too, affirms "design" over reference. The work does not serve "incident" or "events." Incidents and events serve the work. Even the writer and the reader are workmen. What they share are not values or ideas, for they are technicians rather than philosophers. They are artisans more than artists, not creating or even discovering, but "fashioning" the work *as* work, the work as object alone.

Yet what is this work as object alone? Or rather, if it is alone, why does Poe call it an "effect"? For writer and reader, dependent upon it, are also, it would seem, what it depends on in turn. The work is conceivable only in relation to them. They are the center of its structure, determining, in fact, its incidents as a structure, a "whole composition" which otherwise could not even be thought. They give the work a point of reference after all, and internalized, assimilated into the work as they are, we might at first be tempted to say they give it its quality of self-referentiality, as the formalists would call it. Yet the self referred to, Poe thus reveals, "is" not an object but has been objectified. The work, as we noted in relation to Cooper, does work despite itself, the work of objectification. It formalizes the writer and reader as functions of a work that is still, however, function*ing* in a continuous and, since it will not stop, even a vicious cycle. Self and object, asserted as identical, are yet different. Nor will Poe, who refuses either to resolve or to sanction the difference, who incorporates within the object the very self laboring to define the work as an object independent of itself, allow this cycle to stabilize. The identity of what is different is not, in Poe, the solution of a problem but the problem exactly.

The difficulty, of course, is once again that intensity of otherness which we have been at such pains to register. The magnitude of Poe's alienation means the obviation of Franklinian difference with a difference. Differences are not different but opposed. The self is not just *an*other self but *the* other. Poe cannot find anything to mediate his relation with others. He does not, like Cooper, represent his community, but he is excluded from it. Thus like the formalists, and unlike Cooper, he disdains genre. "Keeping originality *always* in view" (14.194) is what he describes himself as doing. His works are to be read not as models, as efforts better than others of their type or as ideal types themselves that others should imitate, but as unique and essentially inimitable. Similarly, like the formalists, and unlike Cooper, it is not as part of a career that he would have us read what he writes. It is "rather by the impression it makes . . . than by the . . . 'sustained effort' which had been found necessary in effecting the impression" that a work must be judged (14.268). An author's total project, incrementally or organically developed, is irrelevant, and indeed, as we have seen, it is in fact difficult to detect any development over the course of Poe's writing lifetime.[33] Quite simply, Poe's otherness is far greater than genre or career will permit. The work is separated from everything, other works included.

And yet, this having been said, it must also be said that the separation of Poe's work, in contrast with formalism's separation, invokes what it is separated from all the more. Thus, in the context of the democratic tradition which we have been following, it is true enough that othering turns writing as one pleases into writing within the context of generic conventions. Genre is the sign of a certain compromising of the possibility of originality as Franklin conceived of it. Yet, in the same context, to deny such genre as has already emerged will not be to recuperate originality but to plagiarize outright. Similarly, careerlessness is properly produced by that appreciation which makes writing at one with living. Again, however, once writing and living have divided, a denial of career does not assert the community's appreciativeness nevertheless, but confirms its lack only more firmly. As we might say, elaborating further the issue of referentiality, what Poe's work points to— its "meaning," if we will—is never Cooper's "theme": the objectification of the self, as we defined it, at a greater or lesser distance from itself. But neither is meaning, as in the formalists, the absence of distance, a property of the object totally unrelated to the self it is distant from. For distance in Poe is rather everywhere than nowhere. It is not absent but only unmeasurable. Poe's work is not, that is, independent of his community. Instead, it frustrates the community's path to it. It "refers," as, since the separation of language and life, it must and as it does even in Franklin, who, as we have seen, merely makes sure to own his reference. But genre and career, born in the condition of such separation, are yet the means by which reference may be retrieved. They are the mode of its ownership, the measure of its owner's distance from it. And Poe, rendering them useless, serves as a reminder of how much the othering of ownership in fact costs.

Poe's attack on reference is double-edged. Critics are wrong, he tells us, in demanding that "every fiction *should have* a moral" (4.213). And yet, since they are so adept at finding them in the least likely works—"a parable in 'Powhattan,' new views in 'Cock Robin,' and transcendentalism in 'Hop O' My Thumb' " —it is rather their own fault in not finding any in his own: "They are not the critics predestined to bring me out" (4.214). Damned if he does and damned if he doesn't, how should the reader read? The critic who is continually finding fault, Poe warns, should remember the fable of Zoilus. Remarking, in response to Apollo's request for the beauties of a work, that he busied himself only about the errors, he was given a sack of unwinnowed wheat and bade pick out all the chaff for his reward. Yet the critic who praises instead is equally wrong, for "excellence . . . may be considered in the light of an axiom, which need only be properly *put,* to become self-evident. It is *not* excellence if it require to be demonstrated as such:—and thus, to point out too particularly the merits of a work of Art, is to admit that they are *not* merits altogether" (14.281–82). Morals are unnecessary. Indeed, interpretation as a whole is unnecessary—our justification, in fact, for not interpreting, in this chapter, the "meaning" of any Poe work. Yet as Poe's own criticism makes abundantly clear, not looking to interpret produces a certain gap between the work and the critic's reading of it. Or better, it produces a gap within his reading. On the one hand we have reading which becomes its own work[34]—like, say, "The Philosophy of Composition," Poe's unbelievable description of how he wrote "The Raven," where, as he himself admits, "the

interest of an analysis . . . is quite independent of any real or
fancied interest in the thing analyzed" (14.105). On the other hand
we have reading as little more than quotation, Poe's usual way
with the works of others and presumably a surrender *to* the other.
It is the gap, as we might say, of the impossibility of ownership, a
gap between practice and that theory—that elaboration of conventions of the object—without which, in a universe of formalized
works, reading will be stymied:

> "The Haunted House," by the same author, is one of the truest
> poems ever written—one of the *truest*—one of the most unexcep-
> tionable—one of the most thoroughly artistic, both in its theme
> and in its execution. It is, moreover, powerfully ideal—imagina-
> tive. I regret that its length renders it unsuitable for the purposes
> of this lecture. In place of it, permit me to offer the universally
> appreciated "Bridge of Sighs." (14.284)

The sheer inauthority of this passage is stunning. Quite literally,
no reading gets done. There are terms of praise—"true," "artistic," "imaginative"—but nothing that the terms really render.
Even the poem that is praised is not rendered, and the one Poe
substitutes for it is substituted with the flimsiest of excuses, un-
justified by the remotest rationale for substitutions. "Self-evident"
—the "excellence" of a work that need not be demonstrated—
comes to seem more and more an honorific name for arbitrary.
The relations of particular to general, one thing to the next, are
unmeasurable. There is no way of determining what should be
praised or criticized. There is no way of choosing one poem rather
than another. Indeed, as Poe's habit of singling out two lines of
this poem or three of that indicates, there is not even any way of
determining what constitutes the poem in the first place. Poe is
not quite the formalist he sometimes portrays himself as being. Or
rather, his "self-evidence" appearing as arbitrariness, his formalism as a failure or, better, a reminder of the failure which creates
it, he is a reminder to those selves who seek a safe oblivion in the
security of form that their disappearance is impossible after all.
Poe's objects, finally, are not constructed according to some inde-

pendent aesthetic but are fragments of a discourse, of a community constituted in its fragmentation, precisely.

Consider Poe's elaboration of some common phrases into full-scale stories. Thus he tells us the tale of "The Man Who Was All Used Up." It is a tale of a larger-than-life war hero, broad shouldered, large limbed, deep voiced, whose shoulders, limbs, and voice, however, are prosthetic devices supported by a figure almost too small even to be seen. He tells us of "Loss of Breath." It is the story of a man characterized by his violent shouting outbursts, who searches for his character, who loses his shout and must pursue it everywhere. He tell us "Never Bet the Devil Your Head." It is the adventure of one Toby "Dammit" whose profane self-rendering in the phrase of the title results, predictably, in decapitation. Members severed from the larger organism go off on their own. Pieces struggle to assert themselves as whole. As in "The Pit and the Pendulum," where a scythe threatens to cut the narrator in half, or "The Tell-Tale Heart," where a murder victim is carved into little pieces, or "Morella," where the loved one's teeth are prized even above the loved one, Poe worries fantastically over the difference between separation and independence. It is a worrying we have seen in less graphic terms in Brown too, and which, in almost the same terms, as Sharon Cameron argues in relation to Hawthorne's and Melville's various dismemberments, is a central feature of the American nineteenth century.[35] Yet as always, Poe's exaggeration of the concern takes us to its heart. We might be tempted to say, perhaps, that Poe here demystifies Coleridgean symbolism once and for all. His literalization of the idea that the part stands in for the whole, by collapsing synecdoche back into metaphor, makes symbolism as arbitrary as the allegory to which Coleridge thought it superior.[36] But then it should also be noted that this literalization depends upon a construction of the phrases "all used up," "loss of breath," even "never bet the devil your head"—a common expression of the period, as recent scholarship has found—in which Poe forgets their discursive status, their use as common phrases with which he starts in the first place. The "gold bug" is not, properly, a yellow beetle, but the name we give a certain greedy desire. Legrand, who has been "bitten" by it, is not physically sick, but terribly desirous. It is folly, as Jupiter and the narrator do, to allegorize such ordinary terms. Or rather, they do allegorize them only because they think Legrand, isolated so long from society, is necessarily mad. Neither metaphors nor symbols—not really tropes at all, in fact—phrases such as these are what are technically called "figures." They are the forms *of* thinking, not the forms in which thinking is arranged after it is already thought. They are elements of a dialogue not determined by reference but, in fact, determining the conditions of such reference as society demands. Thus they are free of the dialectic of metaphor and symbol, arbitrary and ideal on which reference isolated from dialogue is inevitably caught up. They are colloquialisms, language as it is spoken, "meaning" as its speakers mean it, and it is but that alienation which makes Poe put common speech in quotation marks that causes all the difficulty to arise. Poe the journalist, Poe, even, the regionalist, as some have argued,[37] is a formalist only by default, and his formalism, accordingly, reminds us of the breakdown of an America that, for all his pretended aristocratic superiority to it, he cannot quite leave.

It is no wonder that no less a formalist than T. S. Eliot, who did, after all, leave, should have tried so hard to forget Poe. Why, he wonders, can't he get Poe out of his head?[38] It is Hoffman's question, as we noted early in this chapter. It has been our question. It is the question of most Poe readers who find themselves drawn to, but skeptical of, Poe simultaneously. Eliot, however, refuses to examine his own implication in the question, deferring the rhetorical dilemma Poe engages by taking the European route we have already traced. Poe is in him not as an other, but because he influenced Baudelaire who influenced Mallarmé who is somehow international and modern enough, free of genre and career, of this culture or that era, so that influence is resolved into an existential condition never threatening but authorizing authorship all the more. Do our emotions lack any "objective correlative," as Eliot says in "Hamlet and His Problems"? But, then, that is not a problem *of* representation but one which may, unproblematically, be represented. Do we suffer a "dissociation of sensibility," as he calls it in "The Metaphysical Poets"? But then this was suffered so long ago that it has been naturalized and is nothing, anyway, that a little "wit" cannot resolve. Do we lack "tradition," as he claims in "Tradition and the Individual Talent"? But then the writer may still proceed, confident that tradition will realign itself to support what he has written. Most of all, does a writer steal, as he admits in a famous aphorism?[39] Yet stealing, if it be bold enough, is perfectly acceptable, for it is authorized ultimately by the ultimate author, God himself, who will join our separate writings in the grand logos of final revelation. Eliot's religious conversion toward the end of his career is no happenstance. He is afflicted as was Poe by a world fragmented, by language in pieces, become, even, nonsense, as his own nonsense verse—"Five-Finger Exercises," say, or "Old Possum's Book of Practical Cats"—demonstrates. But the fragments, he becomes increasingly sure, will come together. The ethics, as we may call it, of his writing becomes an aesthetics only that the aesthetics may become a metaphysics. These dry bones will bear flesh. These dead bodies, in his own often repeated image, will live. For deadness, what we might say is the ultimate otherness, transcended is not confronted. And, accordingly, we are returned to Annabel Lee, whom, we may recall, Poe insists we must know, a loved one ultimately estranged, whose estrangement itself Poe would hug close.

IV. "The Burial of the Dead"

"The death, then, of a beautiful woman is, unquestionably, the most poetical topic in the world" (14.201). Thus Poe explains "The Raven," what he presents as the ideal poem, an explanation which itself is a kind of ideal, both in its prescriptiveness for future poems, as we have already discussed, and in its design to demonstrate that poets, despite prevailing opinion, can indeed explain how their poems were constructed (14.194–95). And yet, as so often with Poe's ideals, the absolute and the arbitrary meet. The grandness of the pronouncement cannot conceal its too evident absurdity. The "unquestionably" poetic is questionable with a vengeance. The "then" of the statement, ringing with the force of a mathematical "ergo," only points all the more to the separation of what is supposed to be a conclusion from the chain of logic it presumably concludes. Evidently, as Poe explains, beauty is always associated with melancholy. Death is the most melancholy thing of all. And death will be even more beautiful when directly associated with beauty, as in the death of a beautiful maid. Logic circles round and round here, reiterating the word "beauty" in various guises. Repetition is presented as inference. In linguistic terms we should say that the paradigmatic appears as a syntagm or, more broadly, that synonymy extended becomes difference. And, indeed, it could hardly be otherwise, for beauty, in Poe's understanding of it, is precisely such a synonymous kind of difference. Distinguishing it from love or passion as lacking *"homeliness"* (14.198), he presents it as a kind of extreme unhomeliness— uncanniness, as we should now say—the condition of intimate estrangement he can only pretend to escape.

No wonder death is everywhere in Poe. There are songs to the dead. There are songs of the dead. There are characters dead. There are individuals who murder deliberately and plagues which kill indiscriminately. Finding these dead beautiful, Poe gives a necrophiliac turn to the Emersonian dictum "Even the corpse hath its own beauty."[40] For Poe, finding beauty in its opposite, the ugly—finding life, indeed, in death—does not transform the ugliness or the death, as Emerson in the most common understanding of him does, but proclaims it all the more. Contemplating the slaughter in Poe, we are not vouchsafed the assurance that Thoreau, contemplating the slaughter in nature, receives "of the strong appetite and inviolable health of Nature . . . that myriads can be afforded to be sacrificed and suffered to prey on one another."[41] The dead in Poe do not die into nature or the oversoul, into a life somehow larger than they. They are not buried to become life in someone else, as if that were the same as life in them. Rather, if they return from the grave they return *as* dead with whom Poe would consort directly.

"Not hear it?" asks Roderick Usher of the noise his buried sister has been making as she escapes from her tomb:

yes, I hear it, and *have* heard it. Long—long—long—many min-
utes, many hours, many days, have I heard it—yet I dared not—
oh, pity me, miserable wretch that I am!—I dared not—I *dared*
not speak! *We have put her living in the tomb!* (3.295–96)

We shall return shortly to "living in the tomb," a remarkable
phrase, like the one that concludes the paragraph, *"she now stands
without the door,"* a phrase that itself escapes burying, that stands
out in its absurdity, refusing to die even into the general meaning,
the overall referent or (over)soul of the passage as a whole. But for
now we may note Poe's refusal of the Emersonian evasion concerning death, his presentation of it in the fullness of its problematic.
Is it hearing or speaking that is at issue here? What is so hard to
believe, that the dead should live or that, knowing they live, the
living should have remained silent? Who has been the sufferer?
Who is the "miserable wretch," the one presumably buried or the
one presumably free? Most of all, why "dared not" Roderick
speak? For evidently his complicity in killing Madeline is just
precisely what speaking would declare. He is as dead or as alive as
she, as passive or as responsible. Indeed, he is, in the condition of
things, passive and responsible for his passivity, dead and living
the life of the dead, whose deadness, accordingly, spilling over
from the thing represented to the means of representing it, is
overwhelmed by a rhetoric of representation Poe could never quite
forget.

Poe's old, productive confusion returns. No more than any
other matter in his writing is death merely a Poe theme. The
uncertainty of objectification, the blurring of the distance of the
object from him, remains as strong as ever. Accordingly, though
we are saying that Poe's stories again and again are about death,
yet the meaning of "about" is just as much in question as the
meaning of death. We say, for example, that "The Pit and the
Pendulum" is "about" a pit. "The Raven" is "about" a raven.
But in the first case the primary sense of *about* would seem to be
geographic—the territory around the pit in which the story takes
place—while in the second, with the raven in part an image of
death but in part only a body given significance by the bereaved

lover who pursues it, *about* has a sense midway between geography and spirit. Like death or anything else in Poe, even the means of pointing to it are caught up in the opposition of the metaphoric to the literal. Alienation which separates writing from living separates writing even from itself. "We have put her living in the tomb!" Is it a living "her" he has put in the tomb, or is the "her," really dead, now in the tomb making a life of it after all? "She now stands without the door." Of course, Poe means "outside" the door. But it is not the mere archaism of such a usage of *without* that makes us wonder how Madeline might stand "with" the door. Poe's discourse fragments. His words, even mere connectives like prepositions, keep invoking objects upon which, to be intelligible, they must seem to depend. But it is a dependence Poe cannot help but reverse. They are objects again and again recaptured by words which, unlike objects, cannot be so easily disclaimed.

"I dared not . . . I dared not." Roderick's language takes charge. Pointing to passivity, it becomes passive. Reporting the other, it becomes other to itself, repeating itself, quoting itself, from which, therefore, it is split too. Yet, as Roderick continues, "I *dared* not." The split, never healed, is, however, asserted as active. Otherness, italicized, becomes a self not only without loss of, but because of, its otherness. Its passivity is activated. It trembles with a vigor of its own. It becomes its own transcendence itself, its own essence, so that speaking death, Poe makes it live. As we find in the detective stories, death is not life's opposite but, in its horrific melodrama, its grinning luridness, as Thomas Mabbott finds it invariably rendered,[42] a more or less grotesque image, allegory, or, to use Poe's word, a "masque" of life (4.250). This masque, however, is no mere imitation, either. No more duplicating life than entwined in it, no more doubling life than connected to it—to the murderer, his activities, and the circumstances of his involvement with the murdered—it is a clue as well as a copy. Accordingly, if it represents life, it reconceives the life it represents as itself a series of representations, a linked chain of signifiers whose meaning is rather the chain itself than any end it might be said to signify. It takes a C. Auguste Dupin, who reads the chain, to recognize that no simple self has spoken it. Its author is not, as the witnesses in "The Murders of the Rue Morgue," for example, take him to be, a Spaniard, or a Russian, or whoever needs merely to have his language translated to be revealed, but something not quite human, an orangutang, too other for translation ever to take place.[43] It takes a madman like Poe, who writes Dupin's story, to claim this otherness as himself, nevertheless. It will take, as we shall see in the next chapter, Nathaniel Hawthorne, who domesticates the alienation that generates the opposition of self and other in the first place, to rewrite the life of otherness as sane after all.

5   Hawthorne and the
Responsibility of Outsidedness

There is a curious early Hawthorne story, "Roger Malvin's Burial," whose rigidity of form—whose compulsive formalism, even —rises up out of the loose, meandering sketches otherwise characteristic of this stage of Hawthorne's career like literature out of life. In place of open-ended rambling, we find tightly articulated structure. In place of genial, almost folksy narrative, we have analysis, dissection, stricture. Still, the formalism is hard to motivate, the compulsion difficult to account for. Structure and stricture do not quite seem as real as they ought, for the logic of the piece, somehow not sufficiently its own ground, can yet not quite find any other in its stead.

The story has become well known in recent years. The context is the Indian warfare of "Lovell's Fight." Roger Malvin has been mortally wounded and left alone in the forest with one of the few other survivors of the battle, his son-in-law to be, Reuben Bourne. Reuben's first impulse is to remain with Malvin to the death, but persuaded by Malvin that such a course is foolish and even irresponsible, he goes back to the settlements, vowing to return to give his father-in-law a proper burial. Once back in the settlements, however, Reuben finds it difficult to fulfill his vow. His fiancée and the rest of the settlers assume that Malvin has died and been buried already, for they know Reuben to be honorable, and Reuben finds himself in an untenable position. He marries, takes up farming, fathers a son, but his guilt keeps him morose and unprosperous. Finally, after many unhappy years, he packs up his family and journeys to start anew somewhere else. In the course of the journey, while hunting, an accident occurs. On the very spot where his father-in-law died, Reuben, shooting into the bush, kills his son, and, as Hawthorne concludes, "The vow that the wounded youth had made, the blighted man had come to redeem. His sin was expiated, the curse was gone from him."[1]

It is as neat and as symmetrical a story as even Poe might wish. We end where we began. The head bites the tale. Reuben's quandary, his suffering, his life experience rounds itself into an aesthetic whole, a form in which the self is othered about as far as it can be, and in this othering, in fact, Hawthorne, in an access of apocalyptic violence, even outdoes Poe by calling it redemption. Yet what sort of redemption, exactly, can killing a son really provide? In what sense is the curse lifted? Reuben's otherness is a difficulty not to be so easily conjured away. He is rendered in sufficient density—he lives and he loves—to make us wonder at the readiness with which he turns his life into an aesthetic in the first place. Quite clearly, that is, this is—or ought to be—Reuben's story. If it has a moral, it is a moral concerning Reuben. If there is a lesson to be learned, Reuben should learn it. And yet so much of what happens to Reuben would not seem to have to do with him at all. So much of what he does seems, indeed, utterly beyond his control and even his consciousness. It is "attributable to no care of his own, that his devious course kept him in the vicinity of the encampment" (10.355). Reuben does not of his own will return to the scene of Malvin's death, but is compelled. And yet, therefore, precisely where is the compulsion located? What causes his return? What motivates the formalism into which he enters—something which is "his own" or something else?

This has been the problem on which most interpretations of "Roger Malvin's Burial" have foundered. There is a gap here, a discrepancy between Reuben and his story to which traditional interpretations, tending rather to explain it away than explain it, do not quite lend themselves. Thus it is not quite to the point to claim, say with Frederick Crews, that events may be given a psychological account.[2] Crews's oedipal reading, his tale of a guilty boy punishing himself in the form of his own child by returning to the scene of his disobedience in a kind of return of the repressed, is internally convincing. But it is difficult to understand the social expectations with which Reuben contends, the communal norms which cause his difficulties in the first place, as mere projections, as we would have to do for a complete reading. No projection can account for so externally validated a matter as the Indian warfare with which the story opens. No projection can deny the quite explicit context seemingly offered for the story's wider understanding. On the other hand, how much are we to make of this wider context after all? Historians, such as Michael Colacurcio, take the tale as Hawthorne's reminder to his American public of its guilt for extirpating the Indians.[3] Reuben is a victim of collective sin, his story the story of a man caught in the operation of a retributive history. Yet the gap remains, for the providentiality of such a history seems quite to contradict the singularity which, *as* story, Hawthorne gives Reuben's life. As Hawthorne is careful to distinguish, "This battle, so fatal to those who fought, was not unfortunate in its consequences to the country." The congruence of Reuben and his context is denied. The history *of* this story is useful *in* the story, as Hawthorne puts it, rather for its susceptibility to "the moonlight of romance" than for the light it sheds on history in general. Its actual circumstances are to be set aside by the "imagination" (10.337).

It is tempting to see Hawthorne denying history as well as psychology in "Roger Malvin's Burial." It is tempting, since both seem inadequate, to see him marking out in the form of the story another bit of his famous "neutral territory" in which neither the one nor the other quite intrudes itself. This would be a territory prior to the divisions of internal and external. It would be a space, in Hawthorne's more usual formulation, neither exactly actual nor imaginary, neither bound by materiality nor yet given over to fantasy. It would be a moral or ethical space, rather—to speak in our own terms, the ground of a true selfhood, the basis of action democratic, action truly free, such as we have seen it in Benjamin Franklin, that is, freely granted by a community which has not fully formalized action psychologically or historically, and, as such, particular, responsible, self-motivated. It is only that such action would stand in denial of the very formalism to which Reuben is explicitly subjected and which, in fact, seems rather to motivate *him*.

To put it another way, Reuben is in a hopeless bind. He would save his life rather than risk it on a man who cannot be helped. He would become the husband of the man's daughter, providing a life for both of them, rather than sacrifice life to what is as good as dead. And yet the "he" who would thus be saved—the Reuben who abandons his father-in-law—is, in the communal circumstances in which he finds himself, no one who really can be a proper husband any longer. As Colacurcio, attempting to resolve the dilemma, even against the necessity of his own historicism, argues, Reuben's trouble is not that he fails to live up to the demands of his society, but that he does not decide what demands he has of his own, that he does not "settle his intention."[4] And yet, precisely by the light of any serious historicism, Reuben's desire is never his own. He can have no intention that is properly "his." In the terms of our argument, Reuben both is and is not the author of his life. What he writes is yet not his, nor can possession be either full or fully repudiated. And yet Hawthorne would avow the possibility of authorship nevertheless. In the light of a consciousness beyond Reuben's, he ratifies Reuben's dilemma. He writes it. And, writing it, he thus declares that such is what authorship really is. Self-motivation is, indeed, maintained in "Roger Malvin's Burial." The space remains ethical despite all problems. But it is Hawthorne who, by a certain act of will, maintains it. It is he—over and against Reuben—who establishes it as such, and indeed through an act that thus might be termed a kind of "redemption" after all:

> A mournful smile strayed across the features of the dying man, as he insinuated that unfounded hope [that help might be brought if Reuben left him]; which, however, was not without its effect on Reuben. No merely selfish motive, nor even the desolate condition of Dorcas, could have induced him to desert his companion,

at such a moment. But his wishes seized upon the thought, that Malvin's life might be preserved, and his sanguine nature heightened, almost to certainty, the remote possibility of procuring human aid. (10.342)

As a consideration of selfhood, this passage, in its overnicety, might seem no less than Reuben under a certain compulsion. In its attempt to distinguish between altruism and self-interest it is corrosive and inhuman. It is Ramist analysis rather than constructive understanding. It is Puritan logic, judging a person's activity in terms not *of* his activity but of external moral standards, justifying the particulars of what he does on the basis of fixed principles rather than the disposition of his freedom. Hawthorne, it would seem, like Reuben, is bound to the inhumanity of such standards. He cannot evaluate Reuben's behavior—any more than Reuben can behave—outside the terms of so strict and unforgiving a moral calculus. And yet Hawthorne, thus doubling Reuben's condition in his rendering of it, renders a certain significant perspective on Reuben as well. As we might put it, Hawthorne also is in the grip of what is not him. He too is formalized and at a certain distance from himself, whether an internal or external distance. But, in a way that Reuben could not, Hawthorne would grip what grips him in his own turn. He would assert the distance as a kind of freedom. He would not so much declare any intention as his rather than his community's. Yet he would, from the perspective of a certain remove never elided, declare such or such an intention as belonging to a "he" whose communalization he openly adopts. Selfhood in "Roger Malvin's Burial" is, indeed, compelled. It is, as in Poe, not only itself but an other. And yet this otherness is not, as it was in Poe, what the self has become, but what it has chosen. The compulsion is a "curse." But in accepting it, in acknowledging, even, a certain complicity in constituting it, Hawthorne sees a hope for expiation at last.

To put it as Lionel Trilling has most exactly, Hawthorne is "our Hawthorne."[5] His stories are not his own but ours. They represent not a personal vision. They speak not a private language. They are cut and finished, formed in the form of speech as we

speak it already. Is psychology what we demand—as did, say, the
impressionists who first established the American canon before
Crews? Then Hawthorne is a *poète maudit.* [6] Is history in fashion—
as it was, say, for the second generation of Americanists who
consolidated the canon as well as for Colacurcio? Then Hawthorne is a sharp-eyed social critic. [7] Of all his contemporaries,
indeed, we seem to have been able to accommodate Hawthorne
almost too comfortably to whatever the reigning critical discourse.
From his own time to ours, through all the valuations and revalua-
tions of the American tradition, Hawthorne's reputation as somehow central to the writing of his era has remained virtually un-
challenged. And yet this is not the whole story either, for "our"
Hawthorne is yet "Hawthorne" as well, and accordingly the implications of his unchanging centrality are not so comfortable as
historical or psychological readings of him generally pretend.
Hawthorne, adapting himself to us almost too deliberately, yet
signs himself in the act of adaptation. He is not passive and
approving, but active and self-critical. His writing "is" not, simply, our writing, as conservative readers might like to assume. Nor
even is it simply "his" writing—that is, a writing opposing ours
that, to make him seem like us, we or he have misread, as radical
readers have more recently seen it. Rather, accommodating his
writing to us quite openly, freely admitting his accommodation,
he acknowledges us as what he must write if he would even be a
writer at all. Hawthorne, as we should say, exposes the burden as
well as the freedom of democratic authorship. Addressing an other
no longer pleased by nor pleasing the self, he cannot reject it for
the self. But he does not make himself quite other either. Rather,
he accepts otherness as what, for the self, there is and in which, by
taking it responsibly up, he would become himself after all.

I. Outsidedness

Hawthorne is "our Hawthorne." Trilling's formulation is rich
enough and close enough to our concerns to warrant some further
discussion. It is, indeed, something like Tate's formulation that
Poe is "our cousin." In both, closeness and separation are con-

joined. In both, a certain distance is asserted even while it is being bridged. And yet the difference between "our author" and "our cousin, the author" is notable too. For the shift to a familar, as we might put it, from a familial form of description exhibits nicely just what the additional freedoms and burdens that Hawthorne takes up entail. As Hawthorne puts it, "It is a little remarkable, that—though disinclined to talk overmuch of myself and my affairs at the fireside, and to my personal friends—an autobiographical impulse should twice in my life have taken possession of me, in addressing the public" (1.3). Consanguinity has disappeared here as a context for self-definition. The home and the hearth—places Hawthorne laments, in "Fire-Worship," having himself displaced with so alienating a mechanism as the modern stove—yet have been displaced, and it is now to strangers, in the context of what is "public" rather than "personal," that the self would be rendered at all. This is alienation, indeed. No ties of nature or spirit, no god of family or fire binds Hawthorne to those to whom he would tell his life. He is (to his reader, at least) no brother but an orphan writing to other orphans (orphans to him, at least) as well. And yet, it must also be pointed out, thus Hawthorne has not been, like Poe, orphaned. He does not project a state of relations prior to orphanhood which might be recaptured. Or, at least, his nostalgia for such a state is only nostalgia. This is a matter we will deal with shortly, but meanwhile, we may note, it leaves him in the state in which he does find himself, living what we might call life enough.

Hawthorne's otherness, we should say, is both more and less intense than Poe's. With no attempt to recover any even forgotten unity of himself and others, with no assumption of any necessary connection between them, his words might just as well not be written altogether. On the other hand, since his otherness is not, therefore, oppositeness, any conjunction of his words and the words of the other need not obliterate him in oppositeness' own opposite, identity, but may constitute a kind of self-realization instead. For twelve years after college, in his mother's attic, while his classmates, as he complained, were making names for themselves, Hawthorne remained, unsought and unknown. As numerous biographers who would know him nevertheless have, accordingly, construed it, he was no such unsearchable recluse as his earliest interpreters assumed, but followed a path worn well by presumed loners like him everywhere. And yet the significance of the country wanderer, devotee of cigars and a social drink or two that, say, Randall Stewart first gave us, is not that the path he followed is social, but that his reclusiveness is itself socialized.[8] The self, in Hawthorne, neither denies nor becomes the other. We have in him no doubles, no William Wilsons or Fortunatos and Montresors, two characters so much alike that only one may exist. But instead there is Gervayse Hastings, the protagonist of "The Christmas Banquet," whose inability to feel sympathy even for himself is itself a kind of doubleness, or Richard Digby, "The Man of Adamant," whose rocklike otherness makes one character always two. There is no "Man in the Crowd," as there is in Poe, who, nameless and homeless, loses his identity in the general stream of humanity. But instead there is a character like Wakefield, who, even within the general stream of humanity, finds his identity in his being outside his home, whatever home he happens to take up.

As we might put it, "outsidedness" is, in fact, a better term than "otherness" for Hawthorne, suggesting, as it does, a kind of otherness only without any positivity. The relation into which selves and others enter precedes the self and the other. The outsider has not been thrust outside. His goal is not to obliterate or become the insider. Individuality is not conceived of as a nature which must envelop or be enveloped by another nature, as it sometimes seems to be in Poe. It is not even conceived of as a nature enveloping or enveloped by that second nature to which Cooper promotes culture. As Hawthorne puts the issue in *The Scarlet Letter,* has Pearl been plucked off a bush, as she explains her origins (1.112)? Yet her giving this explanation is a sign not of her naturalness but, as the Puritan fathers conceive it, of her bad upbringing. Should Pearl, then, be taken away from Hester and brought up better? Yet this would not be good upbringing after all but, as Hester knows, the unnatural taking of a child away from her mother. Categories are confused and rearranged here. In the place of Cooper's natural,

Hawthorne puts the eccentric. In the place of Cooper's cultivation, he gives us the *un*natural. Self which has been othered, selves which have moved, in Poe, to a kind of dialectic, are pushed back toward a diacritic. And while this is not yet, nor ever can be, Franklin's prediacritical difference with a difference, while it does not abolish the alienation whose consequences we have been tracing, it does, rather than merely hold the line against it, actually use alienation, as it were homeopathically, to cure itself. In effect, Hawthorne cannot return to the preconscious state of selves authorizing, rather than denying, each other. Their division has been thought past the possibility of unthinking. And yet, *re*thinking division, thinking it, that is, self-consciously, he authorizes it on the basis of a kind of deliberation, a responsibility carried by a self which is therefore indispensable.

Hawthorne, let us say, is caught in that circle of alienation we described in relation to Poe. Yet, as it were, he squares the circle, turning his limitation into possibility instead. Poe's first third-personness becomes a kind of third first-personness. That is, in Poe the self is othered in what, because he conceives of otherness so starkly, threatens an infinite regress away from communality. This is why, as we have seen, otherness must in effect be what we called transcendentalized to remain conceivable as communal after all. And it is why, too, critics who define community rather as what has no place for the other have struggled with what appears to be Poe's triviality. Poe's writing is formalized, reduced to the status of case history or, to save it, phenomenologized, the lost communality of its too-objectified "I" recast as a globally subjective cogito. In Hawthorne, however, the self as outside rather than other must labor to communalize itself in order even to be itself. Hawthorne is threatened not by objectification, but by disappearance. And the formalization of his writing, accordingly, is the sign not of his isolation but of his integration, his decision to commit himself, from a position of alienation, to such forms as he finds in his community already in place. The self, as we might say, achieves selfhood by very virtue of its outsidedness. It establishes selfhood in the choice of what is outside it, freeing it from being bound to either a phenomenological or a material self which would not be itself at all. That is why, even though no Rufus Griswold has intervened with false information to complicate the task, biography of Hawthorne has been so varied. On the one hand, the facts of his life seem so incompletely his life that, unlike Poe's, even their fullest rendering is never claimed as his authoritative biography. On the other hand, against the fictions which others have taken as Poe's real expression, even Hawthorne's presumably expressive autobiography, the voluminous yet so uninformative pages of the English, French and American Note-Books, seems to express nothing at all.

Indeed, if anywhere, we should say that Hawthorne is rendered most authentically in that sort of bio-autobiography which are his remarkable prefaces. Here, in what he called his "attempts to open an intercourse with the world," self and other which "are" not in themselves are created by disposing each toward the other. Here, in a discourse frankly mixed, are neither the individual nor his community, but the relation between them, their not being each other which is the condition of relation and which guarantees their individuality even when most—formally or expressively—they seem the same.

> Has the reader gone wandering, hand in hand with me, through the inner passages of my being, and have we groped together into all its chambers, and examined their treasures or their rubbish? Not so. We have been standing on the green sward, but just within the cavern's mouth, where the common sunshine is free to penetrate, and where every footstep is therefore free to come. I have appealed to no sentiment or sensibilities, save such as are diffused among us all. So far as I am a man of really individual attributes, I veil my face; nor am I, nor have I ever been, one of those supremely hospitable people, who serve up their own hearts delicately fried, with brain sauce, as a tidbit for their beloved public. (10.32–33)

This is an easy passage to misconstrue. It is such a mixture of giving and taking, of courtesy and hostility, of frankness and withholding. What is Hawthorne saying? If "the inner passages" of his being remain concealed, why boast about it? Is Hawthorne proud of his superficiality? Or does he indict us for ours? Is "he" unreal, or are "we"? It is tempting to resolve the difficulties here, to search out, beyond the "I" that is manifest, a deeper "I" who might be known more intimately. We are impatient with the "I" dispersed across the passage and so hypostatize an "I" unified behind it. Hawthorne, we imagine, is not really in the surface he speaks. The "common sunshine" exists only to conceal the uncommon darkness, the real self he invites us to learn.[9] Or we imagine, perhaps, that Hawthorne does not himself understand this real self. In his squeamishness about "hearts" with "brain sauce," he turns from what we, however, must relish in despite of his taste.[10] We presume a Hawthorne behind Hawthorne—revealing himself, concealing himself—but the true object of our reading.

And yet the hard truth which Hawthorne is asking his readers to face is that, despite any longings to the contrary, they must take the passage at "face" value precisely. It is *in* the difficulties the passage raises, not in resolving them, that Hawthorne exists. It is as responsible for how he appears that he would be read. Or better, if he appears to conceal himself in the face he puts on, then as one declaring his concealment exactly, he takes responsibility for himself all the more. "I veil my face." Hawthorne does presume a self behind himself. This is the nostalgia which we mentioned, the lost faith in self-identity after which lesser writers run. Yet Hawthorne, taking the loss as the condition of such selfhood as is available to him in the first place, recreates it. He accepts his alienation. The self-identical self, relegated to nostalgia, loses its force, making available a self with whom intimacy is possible all the more. As Jonathan Cilley, Hawthorne's college friend put it, "I love Hawthorne, I admire him: but I do not know him."[11] The veil separates. The veil disrupts community. Putting it on, like the Reverend Hooper in "The Minister's Black Veil," Hawthorne calls attention to his distance from us which we had, perhaps, been far better never noticing. Yet noticing it, we can do worse than exaggerate it, as the minister's parishioners do, in their refusal to continue their relations with him. We can, like Elizabeth, the minister's fiancée, attempt to see beneath it, to pretend to a relation of selves at a depth in which, however, the only selfhood that matters would be destroyed.

That is why "though this veil must be between us," as Hawthorne has the Reverend Hooper insist, he nevertheless has him entreat Elizabeth, "Do not leave me in this miserable obscurity" (9.47). It is why, in the passage quoted above, though he fancies a self that, indeed, is obscure, he asks us to accept a self almost too obvious, instead. "I have appealed to no sentiment or sensibilities, save such as are diffused among us all." Must this really be stated? What would a sentiment not so diffused be? How would *it* be stated? In what language? Spoken by whom? Rather, even obscurity is stated in language "among us all," so that putting selfhood off as obscure is but to establish for it, in what is not obscure, an identity that may be picked up after all.

II. Writing Once More

As we might put it in the context of our book so far, Hawthorne too engages the issue of representation. The audience's refusal to grant the author authority drives him, no less than Brown, Cooper, and Poe, further and further away from what he writes. Speaking to his community, he appears no longer to be speaking himself, and, since we cannot quite readily accept the notion of speech without the self, we invent a self beyond speech instead. Alienation, as we should say in current linguistic terms, threatens a split between signifier and signified. The self represented and the language which would represent it separate. Language becomes merely conventional, and the self which speaks convention, accordingly, an "obscure" self indeed. Still, Hawthorne's treatment of this obscurity differs from those of the others. Unlike Brown and Cooper he does not resist it, and unlike Poe he does not idealize it. More comfortable with his otherness—outside, as we have said, rather than other—he accepts it, acknowledging his alienation and so recovering himself as one for whom acknowledgment is the beginning of such speech as he can engage after all. As we might put it, the difficulty against which Brown, Cooper, and

Poe struggle becomes its own solution. Allegory, symbolism, the variety of problematical responses to the uncertain connection of language with its referent, are so clearly foregrounded, so openly displayed, that they lose their force *as* problems. We will discuss these matters in more detail later. Contemporary theory has been much vexed by them, and that Hawthorne is not also vexed needs further elucidation. For now, however, we may note that even early on in the history of Hawthorne criticism, when Yvor Winters praises what he calls *The Scarlet Letter*'s "alternative possibilities" as yet, surprisingly, "unobscurantist," he is thus pretheoretically acute.[12] For Hawthorne approaches the difficulties of representation from the vantage point of an outsidedness from which he would embrace rather than end them. He engages a writing whose clarity and obscurity he would not settle but domesticate. Accordingly, in the midst of barriers to representation, Hawthorne can yet be successfully representational. But he can be because he acknowledges representation as rather a kind of will to represent. He can be because first and foremost he conceives of representation in the context not of some assumed closeness to what is represented, but of a certain commitment he is willing to make to what he takes, precisely conventionally, to be close enough.

To put it in other terms, Hawthorne's writing, like the writing of the others, as we have defined it, is writing indeed. No more than it is independent of his life does it refer back to his life, taken to be somehow anterior to it. But engaging less defensively than the other writers we have discussed the threat of such anteriority, admitting the split of representation and represented *as* a split, Hawthorne would write it without apology as a split which, therefore, he lives all the more. In these terms, it does not matter that life no longer appears to be quite what he describes it as. It does not matter that description appears to have fallen away from life. For in Hawthorne's case, the fallen life is conceived as life also, and so he would give himself over to description just the same. As we might admit, following Winters, *The Scarlet Letter* is thus, indeed, Hawthorne's great representational achievement. In it, let us agree, Hawthorne appears to resolve the great cognitive difficulties of his age. In it, let us say, he brings together what some critics have seen as the ideal and the real or the interior and the exterior. Yet bringing them together, we must also say, in a letter, in a representation whose standing as a resolution is established only by hearts committing themselves to it in the first place, he thus establishes commitment as representation's very ground. In the terms with which we began, the self, neither a self nor an other, becomes itself by committing itself *to* the other. Cognition, in the terms we introduced in connection with Cooper, becomes a matter not of epistemology but of ethics. Or in the terms we have been using since Franklin, representation becomes a rhetoric, and the establishment of rhetoricity as more real than the very alienation which would replace it with cognition becomes Hawthorne's greatest achievement.

As Hawthorne puts it in *The Scarlet Letter* in a much quoted passage: "Be true! Be true!" Yet the "truth" of *The Scarlet Letter* is only apparently the revelation at the end. For the wonder of what is revealed—a secret, after all, to which we are privy from almost the beginning—is rather that something so unrevealing should even count as revelation, that the letter whose meaning remains even at the end so much in doubt should be deemed meaningful nevertheless. As Hawthorne continues, "Be true! Show freely to the world, if not your worst, yet some trait whereby the worst may be inferred!" (1.260). Truth just precisely is the inference *of* truth. But thus inference, not secondary to what is inferred, is redefined as primary by the force it is made to carry of an insistent moral imperative. "You [understood]," "be [an act, not an existent]" "true [a predicating, not descriptive, adjective]." Representation neither "is" nor "is not" adequate to truth. But as just the kind of truth that has, in fact, been represented, it must be owned by anyone who would truly "be" in the first place.

Hawthorne, we might say, like Hester, putting on the scarlet A because there was more "real life" in it than without it, puts on the letters of his community as his life too. Of course, like Hester, he would rather be not his community but himself. Like Hester, if we might put it this way, he would be himself, that is, independent of other selves. Yet like Hester too, he knows that the basis of independence is dependence precisely, that if the self cannot be prior *to* the community's representation of it, yet it may be prior *in* it. Accordingly, though Hawthorne has difficulties in speaking of himself, he conceives of these difficulties not as a limit of self-articulation, but as its ground. Thus Hawthorne speaks openly of his difficulties. As we have seen, he is embarrassed about speaking, as he tells us in *The Scarlet Letter* (1.3–4). Or if, despite embarrassment, he does speak, he worries that no one may listen. Thus he imagines that his reader may be under some mossy gravestone, in *The Marble Faun* (4.2). Or, if his speech is heard after all, he doubts that it will be understood. Thus he fears that the story of *The Blithedale Romance* will be taken as a roman à clef about Brook Farm (3.1–3). Finally, however, it is in the speech that it generates that his fear is also confronted. Hawthorne does not, like Franklin, address himself to his "Dear Son." He assumes no interest on the part of the reader, no confidence that will make him articulate whatever he says. Instead he addresses himself to a distant, to an alienated or "Gentle Reader" (4.1) so *un*assuming that he may even prefer, like the Reverend Hooper's parishioners, that nothing, finally, be articulated. It is only that readers, gentle or otherwise, are addressed only as they do read, and because they cannot be assumed to read as a matter of course they must perforce read independently or not at all. Readers, no more than the writer, are independent of their reading, but they are independent by virtue of it. Writing and reading, writers and readers are thrown back on themselves. Writing and reading, they take hold of themselves, come home to themselves. And so Hawthorne comes home to himself too. The "obscurest man of letters" (9.3), as he called himself, writing in his garret, alone, composing his stories to burn them, he preferred a life of pseudonymous or even anonymous composition to a public career as man and author in the world. And yet, by what can only be seen as sheer force of self-creation, he came out, married, and published under a name indeed assumed, but therefore precisely as his own.[13] Hawthorne would be a writer. Accordingly, he took upon himself the burden of writing, to live *in* his work, not behind it. He bound himself to the conventional way of speaking, to speaking which, he admits, is always a convention. And yet, binding himself rather than being bound, he assumes, from the vantage point of an outsidedness which might instead have remained outside, the responsiblity for conventions, himself.

III. History and Responsibility

Let us frame the issue forthrightly. What is the status of this writing in which the writer might live? Who is this Hawthorne who lives in his work? From what does his authority derive? How does his outsidedness, no life in itself, establish his life after all?

> The Author, who, on the internal evidence of his sketches, came to be regarded as a mild, shy, gentle, melancholic, exceedingly sensitive, and not very forcible man, hiding his blushes under an assumed name . . . is by no means certain, that some of his subsequent productions have not been influenced and modified by a natural desire to fill up so amiable an outline, and to act in consonance with the character assigned to him. (9.7)

Author and work circle around each other here, serving to cancel each other out. Who—or what—authorizes what—or whom? We are far removed from the certainties of psychology or history that finally what works refer to is someone or something beyond themselves. Hawthorne refuses us the comfort of a world which is not words, of a life which is not writing, for all its difficulties.

And yet we are far too from asserting that writing, therefore, is "only" words. This has been the growing view. The veils to which we have referred have loomed ever larger in recent Hawthorne studies, and, since they can be taken no longer as masking a reality which must be our true end, they are deemed to deny truth for a shadow world to which, instead, we are condemned.[14] Still, the world's shadowiness—as but outsidedness as it were existentialized, the author's outsidedness extended onto what might otherwise be the inside as well—thus denies the very distinction between truth and shadow, outside and inside that seems to be a problem in the first place. We should remember the response of Miles Coverdale confronted with a similar mask, the Arcadian "masquerade," as he calls it, of the Blithedalers playing at utopia. Zenobia's rich circumstances in Boston cast doubt on the authenticity of the linsey-woolsey she wears on the farm. "To this day," as Coverdale remarks, "I hardly know whether I then beheld Zenobia in her truest attitude, or whether that were the truer one in which she had presented herself at Blithedale." He despairs of knowing the truth: "In both, there was something like the illusion which a great actress flings around her." He supposes a truth which is unflattering: "I malevolently beheld the true character of the woman, passionate, luxurious, lacking simplicity, not deeply refined, incapable of pure and perfect taste." And yet, "the next instant," as he acknowledges, "she was too powerful for all my opposing struggles. I saw how fit it was that she should make herself as gorgeous as she pleased" (3.165). Indeed, why should Zenobia not make herself as gorgeous as she pleased? Why does not everyone make himself gorgeous, or since, manifestly, everyone does not, why not? No throwing up hands at "illusion" will do. No recourse to "true character" is an excuse. The world as words, if it is a constraint, yet is a possibility as well. It is—must it not be seized?—a freedom. Or if, free to write what it will, the nation has written so badly this, then the freedom of writing has become—and must this too not be accepted?—a responsibility.

Miles Coverdale, we might say, is Hawthorne's figure of the skeptic. He spends his life looking and, as a consequence, wondering if what he looks at is real. Alienated from his environment, retreating to the distance of his parlor window or his hermitage, he views the world from the vantage point of cognition itself, where it becomes, as it must, an epistemological conundrum. Unrepresentable in himself, Coverdale narrates the other, in itself equally unrepresentable, and so his narrative is shadowy, unreliable, untrue. As he himself admits, however, it is only in the bringing together of such untruths that truth may be created. What has made the world unreal is his own lack of commitment to it. It is an ethical absence, the "lack [of] a purpose," as he frankly acknowledges, that has ruined his life (3.246), for it is by committing himself that the reality of what he is committed to is in fact established.

I cannot agree with recent deconstructionist-inspired skepticism that unreality is anything more for Hawthorne than—however difficult—an opportunity. The vantage point of such a critique is too manifestly another hermitage such as Hawthorne exposes. Nor, while I sympathize with that critique of certain of Hawthorne's bourgeois values leveled by the New Historicism which claims, in a sort of strategic retreat from deconstruction, that such values, at least, are unreal, do I suppose for a moment that Hawthorne would allow, in that case, any other values the status of being somehow more real.[15] To reconsider, for example, Hawthorne's coming out from his attic which we have praised, it is true enough that thus he joined his art to the capitalist world of publication and trade. He married too and in the conventionality of his marriage allied himself to the sexism of mid-century gender relations. Indeed, as the intensification of those conventions in his love letters, with their "Sweetest Dove" and "Dearest Phoebe," demonstrates (15.290ff., 699), Hawthorne more than passively slid into mid-century sexism. He helped establish it. But what he thus established was a life not only for himself but for his "Phoebe"— Sophia—who prior to the role of bourgeois wife and mother he provided for her had not really lived, but remained an invalid in her attic too. On either side of the equation was, equally, what he might make of it—as it presented itself to Hawthorne, life for women or life for this woman. Nor, though we might have chosen the former, though we might legitimately criticize Hawthorne for choosing the latter, may we absolve ourselves of the responsibility for what our choice would have entailed for Sophia, the level of "reality" it assigns her, as if it were not in fact what we assigned at all.

Hawthorne, as he tells us, writes plainly. His words have no "abstruseness." "They never need translation." "Every sentence, so far as it embodies thought or sensibility, may be understood and felt by anybody, who will give himself the trouble to read it, and will take up the book in a proper mood" (9.6). Yet the appeal to what anybody may feel and understand is an appeal not to truth but to the "trouble" taken with precisely what is plain in order to establish the thinking and feeling in it *as* true. The "proper mood" is not the conservative temperament evident in the decisions Hawthorne everywhere makes, but the ethical basis—the philosophy far more radical, despite its lack of abstruseness, than his most radical critics have yet come up to—on which a proper American politics, conservative or not, may be founded. In an act similar to his marriage, Hawthorne writes a campaign biography to help Franklin Pierce, his friend, but a terrible waffler on slavery.[16] Hawthorne preferred union to abolition. Or at best, he preferred abolition later to war now. But if, as we must today, we prefer the reverse, we must be willing to take responsibility for war now, from which no distinction between real and unreal living, no appeal—say, to historical inevitability—will exonerate us. There is in Hawthorne no unreality save that which is not lived altogether, nor is there life for which those who live it are not to blame. There is no history save that which is dreamed. But dream becomes history precisely as the dreamer is held to account.

It is no wonder that it is so difficult to distinguish history from dream in Hawthorne. Nor does Hawthorne, of all American writers the most historically well read, wish to deny that distinctions need to be made. It is only that admitting that he makes them, accepting them as difficult, he takes on what he regarded as the democrat's burden, which no preexistent distinction would ever make easy. Hawthorne's inconsistency in the matter is here wonderfully precise. Is "The Great Carbuncle" a foolish illusion? Yet the vision of "The Artist of the Beautiful" is realized in even a material form. Does Aylmer of "The Birthmark" do evil in striving for perfection? Yet the couple of "The Shaker Bridal" does as badly by refusing to strive altogether. Dreams are too much or too little, and there is no certain test of which is which. But the uncertainty is no exoneration either, for tested and tester alike are to blame. "Accursed one. . . . Thou hast blasted me. . . . Thou hast made me as hateful, as ugly, as loathsome and deadly a creature as thyself," cries Giovanni, in "Rappaccini's Daughter," rejecting Beatrice's contention that "though my body be nourished with poison, my spirit is God's creature" (10.122–23). And yet, as Beatrice quite properly counters, "Oh, was there not, from the first, more poison in thy nature than in mine?" (10.127).

Beauty and loathsomeness, body and spirit—distinctions are inevitably wrong. But criticism of them is wrong too, nor, if the world is wrong, can any place be right, can there be any refuge from wrong distinctions, which implicate everyone.

Thus it is that Hawthorne's first important "historical" tale, "The Gray Champion," deals not quite with history, after all, but with what he insists is "our" history. It is "our liberties" and "our religion" that are involved, "our ancestors" and "our shores" (9.9–10). It is even, as we may say, "our" myth.[17] For the figure of the champion himself, the "type of New-England's hereditary spirit" (9.18), though differentiated from genuine historical figures—James II, Edward Andros, William Bradstreet, Edward Randolph, all made to appear in a blatant show of historical fact—is yet differentiated not in fact's service but in its own, as what might be made historical, perhaps to New England's peril, but also, perhaps, to its credit, if it so chooses. As Hawthorne saw it, the problem is not really that America has been living a dream, but that in its not having chosen this dream, it has not really lived it at all. "There was once a time, when New-England groaned under the actual pressure of heavier wrongs, than those threatened ones which brought on the Revolution" (9.9). History undoes the revolutionary mythos. The momentous event was produced by small causes. The injustices for which Americans acted were not so unjust after all. And yet, too, there were injustices enough—the "heavier wrongs"—for which Americans did not act, so that the question, as in "Roger Malvin's Burial," is rather which injustice they should decide to make momentous and when. Again, is the Gray Champion actually to be believed? Surely he is too heroic to be real. He cannot be New England's true representative. He walks "solitary" and at a "distance from the multitude." His dress is "antique" and of a fashion thoroughly outmoded (9.13, 14). Yet Hawthorne's plea at the end of the tale, "still may the Gray Champion come" (9.18), does not recant the doubts fed by the body of the story, but enlists them in a call, therefore, to realize him. It separates the representative from those he represents so that he may become their representative by the force of their, even, heroic choice. The Gray Champion is not quite a myth in the manner of Cooper's Natty Bumppo, but America's tendency to see itself mythically. Or rather, if Natty is, as we have said, a myth of America preserved from mystification only by unconsciousness, the Champion is so blatantly mystified that the agency of Americans in his making is manifest. He is America as Americans might hope to create themselves consciously once more.

As we might sum it up, for Hawthorne, history is what a community writes. It is its convention of itself, its version of itself seen from a certain distance, from a position of alienation which, by strict philosophical standards, removes it from what it truly is. Yet Hawthorne's concern, for all of his criticism of his community's writing, is not, thus, that it will whitewash, that it will conventionalize out of existence those truths which are too unpleasant for it to face. This is a really too philosophical concern. Of course whitewashing occurs. People will always be blind. They will see badly. They will write and read badly too. But it is hard, given Hawthorne's democratic assumptions, to know how to prevent this, for he does not so simply presume he is any less blind than anyone else. He does not, after all, presume to write any better than his readers read. Rather Hawthorne is concerned that without a critical or, as we have called it, an outside perspective, "truths" of all sorts—whitewashed or not— can have no ethical force. He is concerned, that is, not to rectify this or that record of an event in national history, but to make the nation's practice of conceiving of events historically admittedly its practice. "To us," as he meditates in a historical essay, "the wisdom of the politician appears like folly, because we can compare its prognostics with actual results":

> the old merchant seems to have busied himself about vanities, because we know that the expected ships have been lost at sea, or mouldered at the wharves; that his imported broadcloths were long ago worn to tatters, and his cargoes of wine quaffed to the lees; and that the most precious leaves of his ledger have become waste-paper. Yet, his avocations were not so vain as our philosophic moralizing. In this world, we are the things of a moment, and are made to pursue momentary things, with here and there a thought that stretches mistily towards eternity, and perhaps may endure as long. All philosophy, that would abstract mankind from the present, is no more than words. (II.133)

History provides its wisdom. With living turned into life already lived, the true proportions of things seem evident enough. But thus such wisdom is a loss precisely of living, and accordingly, heroic or venal, history *as* history will not help. It is dead rather than alive, past rather than present. And the important thing, since historicizing would seem, like mortality, to be man's lot, is to revivify it, to make it human again.

Hawthorne, we should say, is fallen *into* history. Like Franklin and the others, he would live now. He would found existence in life as it is made in the moment rather than as it was made long ago. Yet unlike the others, he does not so much resist his fall, he does not deny the past, but re-presents it, and, if not exactly as new, yet as what he calls "Old News," balancing the two perfectly:

> Happy are the editors of newspapers! Their productions excel all others in immediate popularity, and are certain to acquire another sort of value with the lapse of time. They scatter their leaves to the wind, as the sybil did, and posterity collects them, to be treasured up among the best materials of its widsom. With hasty pens, they write for immortality. (II.132)

Here is history, like identity as we discussed it earlier, in the shape of a letter. Hawthorne's remarks are like the passage we quoted before from "The Custom-House" in which, much to his surprise, he finds himself addressing strangers rather than intimates, but whose strangeness is what enables intimacy nevertheless. The leaves scattered to the wind here are the "book, thrown at large on the wide world" there (1.3). The hasty pens writing for immortality are the writer prating autobiographically to a general public. Distance between eras is distance between selves. And the public's acceptance of that distance, a certain determination to send itself across a space it knows it cannot eliminate, is the only assurance of such humanity as it may hope for its history to have.

IV. Craftiness

Now the name we may give to this peculiar determination is, in Hawthorne's term, "craftiness." "Craftiness" is outsidedness as a praxis. It is, that is, as Kant defines praxis, "what concerns our freedom."[18] In Hawthorne's case it is outsidedness, which is the freedom of being at a distance from what he writes, committed to what he writes nevertheless. It appears in its purest—or, at least, its most egregious—form in "Wakefield," the story in which Hawthorne uses the term and to which we shall return shortly. But it may do well, here, to continue with "Old News" and in particular its concluding section, "The Old Tory." Here, in a device that will be repeated—in "Legends of the Province-House," for example, or even, to an extent, in "My Kinsman, Major Molineux"— Hawthorne gives us his world as an outsider caught up in it sees it, democracy triumphant, but as an old King's man yet demurs.

The situation is that of an aging loyalist left behind in America to meditate on the growing success of the Revolution. As we might expect, Hawthorne's point is to develop a certain critical perspective. The Tory exposes what is wrong. He is able to point out what democrats, lost in their triumph, have refused to grasp. He demystifies the democratic mythos, insisting on everything wonderful over which democracy has triumphed. And yet it need hardly be said that, for all that, the Tory's perspective, as ideological as is democracy, is not founded in anything true in itself. And, indeed, as Hawthorne renders it, the Tory's authority to criticize, the force of his criticism, is a consequence less of its expression of the culture of Torydom than of its engagement with democracy, its use of a democratic rather than an aristocratic language, only aristocratically twisted. "Here are prize-vessels for sale," the Tory comments, as he reads from the columns of the latest newspaper,

> no French nor Spanish merchantmen, whose wealth is the birthright of British subjects, but hulls of British oak, from Liverpool, Bristol, and the Thames, laden with the King's own stores, for his army in New-York. And what a fleet of privateers—pirates, say we—are fitting out for new ravages, with rebellion in their very names! The Free Yankee, the General Green, the Saratoga, the Lafayette, and the Grand Monarch! Yes, the Grand Monarch; so is a French King styled, by the sons of Englishmen. And here we have an ordinance, from the Court of Versailles, with the Bourbon's own signature affixed, as if New-England were already a

> French province. Everything is French. French soldiers, French
> sailors, French surgeons. . . . Everything in America is French,
> except the Canadas—the loyal Canadas—which we helped to
> wrest from France. And to that old French province, the En-
> glishman of the colonies must go find his country! (II.156)

This is as nearly what Bakhtin calls "dialogism" as it is criticism.[19] If the various voices disagree, they also blend. If the
perspectives conflict, yet they also intermix. Hawthorne, rendering his own views, speaks not in the anonymous speech of one
risen above the argument, but in the speech of a loyalist in turn
using the words of revolutionaries. It is a speech not quite, as
Bakhtin sees dialogism, of selves fulfilled. We get not quite what,
in a Marxist thesis, appears as the dissolution of perspectives into
one another, a sort of collective discourse of the unified folk in
which the formal boundaries that separate us, the divisivenesses
of ideological speech, wither away. But we do get, based on the
even-handedness rather than the elimination of such division, a
collective, nevertheless. Ideologies do not disappear, but remain
intact, rendering each other, now, equally ideological by the equal
force with which they oppose each other. No one agrees with
anyone here, but everyone is dependent on everyone nevertheless.
The Tory's praise of loyalism is precisely his criticism of what he
calls rebellion, and by extension, so therefore is praise of the rebels
no more than criticism of loyalism. The hierarchy of loyalist and
rebel is destroyed. Metalevels of discourse are collapsed. But the
discourses still remain. No folk ever emerges. Persons and perspectives do not dissolve. But they are made to occupy the same
space.

As we ought to recall, Hawthorne early abandoned his attempts at unified collections of stories under rubrics like "Tales of
My Native Land" or "The Story-Teller."[20] The idea of himself as
a sort of New England minstrel was attractive, perhaps, as an
antidote to his anonymity. Yet threatening, in its own turn, to
reestablish anonymity by overwhelming his voice with the voice of
his culture in general, such an idea would appeal to him not much
longer than it did to Cooper. Accordingly, Hawthorne rather

re-presents than presents his tales. Offering them but as "Fragments" or "Passages from . . . ," as he called them, parts of collections which, in the unfinished form that he kept invoking them, exhibit their formalism, their distance from him, all the more, he presents the culture he will not tell as a form that might yet be "twice-told," instead.[21] Community speaks, but in an individual speaker, Hawthorne, whose simultaneous distance from it guarantees both community and that the community will remain one of individuals, precisely. Such individuals must always interrogate their community. Indeed, their community *is* their interrogation of it. Yet it is a community, accordingly, whose interrogators bear a certain communal burden and even guilt, and whose progressive assumption of that burden is, in fact, the pattern of Hawthorne's career. It is a pattern which might be followed in very elaborate detail. Moving from the tales to the more fully extended structures of the four novels, it exhibits a Hawthorne taking up an increasingly articulated formalism, the rendering of which, in its full range, must be beyond the scope of this chapter. But something of its nature is projected even within the stories themselves, which may, accordingly, be taken as providing a convenient capsule of what is to come.

As we have discussed already in connection with "Roger Malvin's Burial," then, Hawthorne, in what we shall now call his first phase, rises out of the looseness of his provincial sketches to identify the patterns of his culture and master them. As in Poe, that is, separation leads to formalism. Hawthorne's alienated relation to his audience is projected onto the field of relations. Telling is objectified, and the "work" is born. Unlike Poe, however, Hawthorne is not protective of such a work. He does not exalt separation but acts upon it. As we have put it, the self in Hawthorne is not bound to form but binds itself to it, so that form is not his end but his beginning. All is not, as it was in Poe, complete already. Career, development, is not stymied. But development is itself not so much *in* Hawthorne's form as in his attachment *to* it. That is, it is in his investment in the works, his assumption of his culture *as* his and increasingly, therefore, his pronouncements on it as a kind of self-pronouncement as well.[22]

Thus, for example, in what may serve to mark the beginning

of this phase, "The Wives of the Dead," Hawthorne seems to uncover the very idea of form and to experiment with it. The story takes the shape of a simple O. Henry-like criss-cross. Two sisters, bound together by affection and a common lot, wait for news about their husbands, whom they fear dead. When each, in turn, hears, while the other is asleep, that her husband alone is safe, each sensitively refrains from sharing the information, and thus the same sympathy which worked to their comfort now prevents a full communion of joy. It is a finely wrought little piece, an exquisitely formed jewel. But its main point would seem to be no more than a formal description of form, if we may call it that, and accordingly what emerges from it is irony which, thus, Hawthorne discovers *is* form. Meaning—what we called in Poe meaning as the community means it—is, in the absence of any community, frustrated. As the story circles back on itself, readers and writers find their expectations of significance denied. A corrosive irony is begun which finds its end in "The Devil in Manuscript," where the work collapses into itself in a sort of early deconstruction of formalism that will obviate the necessity of his ever deconstructing his work again. As the anonymous author burns his manuscripts, as his stories, unpublished and unread, become fuel for the fire that consumes them, the fireplace, and then the city, the whole world from which they have been excluded is, in his pun, "set ablaze." The work establishes nothing. Or rather, invoking a readership who might make it meaningful *as* nothing, it disestablishes readers, creates their presence as an absence, nothingness as their only positivity, which thus self-destructs. As Hawthorne discovers in "Alice Doane's Appeal," perhaps the central tale of this phase, only as he tells it can a tale have any significance. The old story the narrator-author carries with him in his pocket will in itself have no effect. This work written yesterday cannot wring tears from the ladies he presents it to today. And so he must take hold of it anew. He must redirect it. He must reframe—as, indeed, he does in the frame which presents the lady listeners in the first place—the gothic conventions which, in their original (as, say, in *Fanshawe*) rather framed him, and thus he may advance to the second, more serious phase of his writing.[23]

Typical here are "The Gray Champion" and "Old News," that

mode of formalized telling we call history and in which, as we have seen, Hawthorne takes up the ethical problems which the nation's historicization of itself produces. Even more characteristic, however, are the more famous histories, "The Legends of the Province-House," "Endicott and the Red Cross," and "The May-Pole of Merry-Mount," in which, following through such an ethical determination, Hawthorne converts the problem of history into a problem of telling, quite directly. In these stories, history is not only problematized but embraced, or rather, by embracing it Hawthorne implicates himself in the problems raised and thus authorizes them on a new basis. Form, as we should say, is here not, as it was in the first phase, formal alone, but as a culture's formalization of itself, it is a content too. In the terms of these works, we should say that history so called is fictionalized. And yet these works, neither ceding their ground to history nor yet exalting fiction as a ground itself, instead preserve both terms and achieve a kind of historicity of their own. Outsidedness is internalized. A double perspective is always present. The story poses a question. It is only that questioning itself, asserting itself *as* a question, it defines questioning as what a culture's histories really are. As Hawthorne puts it in "May-Pole," "In the slight sketch here attempted, the facts, recorded on the grave pages of our New England annalists, have wrought themselves, almost spontaneously, into a sort of allegory" (9.54). Or again, as he portrays it in "Endicott": the mirror-shiny breastplate, by embodying the world of Salem rather as a reflection than as an engraving like its model, the shield of Achilles, yet thus makes reflecting embodiment after all. Indeed, as he frankly admits in "Legends of the Province-House," the legends are not narrated directly. They are told "at one or two removes" and by a narrator whose "oddity" of name and "individuality" of telling Hawthorne insists upon (9.243, 258). And yet such oddness and individuality do not undermine the truth of the legends, but establish them truly *as* legends, as told by Hawthorne's "legendary friend" (9.257), who thus individualizes community, whose removed perspective may even constitute a sort of doubt of community, but all the while is a perspective which owns its communality itself.

Of course, nowhere in this second phase is such a perspective realized as well as in "Wakefield," the story, as we have said, in which "craftiness" is defined.[24] Wakefield is the classic alienated man. Leaving his wife one morning, for no particular reason, he moves into an apartment around the corner meaning to return in a few days. Days turn into the better part of a lifetime, however, and only after twenty years have passed and all expectation of him has disappeared does he walk through his front doorway and take up his life once again.

Here is a perfect case of outsidedness. Wakefield's effect is to set everything beside itself, and it is difficult, insofar as we identify with him, to know, therefore, on which side we are. His story "appeals to the general sympathies of mankind," yet it is at the same time "unexampled." "We know, each for himself, that none of us would perpetrate such a folly, yet feel as if some other might" (9.130–31). We, like Wakefield, are othered, and accordingly, when he leaves his life and in effect formalizes it, it becomes impossible for us to evaluate the form in any undivided way. On the one hand, Wakefield turns us into objects. We live—those of us who remain in our lives—in a rut. We tread a round of existence, a convention to which we are doomed and from which Wakefield, simply abandoning it, would free himself. On the other hand, how can we criticize that abandonment, how make a case for our subjectivities without repeating the very activity we otherwise are attempting to discredit? To put it in nearer terms, Wakefield's actions cannot be condoned. If our lives mean anything, what he does must be held irresponsible. It is a dereliction of his duty, a "folly," indeed. Yet the nature of the folly, or rather our argument in calling it folly, if it is not to be a mere repression of our sense of our life as a rut, must be based on the same dereliction, on the selfhood won only by stepping outside the rut in the first place. After all, no other option, no higher argument exists. As Hawthorne constructs it, Wakefield really does no more than hold a spotlight on what everybody does. There is no positivity in his leaving, no principled opposition which might, in its own turn, be opposed by yet other principles. His "craft," no more than Hawthorne's, is some alternative vision of life, but a "quality . . .

indefinable, and perhaps non-existent," best described, as Wakefield's wife puts it, as "a little strangeness" (9.132). For Wakefield
does make the world strange. He does not create a new world. He
only repeats the old. And yet this repetition ought to be a creation
too. Or, rather, because for Wakefield it is not, what he does is
something we can call a dereliction, indeed.

This is why, in the terms of the story, Hawthorne calls Wakefield not only "crafty" but a "crafty nincompoop." It is why his
decision to abandon his wife is termed not a decision but a "whim-
wham" (9.135) and why even his going home, as undeliberate as
his leaving, is conceived as going home to his grave.[25] For home
cannot be treated so lightly. Outsidedness and the knowledge,
even, that comes with it of what is wrong with life inside yet must
be committed to insidedness if it is to be a life itself. And this is
why, too, as just such a commitment, Hawthorne, after remarking
that he will give the reader no comforting moral "done up neatly"
to ease the difficulties of Wakefield's story, gives one nevertheless:

> He has left us much food for thought, a portion of which shall
> lend its wisdom to a moral; and be shaped into a figure. Amid the
> seeming confusion of our mysterious world, individuals are so
> nicely adjusted to a system, and systems to one another, and to a
> whole, that, by stepping aside for a moment, a man exposes
> himself to a fearful risk of losing his place forever. Like Wake-
> field, he may become, as it were, the Outcast of the Universe.
> (9.140)

Here is the sort of ending often criticized by Hawthorne scholars,
a seeming recantation, of the kind we discussed in relation to
"The Gray Champion." Wakefield's exposure of the world becomes a defense of the world. Life, whose "system" he finds alienating, becomes, as a "system," precisely something with a "place"
for everyone. And yet, we should note, Hawthorne does not therefore recant anymore than he does at the end of "The Gray Champion." After all, the moral does not so much deny the body of the
story as redirect it. It does not alter the possible reasons for leaving
a community, but restates them as, equally, reasons for staying.

And, indeed, as we might say of the form of the moral in general, which is really what seems the greatest recantation of otherwise so subtle a story, such oversystematization or moralizing as Hawthorne performs in writing it is precisely the sign of his commitment to revalue staying. It is his commitment to the system without denying his knowledge of the dangers of systematization. Or better, it is his assumption of the burden of systematizing, his avowal that he, also, is a systematizer and, accordingly, that he— for has he not warned us against it?—is guilty, too. As he says in the preface to *The House of the Seven Gables,* after protesting his audience's conventional demand: "Not to be deficient, in this particular, the Author has provided himself with a moral" (2.2). Hawthorne will have his fun. He cannot resist a certain superior air. The audience is wrongheaded. The audience would impose a false construction of things on everyone who would speak to it. Yet remembering his avowed superiority, let us not assume a reversal in which he himself forgets it. For it is not that Hawthorne gives his superiority up, but that he integrates it with what he is superior to. Or, to put it in other terms, passing beyond the presumption that a perception of other people's wrongheadedness makes him, somehow, right, Hawthorne knows, as we should rather say, that resting on such a perception is to be wrong as well. It *is* to be deficient. And, accordingly, it is as he ends the deficiency, it is as, democratically, he owns his own wrongheadedness too, that he embarks on the third and mature phase of his career, that phase of extended moralization implicit in the personification of "Outcast of the Universe," which we and he call "allegory."

V. Allegory

Now maturity is, I am aware, a peculiar term to use for a mode of writing that seems to most readers, today, so evidently regressive. It is difficult, in this postromantic age, to conceive of allegory as anything more than, as it were, preromantically superficial. Hawthorne, certainly, in the romantic age itself, acknowledging the tendency of his "inveterate love of allegory . . . to steal away the human warmth out of his conceptions" (10.91–92), seems to admit just such a superficiality, at least at the level of character. So a virtual wall-to-wall consensus exists that, as Poe put it in his famous critique of Hawthorne, "The deepest emotion aroused within us by the happiest allegory, *as* allegory, is a very, very imperfectly satisfied sense of the writer's ingenuity in overcoming a difficulty we should have preferred his not having attempted to overcome."

Still, as should now be clear from our discussion, such an ingenuity is not to be so readily dismissed as we might wish to assume. The "difficulty" presented by allegory is precisely one that Hawthorne, more responsible than Poe, felt he did have to attempt to overcome—or, rather, engage—after all. The appeal to presumably "deep" emotion, as we have said, is just exactly the preference that, as an evasion of the—call it—"superficial" world, Hawthorne would not satisfy. To quote Poe at greater length:

> In defense of allegory . . . there is scarcely one respectable word to be said. Its best appeals are made to the fancy—that is to say, to our sense of adaptation, not of matters proper, but of matters improper for the purpose, of the real with the unreal; having never more of intelligible connection than has something with nothing, never half so much of effective affinity as has the substance for the shadow. . . . Under the best circumstances, it must always interfere with that unity of effect which to the artist, is worth all the allegory in the world.[26]

Poe repeats the well-known objection of Coleridge which we discussed in the previous chapter.[27] Allegory is a product of mere fancy. The relation in it of real to unreal, of tenor to vehicle, is conventional, factitious, a series of "ases," so to speak, rather than "ises." As we have seen it argued, metaphorlike allegory compares unfavorably with the more synecdochelike symbolism, the product, rather, of true imagination in which the "as" of the conventional is penetrated by the eternal "I am," and the "is" of the real is expressed directly. As Poe, however, continuing the argument, makes clear, the difficulty that most troubles him about such a metaphorics is a matter of aesthetics more than of truth. It is the absence of "unity" that disturbs him. It is the violation of his cherished formalism by the gap constituted by the metaphoric "as" —the distance between "obvious" and "undercurrent," "something" and "nothing"—that he finds most distressing. So it is out of the alienation in which a formalist aesthetics is born that the distinction between allegory and symbolism is generated in the first place. It is out of a denial of the writer's responsibility for what he writes, a responsibility which saying "as" invokes, that a difference between fancy and imagination is even thought.

No wonder Hawthorne, though he regretted it, committed himself to allegory over and against Coleridge and Poe. No wonder that, eschewing imagination, he wrote fancifully quite deliberately. For his point, precisely, is that imagination is after all but a mystification of fancy. His point is that the way out of conventionalization must be not through concealing the conventionalizers in the projection of some mysteriously unified work, but instead in a return of the work to its projectors as they, all too manifestly, can or cannot unify it. His point, in other words, is that all, indeed, is factitious. But his point too is that the factitious is nevertheless real and that this reality must be attended to beyond the possibility of concealment or mystification once and for all.

As we might put it in summary terms, allegory as Hawthorne writes it is the realism of a romantic age. Like the better-known realism of the age succeeding, it speaks of what is all around, of what is actual rather than ideal. It is only that since the ideal, in an age of imagination, is conceived of as itself actual, allegory speaks, to phrase it better, of what is "imagined" as all around— and, indeed, *that* it is imagined—instead. Of course the trouble with such allegory is a certain limitation it imposes. The allegorist, telling his readers in effect only what they already know, confines them and cannot offer them imagination's great promise of liberation into knowledge which is beyond them. It gives them at most the consolation of a sort of pat on the back liable to become, at its worst, the sentimentality we find often in Hawthorne and which we might define as a certain shared smugness about what they know. But in allegory at its best, such smugness disappears, becoming a reminder instead of how much of what they know is nothing to be smug about at all, becoming a reminder of what Hawthorne in a theological vein called, even, sin. It is man's "original" or "unpardonable" sin, which is his responsibility for having established such stuff *as* what he calls knowledge in the first place.[28] For as we might phrase it, Hawthorne, wishing he might write on the basis of a knowledge more luminous than what he knows, yet knows as well that knowledge as he has already consented to it is damning enough. Hawthorne is conventional with a vengeance. He would write conventionally, indeed, daring not only conventionality but the banal. And yet, as we should say, the problem is not that his writing *is* banal. It is not that he would know only what his community allows he *may* know. Rather, the problem is that he fears he does not know what he may know quite sufficiently. He fears he has not taken hold of his knowing, has not suffered the life that knowing thus or thus, in fact, really means.

As he comments in "Chippings with a Chisel," reviewing the tombstone maker's inscriptions:

> But, when we ridicule the triteness of monumental verses, we forget that Sorrow reads far deeper in them than we can, and finds a profound and individual purport in what seems so vague and inexpressive, unless interpreted by her. She makes the epitaph anew, though the self-same words may have served for a thousand graves. (9.414)

It is tempting enough to reject trite writing. Hawthorne, too, would hold himself apart. He would separate himself from his community which is trite and, preserved from its language "so vague and inexpressive," suppose that he might thus give his individuality access to greater meaning than a communal language provides. But he knows that such a language is what the individual must speak in any case. The epitaph is what he is destined for one way or another. And so he would rather make sure to individualize it, to take it on himself *as* an individual, for its meaningfulness is his responsibility as well.

As Hawthorne instructs us in his most extended excursis on

allegory, by way of introduction to a minor tale, "The Threefold Destiny":

> I have sometimes produced a singular and not unpleasing effect, so far as my own mind was concerned, by imagining a train of incidents, in which the spirit and mechanism of the faery legend should be combined with the characters and manners of familiar life. In the little tale which follows, a subdued tinge of the wild and wonderful is thrown over a sketch of New-England personages and scenery, yet, it is hoped, without entirely obliterating the sober hues of nature. Rather than a story of events claiming to be real, it may be considered as an allegory, such as the writers of the last century would have expressed in the shape of an eastern tale, but to which I have endeavored to give a more life-like warmth than could be infused into those fanciful productions. (9.472)

Here is allegory as most of its critics understand it too. It is a representation of the "sober" in terms of the "fanciful." If written in the present century, it is an anachronism looking back to the century before. Insofar as it deals with presumably real people, it is in danger of robbing them of all their "warmth." Hawthorne knows his form. He knows its limits and its difficulties. Yet his concern is not to overcome such difficulties, to connect a limited form with a content it cannot quite reach. Rather it is to instruct his audience on the uses of such limits themselves, on the "train of incidents" it must follow, the "mechanism" it must accept to read at all. The passage, that is, is not after all about the truth or falsity of allegory, but about the community in which an allegory so manifestly false might be established as true enough. It is about the "I" who has "sometimes produced" it and the "we" for whom "it may be considered." It is about "the writers" who used to write something like it and the writer who now writes this in particular. It is about reading and writing, about learning the language of reading and writing, say as Hawthorne himself learns it in such allegorical catalogues as "A Virtuoso's Collection" or "The Hall of Fantasy" or "The Intelligence Office." In these sketches, Hawthorne piles metaphor beside metaphor: Father Time's hourglass with Prometheus' fire with Death's dart, the man looking for "his place" with the one looking for a different heart with the one looking for his "pearl of great price." Metaphor, here, no longer tells truth but its own metaphoricity, constituting with other metaphors a kind of storehouse whose truth, rather, will be Hawthorne's decision to choose from it. And so we might turn to a story in which, perhaps for the only time in his career, Hawthorne is tempted not to choose, "My Kinsman, Major Molineux," in which, however, the lesson is that this temptation too must finally be resisted.

Now "My Kinsman, Major Molineux," though it is today regarded as one of Hawthorne's best stories,[29] was not especially noted in his own age. Though he wrote it early, Hawthorne waited for twenty years to collect it and thus seems to have had considerable misgivings about it himself. Still it was canonized in the twentieth century after the consolidation of romantic aesthetics, so that we might say "My Kinsman" is not so much a great Hawthorne story as a great romantic story which Hawthorne was talented enough to compose but worked hard to overcome.

Here is its climax, when Robin, a boy visiting Boston from the provinces, at last finds the patron on whom he has been counting for preferment, tarred and feathered and being ridden out of town in disgrace:

> "Haw, haw, haw—hem, hem—haw, haw, haw, haw!"
> The sound proceeded from the balcony of the opposite edifice, and thither Robin turned his eyes. In front of the Gothic window stood the old citizen, wrapped in a wide gown, his gray periwig exchanged for a nightcap, which was thrust back from his forehead, and his silk stockings hanging about his legs. He supported himself on his polished cane in a fit of convulsive merriment, which manifested itself on his solemn old features, like a funny inscription on a tomb-stone. Then Robin seemed to hear the voices of the barbers; of the guests of the inn; and of all who had made sport of him that night. The contagion was spreading among the multitude, when, all at once, it seized upon Robin, and he sent forth a shout of laughter that echoed through the street; every man shook his sides, every man emptied his lungs,

> but Robin's shout was the loudest there. The cloud-spirits peeped
> from their silvery islands, as the congregated mirth went roaring
> up the sky! The Man in the Moon heard the far bellow; "Oho,"
> quoth he, "the old Earth is frolicsome to-night!" (II.229–30)

Everything comes together here. All the discontinuities of the
story are harmonized: the people who have frustrated Robin's
search bring it to a close; the man he has been looking for is found
and becomes, now, the focus of all—of all nature, even, as the
clouds and moon too look down upon the scene. The truth of
things, it would appear, is revealed. Life stands unified, truth
revealed beyond our will in a formalized tableau vivant[30] in
which Robin's life, until now at such cross-purposes with everything around him, is made part of the form as well. And yet the
laugh that signifies Robin's integration into the tableau, that joins
his life to the life of the world, is ironic as we have discussed irony,
decreating him, a laughing at himself who must lose himself in the
process. It is a laugh that negates as much as it affirms, proceeding vertiginously not from the old Robin, to whom nothing here is
funny, nor from some new Robin, except as he becomes himself in
a recognition precisely of what he is not. It is the laugh of no one
able to laugh, and so it figures forth a silence, the silence that soon
engulfs the scene, as Hawthorne describes it, in the very next
paragraph.

> When there was a momentary calm in that tempestuous sea
> of sound, the leader gave the sign, the procession resumed its
> march. On they went, like fiends that throng in mockery round
> some dead potentate, mighty no more, but majestic still in his
> agony. On they went, in counterfeited pomp, in senseless uproar,
> in frenzied merriment, trampling all on an old man's heart. On
> swept the tumult, and left a silent street behind. (II.230)

The uproar is "senseless" indeed. The pomp is "counterfeited,"
nor is it a counterfeit that might, this time, be real nevertheless.
For the world of such behavior signifies not itself, but a world it
has negated. If the world is gained, so is it lost. Nor are there two

worlds, but only one that must be either faced or denied. It is the world of "an old man's heart" that only by "trampling all on" ("all" as subject and "all" as object) can "all" (Robin and his associates) hope to make self-denial an affirmation.

To put this another way, why do all the critics ask—and quite properly—why Robin laughs?[31] And we may answer because, as in his moralizations, Hawthorne has taught us to ask, because everywhere else in similar situations Hawthorne not only asks but answers himself, as we have seen, often with several different answers. Hawthorne would remind us that the work *is* such questions and answers, that truth beyond questions and answers is no better than the street's silence. "My Kinsman" is a perfect unity. But what, the critics tutored by Hawthorne still want to know, does it mean? To return to our earlier critics, Crews and Colacurcio, is it as the psychologists say the story of a boy growing up and learning to live on his own? Or is it, as the historians say, the story of the nation breaking its ties with England?[32] Finally, as "My Kinsman" smooths it all over, it is all the same and does not matter. Psychology and history are joined until they are eliminated as what psychologists or historians say, establishing meaning as what remains when saying is finished, instead. Outsidedness is denied. Readings are denied *as* readings. "My Kinsman" is a writing that denies—what we still, thanks to Hawthorne, however, know—that it ever was, in fact, written.

Accordingly, in a story like "Young Goodman Brown," reading seems rather to be forced back upon itself. Differences among critics of "Young Goodman Brown" emphatically cannot be smoothed over. If the story is a fantasy, if the wild events in the forest are the product of Goodman Brown's imagination, for example, then he is morally culpable for seeing his own sinful behavior in others. If they are, on the other hand, actual, say as they would be in a world of Puritan believers, then something like original sin in the orthodox Puritan sense is being rediscovered, and Brown, sinner that he is, is at least more open than his neighbors in admitting that sinfulness in the gloom that marks his every subsequent action.[33] What "Young Goodman Brown" does, then, is disrupt any continuity between readings. It puts the claims of one or the other in doubt. It makes them a matter of opinion. Thus it insists, however, that opinions are really what works are. The reader is put back into the work as making it, and accordingly he must face up to what he has made once and for all.

At the opening of the story we find Goodman Brown saying goodbye to "Faith, as the wife was aptly named" (10.74). Here is expression not vertiginously self-denying but, in its redundance, cloying, almost sickening. It is the reading of a reading, a representation by a self indeed removed from the world it would represent, but whose representation only places it back inside the world all over again. It is a representation signified as the world itself by the transparently allegorical nature of the name "Faith" in the first place. There is no escape from self here. And this is what sickens: the surfeit of a self already known and which Hawthorne would not forget. Hawthorne would sicken before he would hope to be healed. Or, if he might not be healed, he would remain sick rather than pretend to a health that is not his. "No, my good friend Robin," says the kind gentleman of "My Kinsman, Major Molineux," in answer to Robin's request, after the terrible events of the evening are over, that he be shown the way back to the ferry. "Remain with us . . . [and] as you are a shrewd youth, you may rise in the world, without the help of your kinsman" (11.231). The kind gentleman suggests that, as in "Roger Malvin's Burial," a sort of ritual expiation has taken place. He proposes that the destructiveness of the tar-and-feathering might yet be productive. But consider the corresponding passage after the terrible events of "Young Goodman Brown": "A stern, a sad, a darkly meditative, a distrustful, if not a desperate man, did he become from the night of that fearful dream. On the Sabbath-day, when the congregation were singing a holy psalm, he could not listen, because an anthem of sin rushed loudly upon his ear. . . . And when he had lived long and was borne to his grave, a hoary corpse, followed by Faith, an aged woman . . . they carved no hopeful verse upon his tombstone; for his dying hour was gloom" (10.89–90). There is no life after death, after all. There is no praying after blasphemy. There is, as we should say, no writing after that silence that denies responsibility for what has been written. Though as we shall see, Melville will yet try, when it is forced upon him, responsibly to write such a silence as well.

6 Melville's Silence

"Call me Ishmael." Perhaps nothing in our literature rings quite so famously as the opening of *Moby-Dick,* in its own turn perhaps our most famous book. Still, the long period during which it was not famous at all may be heard too in the name Ishmael, proceeding out of a neglect which our latter recognition would thus seem, as it were, to include within itself.[1] *Moby-Dick,* so long unread, is hardly to be approached, even now, free of the circumstance of the nonrecognition that attended it for most of its history. Melville comes to us not like Hawthorne, as "our" Hawthorne, the novelist we have always known. He has been not our "first" novelist, like Brockden Brown, nor our "national" novelist, like Cooper, nor even, like Poe, our "cousin," the author always resisted yet always on our mind. Rather, read, forgotten, then rediscovered, Melville, writing, as he knew even in the midst of his popularity, to an audience which would never respond to him quite as he required, would have his readers read him, accordingly, through his neglect, which he thus may be said to write as well.

"Call me Ishmael." How account for the oddity yet forcefulness of this passage? For it *is* odd, and all the more because its apparent self-negation does not seem to undermine the force with which it makes its appeal. How are we to respond? To whom is the passage actually addressed? Is the reader really empowered to name the speaker? And, if he is, and chooses not to, is there anyone, then, remaining to speak? The problem is not easily solved. In the terms of our argument thus far, the author would seem to give his authority up. The wanderer inscribes his marginality at the center of a work it therefore inevitably undoes. The castoff establishes castoffedness as his metaphysic, an epic skepticism into which the consciousness supporting other, more optimistic novelists—himself, in his earlier works, included—tragically disappears.[2] And yet, carrying such skepticism along, the urgency of "Call me Ishmael" persists. Its force, a call appealing naively *as* a call, demands, despite its seeming impossibility, a response nevertheless. As we might put it, "Call me Ishmael" speaks with a certain colloquial intensity. Its form is the dialogue. Its tone is conversational. And, though we might—skeptically, as well—be inclined to doubt the possibility of a conversation whose negativity undermines the identity of its very initiator, we should say in that case too that negativity is just exactly what *Moby-Dick* would thus conversational*ize*. Here a certain skepticism would be precisely what Melville appeals to his reader *through*. The inauthority of *Moby-Dick* is everywhere. Its improbability, its general air of tall-taledness, as in a fish story about the one that got away, is clear. Yet telling that inauthority so exuberantly, narrating it in a work, of all his works perhaps the most rich and fertile, Melville overwhelms it in a discursiveness, a sheer narrativity that becomes authoritative all the more.

Moby-Dick, we should say, dives deeper than its nay-saying. It presents negativity not as *what* it communicates, but as communication in its own right. As we might put it, its heroics are not quite of the ontological kind of which Melville writes in a well-known letter to Hawthorne,[3] but of the ethical kind, the situation of letter writing precisely, which takes ontology, rather, as its material. "Call me Ishmael" introduces not a metaphysics of Ishmaeldom, but an Ishmaelian rhetoric, as we have termed it, a heroic address not to be heard, an Ishmaelian "call me," exactly. To use an important figure from *Moby-Dick,* it is the call of Job asking not for an answer to his abandonment, but for answer*ing* as itself the answer, or rather, for no answer, even, to be reconceived as but the continuation of a dialogue never—even when carried on alone—wholly despaired of. The colloquialism of "Call me Ishmael" persists as a hope in despair. It is a sort of fictional "Yes, reader as I live" of Melville's first and autobiographical work, *Typee*. It is the "We are off" of the still quasi-autobiographical portion of *Mardi*. Only where, in the other authors we have discussed, the fall of autobiography into fiction is something to be temporized with, Melville, accepting it as a fall, would author it at its very level. The reader, as Melville would acknowledge, does not really call him Ishmael after all. The colloquy is hypothetical. The autobiography is a convention. Yet it is a convention which a real speaker—Melville, not Ishmael—would in that case speak as his autobiography just the same. Melville, proposing to the reader that he call him still, establishes "not really" as something he would write as well.

Moby-Dick is America's epic, indeed, and, coming full circle, because it speaks, like Franklin's *Autobiography*, once more coextensively with its readers. It is just that, having traced the round to "once more," having won its way through a certain disproportion of appeal and response, it treats *as* coextensive even that disproportionality which would otherwise seem to deny it. Is Melville's authority dismissed? But speaking to that dismissal, he in effect authorizes his speech on the same rhetorical basis as acceptance. Is his right of address rejected? Yet opening with a certain nonaddress, he makes rejection the figure of a speech to which his right is all the more incontestable. Most of all, does the reader refuse to read? But, then, Melville writes what cannot be read or, at least, what he owns can be read only passively. Melville writes *Moby-Dick* as an epic recuperation of the story of authorship's alienation—his own and his nation's both. He writes in response to that silence, as we called it in our chapter on Hawthorne, which is the denial of the dialogue of reading and writing on which a democratic authorship is founded. Yet facing more than the mere threat of silence that Brockden Brown faced, not compromising with silence like Cooper, or transcendentalizing it like Poe, or even accepting silence as a kind of limitation, a boundary of authorship, like Hawthorne, Melville writes democratically— and, as we shall see later, quite literally—silence itself.

I. Autobiography and Fiction

Why have we come to Melville so late? How can we account for the failure of his own era to see in him a merit that seems to us now so clear? In one way or another these questions have framed Melville studies since his rediscovery in the 1920s, producing a prophetic Melville, a Melville too deep for his age that the current wave of postmodern revision has tended only to enforce. As students of his specifically literary qualities have long maintained, Melville was too much the modernist to be appreciated in the nineteenth century. In the wild technical experimentations of a *Mardi* or *Pierre* he broke beyond traditional formal convention. In the narrative irregularities of a *Moby-Dick* or *The Confidence-Man* he passed over deeply entrenched assumptions of novelistic point of view. As Henry Sussman, in the contemporary idiom, puts it, "in its critical scenario," in providing "a highly sophisticated and comprehensive mechanism for the deconstruction" of normative representational modes, Melville's work "is beyond its day."[4]

And yet we must not be too quick thus to remove a proper perception of Melville from the arena in which he so intensively worked. It is a little too comforting to see him from the vantage point of a perspective we conceive as outside his history, as, necessarily, outside history in general, the space of a wisdom, a dark illumination in the light of which the illusions of this or that era have at last been penetrated. The problem is not simply that an insufficient cultural context has informed our reading of Melville. As historians, old and new, conceive it, and with reason, Melville's irregularity and experimentation are his deliberate criticism of his age, his assault on mid-century imperialism, say, or bourgeois consciousness.[5] Still, even these historians have missed the imperative which nineteenth-century consciousness presented for Melville, the authority it held for him and with which, as an act of cultural faith, he never fully broke. A certain attempt to do justice to a writer so obviously undervalued by his contemporaries has perhaps made us insufficiently mindful of the credit he gave to the claims of contemporaneity as such. A certain desire to rescue Melville from an uncomprehending public has made us

dismiss the dilemma of incomprehension in itself, either by generalizing it as the end of writing altogether or by trivializing it,
limiting it to the conditions of a time and place whose constraints
have at last been thrown off. It is as if, motivated by certain
laudable, but perhaps too sentimental, humane emotions, we
would assuage the pain experienced by Melville in his writing by
putting him safely beyond writing altogether. Or, more defensively, it is as if, to assuage our own pain, to convince ourselves
that we would not, given the chance, have done the same—that we
do not, in fact, do the same all the time—we would offer an
appreciation that can no longer help as an appreciation sufficient
at last. At best, perhaps, we accept Melville's formulation of the
issue as he presents it in the Dead Letter Office in "Bartleby," that
the conditions of a writer's communication are such that, at a
certain level, he will never find any proper correspondent. But we
do not see the project which Melville undertook—and in "Bartleby," too—of corresponding under such conditions nevertheless.

A certain pervasive rootlessness, an alienation threatening all
the writers we have studied since Franklin and which we have
defined as a not pleasing to, a mutual displeasure of the writer and
his reader, condenses itself in the work of Melville. It is an alienation attacking the writer in the shape of his community, a result,
say, of nineteenth-century repression, and so producing in him a
murderous inclination, a desire of "knocking people's hats off," as
Ishmael phrases it at the beginning of *Moby-Dick*. And it is an
alienation attacking him in the shape of himself, and so producing
a suicidal impulse, a desire to "throw himself upon his sword."[6]
Yet resisting the hypostatization of either community or self, defining reality as neither the one nor the other, Melville finds that
alienation produces in him most of all a desire for a "substitute"
for murder and suicide, an attempt not to die but to live the life of
alienation or, more precisely, to narrate that life in a tale that will
circulate him among the public once again. As Ishmael tells it, in
more detail, "having little or no money in my purse, and nothing
particular to interest me on shore," he goes to sea. An orphan like
Poe, with no settled profession like Brown, an isolato like Hawthorne, he decides to wander around a little "and see the watery

part of the world." Yet unlike Poe and Brown and Hawthorne, he commits himself to the telling of this wandering as providing him with a family and a profession and a world more all-encompassing than the others could ever imagine. From his first work, *Typee,* to his last, *Billy Budd,* Melville gives an account of his wandering. He becomes an author of wandering. And his wide popular acclaim as the author of *Typee,* [7] in fact, provided him with a faith that writing the problematics of wandering might be an acceptable sort of living even when his popularity waned. Authorship, as we might say, was his bridge between the individual even at his most individuated and the community even at its most rejecting. Identity was for him, as for the others, *in* his writing, in writing *as* his living. But in Melville's work, more radical than that of the others, there is never, subsequent to *Typee,* even a suggestion that should rejection make authorship too difficult, abandoning writing might be a better kind of living. For what Melville lived was an authorship which had established abandonment as a condition of the life of his community from the first.

Melville, from the point of view of the dilemma of authorship which we have been tracing, emerges as a kind of Franklin of a more problematical age. Like Franklin he wrote for what he conceived, not wholly oxymoronically, to be a community of individuals. Democratically defining himself as neither prior to nor transcending his community, he would represent himself, in all his alienation, as yet a national figure. To speak in an even more Franklinian way, his effort was to fashion his autobiography as epic, and indeed, since his autobiography was received as a popular romance, his effort was in some measure at least at first rewarded. It is only that as the term "romance" indicates, a certain alienation thus showed itself even in the public's acceptance of him, indicative of the kind of changed circumstances with which Melville would have to deal. The problem was, what did "romance" really signify? On what basis was Melville's story of wandering actually to be accepted, on what authority could he represent a life of wandering as an American life? For with his life so marginalized that it was acceptable no longer simply because he *did* represent it, with authority no longer granted to all representations, he had to contend increasingly with pressure to romanticize, to priorize or transcendentalize himself beyond the individuality where he might be himself after all.

As it was formulated by critics of the time, in a recapitulation of the terms we discussed in relation to Brockden Brown, was *Typee* an account of Melville's actual experience? Was it "true," or, if it was, whose truth exactly was it?

> The style is plain and unpretending, but racy and pointed, and there is a romantic interest thrown about the adventures which to many readers will be highly entertaining. We cannot yield assent to many of the author's remarks about the Missionaries of the Sandwich Islands, which we think are prejudiced and unfounded; but his adventures carry on them an air of truthfulness and fidelity.[8]

Here, in the democratic manner we have described, the writer is granted authority for writing by his community even when it disagrees with him. Though in some measure disposed to quarrel with Melville's un-Christian point of view, this early reviewer yet allows *Typee* the force of its vision. Indeed, he takes that force as authorizing his own vision, an argument against missionaries as validating an argument for them. His "we think"—no more or less "prejudiced" or "unfounded" than what Melville thinks—is offered no further justification than its coexistence with Melville's thoughts despite, indeed even *in,* their difference. In effect, as the reviewer recognizes, he must—if he is to maintain his own standards—allow to *Typee,* equally, standards of its own. *Typee*'s truth is its "air of truthfulness." It is, as another reviewer put it, its *"vraisemblance* that cannot be feigned" or, in the words of a third, its "authenticity" such that "we are not disposed to question it."[9] In our terms, truthfulness, properly, is rhetorical. Authority is "authenticity," indeed, as even those dissenters in effect admitted who, finding *Typee* too well written, too bookish for the pen of a sailor, decided it was inauthentic at last. And yet, as the rhetoric of those who found it inauthentic and those disposed to argue for the missionaries tended increasingly to converge, the ground of authenticity was objectified. The "we" of "we think" grew more and more confirmed, less a matter of what writing itself authorized and more and more of what, authorized already, writing could merely report. Truthfulness was hypostatized as fact. *Typee* was labeled a simple lie.[10] Soon even its defenders could not quite defend it on its own terms, could not praise it without invoking the terms of a presumably objective standard of truth that denied rhetoric altogether.

"Typee is a happy hit, whichever way you look at it—whether as travels, romance, poetry, or humor." "Omoo and Typee are actually delightful romances of real life, embellished with powers of description, and a graphic skill of hitting off characters, little inferior to the highest order of novel and romance writers." "Since the joyous moment when we first read Robinson Crusoe, and believed it all, and wondered all the more because we believed, we have not met with so bewitching a work as this narrative of Herman Melville's."[11] *Typee* might be true. Captivating the reader in no cheap or vulgar fashion, bewitching, but with a witchery long established and of the "highest order," it *was* true. But the truth thus allowed writing was only as fiction, nor would Melville, tempted as he might be to take it as "high," ever quite abandon the rather lower truth of the alienation which made writing fictional in the first place.

Melville, quitting autobiography, as we should say, recapitulates the progress of American writing we have followed thus far. He "falls" into literature as much as he rises up to it. As is well known, his discovery, just about the time of his composition of *Mardi,* of Shakespeare, Browne, and others in what the nineteenth century regarded as the great English literary tradition, marked an epoch in his career.[12] Born again in a prodigious burst of intellectual enthusiasm, "dat[ing] my life," as he put it in almost religious cadences, "from my twenty-fifth year,"[13] he turned from the common self which had proved so attractive to the popular readership in *Typee* and sought to commune, as the argument runs, with the timeless artistic spirits whom he found so transcendently powerful. In the more nativist analysis of Richard Brodhead, he turned to Hawthorne, whom he compared to

Shakespeare, and in whose company he thought he might brave the life of the even prophetic artist, however unpopular the prophet must be in his own country and age.[14] And yet, as we should say, that unpopularity *is* the prophet's spirit. "Literature," as Melville conceived it, was not what transcends its unpopularity, but the discourse of unpopularity itself. As Melville put it in the preface to *Mardi,* obviously exasperated yet writing through that exasperation nevertheless:

> Not long ago, having published two narratives of voyages in the Pacific, which, in many quarters, were received with incredulity, the thought occurred to me, of indeed writing a romance of Polynesian adventure, and publishing it as such; to see whether, the fiction might not, possibly, be received for a verity: in some degree the reverse of my previous experience. (1.661)

Melville will take what "verity" he can get. A certain lack of belief has turned his autobiography into novel. In *Mardi,* Melville, like Cooper in *The Prairie,* confronts the formalization of his career, the formalization of writing *as* a career. And yet, invoking *Typee* and *Omoo* as writing to which, in its reversal, *Mardi* still refers, he neither resigns himself to nor mystifies his form, but includes its formalization within it.

In effect, Melville returns his alienation from his culture *to* his culture. Writing, Melville no longer writes himself. He writes a fiction, not a life, or, perhaps, a life in general rather than his life in particular. His rhetoric is reduced to a kind of quickening decoration. No longer authorizing itself, bound to a self which must, to support it, be taken as authorized already, it is secondary, external. And yet Melville asserts its externalization too. His shift from autobiography to romance is not concealed, but enacted. His change of purpose in the course of *Mardi,* his movement from the early *Typee*-like history to the later allegory, so often lamented as making *Mardi* inartistic,[15] is what, refusing to revise out of his work, he doubles into it, another version of what we have described as telling his wandering. No wonder he might brag mysteriously to the staid Murray, so concerned to publish only verifiable autobiography, that, opening "like a true narrative—like Omoo for example, on ship board . . . the romance and poetry of the thing thence grow continually, till it becomes a story wild enough I assure you and with a meaning too." For the autobiography of *Mardi is* its mystery. It is its unreadability which is its meaning, an unreadability which is commensurate with Melville's audience's refusal to read and, accordingly, which asserts him as a writer who is not read, precisely.[16]

Melville keeps faith with his readers come what may. He takes, as authorizing his work, the assent of his audience to his right of authorship despite his differences with it. It is only that, as different with a vengeance—different, not Franklin-wise, *with* a difference, but different fully oppositionally—he conceives, as included within assent, *dis*sent as well. Melville's epic, unlike Franklin's, is written not before the separation of author and audience from each other, but after it. It is wild where Franklin is calm, tense where Franklin is, as we discussed it, "at leisure." It is important to understand, however, that that tension, the emergence of which signified, as we saw as early as Brockden Brown, a departure from epic integration, is thus incorporated in Melville as a principle of integration itself. The old argument over the curve of Melville's career and, in particular, the temperament of his final years may be recalled. As some critics have argued, in the testament of his posthumous *Billy Budd* Melville finally accepts the demands of a less than perfect society, exonerating Vere for his role in Billy's execution. As others, on the other hand, hold, he protests it all the more, only ironically.[17] We should say, however, that a certain amount of protest between writer and reader, a certain hostility, even—as, say, between Benito Cereno and Babo—is what binds them as well, and the progress of Melville's career, therefore, is only toward an opposition growing so pervasive that it becomes, finally, acceptable itself. This is a matter we shall discuss more fully later. The oppositional rhetoric of Melville's work—not simply its break *with* conventional ways of writing, but the break within it, as a tissue of conventions it thereby simultaneously affirms—is a feature we will need to examine. For now, however, we may turn to irony directly, as Melville reconstitutes it as a mode of democratic solidarity. Nor, like Hawthorne, who fears its social corrosiveness, does he reject it for a more judicious "craftiness" instead.

II. Irony and Allegory

Now the relation between Melville and Hawthorne is well known.[18] They became good friends during their years as neighbors in the Berkshires in 1850 and 1851. They admired each other personally. They admired each other's work. And Melville's dedication of *Moby-Dick* to Hawthorne "In token of my admiration for his genius" (2.772) lends credence to the idea we have discussed of a community of the inspired drawing strength from each other over and against the surrounding and less appreciative community of the common reader. Still, it is important for an understanding of both Hawthorne and Melville not to exaggerate such a notion of inspiration. For a certain asymmetry in their dealings— the fact that our sense of the strength of their bond comes almost exclusively from a reading of the documents on Melville's side of the story—does not so much separate their little community from the community at large as make the one a replication of the other. Melville, we might say, exaggerates the relation, and this exaggeration is a kind of asymmetry in itself. It is an assertion of the unity of his spirit with Hawthorne's, but as well an assertion of himself as having to assert it, as declaring a unity precisely because it does not in fact exist.

As Melville would have it in "Hawthorne and His Mosses," his famous encomium on Hawthorne's stories, "genius, all over the world, stands hand in hand" (3.1165). Those who say "No! in thunder," as he puts it in a letter,[19] constitute a special brotherhood. Melville aligns Hawthorne with Shakespeare and, presumably, himself with Hawthorne. Yet it is not, I think, merely devotion to a higher ideal of self than the ordinary that leads him to hide his identity and pose as a Virginian in Vermont, but a kind of inclusion of the nonrecognition of selves by each other even as he declares the ideal. It is a pseudonymity not self-effacing, but aggressively one-upping Hawthorne's own pseudonymous original publication of the stories. And it is, perhaps even more, aggressive self-assertion rather than devotion that kept him from telling Hawthorne, when they met soon after the review had come out, that it was he who in fact wrote it. Again, as Melville puts it in one of his remarkable letters to Hawthorne, where he declares, but a little too flamboyantly, their solidarity in poetry and philosophy:

> Whence come you, Hawthorne? By what right do you drink from my flagon of life? And when I put it to my lips—lo, they are yours and not mine. I feel that the Godhead is broken up like the bread at the Supper, and that we are the pieces. Hence this infinite fraternity of feeling.[20]

It is, I think, difficult to attribute this kind of language simply to romantic nineteenth-century, or even homoerotic, effusiveness.[21] Melville would seem to espouse a kind of transcendental vision. It is the romantic " 'all' feeling" which he speaks of in another letter to Hawthorne as available to everyone without the toothache[22] and his theological description of which, as being like pieces of the bread at the Supper, is akin to Emerson's description of feeling "part or particle of God."[23] And yet a certain knowledge of the toothache seems to be included *in* his vision of the all, a kind of hyperbole as close to parody as to romantic high seriousness, or perhaps combining both in a way that carries the difficulties of his relation to his readers into his relation with Hawthorne too.

To look at it in more detail, "Whence come you, Hawthorne?" This is not really an invocation of some mystic poetic source, a truth too ineffable to speak. It is not, in other words, quite a so-called rhetorical question—that is, a question not really requiring the reader to answer. But, in our terms, it is a question which, because its rhetoric is not quite externalized, must indeed be answered or which, as we have said, taking nonanswering as itself an answer, internalizes the external all over again. Melville has not given up on the primary force of writing after all. His readership is not quite split—into, on the one hand, his common audience, which does not read and so is given up to nonanswering and, on the other, his intimate, Hawthorne, so understanding that he has as good as answered already. Rather, Hawthorne is his common audience written to *as* intimate, his public *as* personal, his nonreader as reading in his very impersonality.

From this point of view, that none of the letters Hawthorne presumably wrote to Melville has survived takes on new significance. For although it is no doubt too lucky an accident to be credited as evidence for our argument, yet surely what may be credited is a sense, in Melville, that Hawthorne could never write him the kind of letter he really wanted.[24] Hawthorne, we should say, was not so different from Melville's general reader as we might have hoped. Indeed, generally read himself, an established figure, "discovered" already, as Melville himself admits in "Hawthorne and His Mosses," when Melville first discovered him,[25] he served rather as a friendlier version of the establishment—neglectful, but presenting neglect as, yet, benign. He is to Melville, as he was to others, a sort of Plinlimmon figure, a figure of "non-Benevolence," even, as he describes Plinlimmon in *Pierre* (p. 338).[26] But Melville—in Hawthorne, at least—could conceive of nonbenevolence as benevolent, too. He "dash[es] his tumultuous waves of thought up against Mr. Hawthorne's great, genial, comprehending silence," as Sophia describes one of their Berkshire conversations. He makes Hawthorne's reticence the repository of the "rich floods of his mind."[27] He tells Hawthorne's great "No," which is Hawthorne's hardly speaking at all, and "thunders" it himself. He redistributes himself and Hawthorne among each other, and if, like pieces of the Godhead, yet of a God whose nonspeaking he therefore speaks too. For, as he demonstrates in the Agatha letters, where he passes through Hawthorne the suggestion for a story he will undertake to write himself when Hawthorne declines it, what he would write is not a language fully present to him, a language of open and mutual expression, but the language of nonmutuality itself.

As Melville details it, the story concerns one James Robertson, sailor, who abandons his Nantucket wife, Agatha, for another in a different port. Although it comes to him somewhat vague in its particulars, Melville recognizes it as a story which, aided by some reflections of his own, Hawthorne might wish to pursue in his particular line. And, when Hawthorne evinces little interest, he takes it back as his own, asking only that Hawthorne add his notes to Melville's and bless his endeavors in the writing.[28] The whole story—and the story of its compostion—may remind us of Hawthorne's "Wakefield." Like "Wakefield," its subject is the whim-wham of a man who, for no apparent reason, deserts his family. Like Wakefield too it is a story whose outline is from life and which needs to be filled in by the ruminations of the fiction writer jointly with whoever will lend the writer his ear. In a departure from "Wakefield," however, the coming together of the writer and reader of "Agatha" produces no true falseness of a craftily concluding moral, but a series of mutual demurrals and a story itself finally never finished. Hawthorne's "outsidedness," which, as we have said, "Wakefield" exemplifies so well, never comes to rest in Melville in the choice of what is outside. "Outsidedness" exists. It is the reason why Melville does not write the story himself unmediated. It is the reason why he must give it over to Hawthorne first. But outsidedness is, then, inside Melville from the first too, the very condition of a sociality which is consolidated, accordingly, by a certain simultaneous resistance to the social.

As we might put it in our former terms, in Hawthorne outsidedness is a kind of skepticism about his audience's representations that, because it enables him deliberately to take them up, recreates them on the basis of a kind of ethical positivity. But in Melville, skepticism is acknowledged as a part of his ethos from the beginning and so includes the negative, equally, as positive. Melville, to speak morally, protests what Hawthorne can only take as his guilt. To speak politically, he would change what Hawthorne must accept. Literarily, in the terms of Paul de Man, he is an ironist where Hawthorne is an allegorist.[29] He ventures the dismantling of what Hawthorne would make his responsibility for constructing. He risks nihilism where Hawthorne risks sentimentality. And yet, at his best, his irony is no more nihilistic than Hawthorne's allegory is sentimental at *his* best. Or, rather, his irony, at its fiercest, is a kind of sentimentality too, a declaration of his solidarity with his community grounded *in* his disagreement with it, an assertion of the language of his society as the very language of his protest and a refusal to project beyond it, any more than Hawthorne does, a self speaking a truer language from which society would, in effect, disappear.

Melville, we might say, takes us to the limits of democratic writing. He can offer no solution to the evils of his age. He knows, like Hawthorne, nothing his readers do not also know. To repeat the examples we used in our discussion of Hawthorne's politics, he knows no Marxist teleology to resolve the dilemma of abolition and the war which would be consequent upon it, or no transcendental oversoul to resolve the contradiction of gender inequality and the domestic disruption that repairing it would cause. And yet, unlike Hawthorne, he knows too that the knowledge which produces such contradiction is, finally, *not* damning enough. He knows that with knowledge defined no longer as a mutual assent to each individual's knowledge—to difference with a difference— evils will continue, and accordingly he writes his knowledge as a kind of continued ironic protest.

> What are these scrawls in the fly-leaves? what incorrigible pupil of a writing-master has been here? what crayon sketcher of wild animals and fallen air-castles? Ah, no!—these are all part and parcel of the precious book, which go to make up the sum of its treasure to me.
>
> Some of the scrawls are my own; and as poets do with their juvenile sonnets, I might write under this horse, *"Drawn at the age of three years,"* and under this autograph, *"Executed at the age of eight."* (2.157)

This, from *Redburn,* at an early and not too problematized stage of his career, is Melville's protest against paternity and the sort of rigid knowledge it implies. Melville criticizes the repression by parents of youth. Redburn must learn that his father's twenty-year-old guidebook of Liverpool is no map for a modern son in the contemporary city. And yet, as Redburn tells his ostensible growth in knowledge, as he narrates his progress from a kind of innocence to a kind of experience, his irony is directed not only at the ignorant youth he was, but at the wise man he now has presumably become. As Edgar Dryden explains the unsettling tone in passages such as the above: "The time-of-action voice never merges with the time-of-writing voice as it does in *Great Expectations* and most other picaresque first-person narratives."[30] The youth in the grip of the father is not resolved into the man describing that grip. And, indeed, youth and man equally, the self—and, in the language of the passage, the writer's self, writing himself into his father's book—is in both places. It is for neither a transcendent self beyond the father, nor yet for himself grown into his father's substitute that the writer longs, but for the father and himself in a kind of mutual recognition. His desire is for neither independence nor inheritance, but both, for similarity *in* difference, the absence of which has turned a guidebook that might have served as the useful record of experience—the guide as autobiography—into a coercive fiction he will have to autobiographize in *Redburn* all over again.

And so, at even a late stage of fictionalization, in *Pierre,* the same dynamic applies. In *Pierre* the hero's ostensible progress is through a paternity even more coercive. It is toward a self, a psyche so repressed that Pierre's self-awareness, it would seem, may be purchased only by an overthrow of domestic conventions in their entirety. It is not duty, as he must learn, that makes him "marry" his sister, but incestuous promptings. It is not piety that makes him protect his father's name, but the desire to usurp his father's position with his mother. And yet, again, *Pierre's* irony is such that the true Pierre finally produced is not, after all, much less a convention than the ones he overthrows:

> Thou Black Knight, that with visor down, thus confrontest me, and mockest at me; Lo! I strike through thy helm, and will see thy face, be it Gorgon!—Let me go, ye fond affections; all piety leave me;—I will be impious, for piety hath juggled me, and taught me to revere, where I should spurn. (3.80)

Abandoning the Spenserian world of Saddle Meadow, Pierre adopts only the Byronic one of the Apostles. There is, indeed, no Pierre, but in one such conventionalized world or another. Pierre, a writer like Redburn—and writing of a character who, from all evidence, is as much like himself as he is like Melville—dissolves into his book. The nihilistic danger we have spoken of emerges, the *mise en abîme* of subjectivity endlessly deferred. And yet here too, we should say, deferral, finding irony as its voice, is subjectified all over again. It is a "rural bowl of milk," Melville tells Sophia he is writing in *Pierre*. It is a "regular romance," a work "very much more calculated for popularity than anything you have yet published of mine," he tells Richard Bentley and, evidently, quite seriously.[31] For fiction does not so much make autobiography impossible as become autobiography. The work does not banish the writer from it, but articulates him in his very banishment: "Pierre," the writer and his work, alike.

To put this in the terms we used in our discussion of Brockden Brown, "Pierre" threatens to become a book "he" does not quite author. Pierre cannot write himself quite in his own terms, but must use the terms formalized by his culture in advance. A growing objectification afflicts him, a split between writer and the written, ownership and reference, and a consequent difficulty, for Melville as well as Pierre, of self-assertion so long as he refuses to transcendentalize the split, to resign himself to the written or to point beyond it to a self too idealized for writing ever to touch. Indeed, as Melville's career continues, the "self," at the level of both the writer and the written, seems less and less in evidence. Colloquial narrative disappears in favor of disembodied narration. The protagonists of the stories are ideas not men. And, in *The Confidence-Man*, the protagonist, virtually no one at all, dissolves into the representation of a series of ideas no one of which Melville even believes. Still, as we should say, the difficulty of self-assertion is finally asserted too. And at its most balanced, indeed, Melville finds that it is assertion after all.

III. *Moby-Dick*

Now the greatest embodiment of that balance is, of course, *Moby-Dick*. *Moby-Dick* is Melville's epic, as we have said, a summation of his career and, indeed, of the career of American literature in

general. Perhaps nowhere better is the perilous state of the subject
on its way to objectification rendered than in the portrait of
Ahab's growing obsession or Ishmael and the crew's domination
by him. Perhaps nowhere is the loss of authorship so well represented as in the shift of narrative voice from first person to third
person to Shakespearean dialogue. It is worth reiterating, however, what we pointed out in connection with Franklin, that epic is
a matter not so much of *what* a book represents, as of the status of
its representation itself. Accordingly, in *Moby-Dick,* most fundamentally of all his works, Melville readdresses himself to the
question of what authorizes an American book. He recommits
himself to Franklin's "as any one pleases," and this in the teeth of
no one pleasing, of, indeed, a displeasure which has hardened
American books into tyrannical conventions with which pleasing
or not pleasing would seem to have very little to do. The irony of
Moby-Dick, its "desperado" humor (2.1035), as Melville calls it, not
so open as the irony in *Redburn* nor yet as bitter as in *Pierre,* is its
reaffirmation of pleasing in a context in which, Melville realizes,
it ought to have no hope of existing. It is his reconstitution of a
community of individuals in a situation where individuality
means the rejecting of community and community means the
surrender of individuality. It is an appeal by the writer in the
language of an audience which brooks no appeal, but a language
which, quite simply by appealing in it, he rewrites as his language
still.

To whom is *Moby-Dick* addressed? Who does the addressing?
Why should they listen to each other? *Do* they listen to each other?
From the opening, "Call me Ishmael," as we have discussed, these
questions are raised. But most remarkably, having once raised
them, Melville never puts them down. What most writers are
content with, the reader's granting of their initial premises,
Melville understands as a refusal of an ongoing granting. He
understands it as a mystification of his proper authority for writing whose danger, like the danger encountered by the crew and by
Ahab too once the crew commits itself to his mystic purpose, is the
loss of the only authority with which a democratic writer could
really be satisfied. Melville, as we might say, understands the

danger of what Hawthorne takes as a comfort when referring to the "pitch" of *The Scarlet Letter*, in which, once having reached it, he could "go on interminably."[32] For it is the danger of going on in the wrong pitch, of an interminability beyond his authority to terminate even when he wants to, and so Melville interrupts himself, begins over and over again, multiplies his "pitches" to a readership who will have, accordingly, to take nothing for granted but to recreate itself in relation to him continuously. Who tells this book? It is the schoolmaster of the beginning (2.798), but also the "unlettered" sailor of the middle (2.1165). Who are his readers? They are "landsmen," as he assumes when describing the wonders of the sea (2.908), but also those knowledgeable about sailing when he describes the peculiarities of the *Pequod* (2.867). No body of coherent cultural knowledge ever quite takes hold in *Moby-Dick*. No consistent pattern of allusions—like, for example, the allusions to Shakespeare and the Bible that we discussed in Cooper—defines it as the product of a fixed consciousness delivered to a settled audience.[33] Instead, as has been often noted, levels of reality multiply. Representations shift indiscriminately from the realism of whaling details to the "intolerable allegory" (2.1011) of Ahab's search, in effect internalizing the reaction to *Typee*. No wonder that *Moby-Dick*'s contemporaneous reviewers considered it "Bedlam literature" and that the scholars of the Melville revival, more scientifically, insisted that Melville, as in *Mardi*, changed his mind about what he was doing.[34]

And yet the question that needs to be asked is why, then, Melville thought it acceptable to change his mind, or even more fundamentally, what made him conceptualize various representations *as* at different levels. For Melville could no more than the other writers after Franklin speak all levels as one level. For him, as for the others, the writer's authority over his representations was problematized. As he knew, he had been alienated from his writing. What he wrote was no longer unified in all its variety *as* his. It was authorized not *by* his writing but by a referent—himself objectified as a positivity whose relative materiality or ideality, however settled, could prove only coercive and tyrannical. Accordingly, he unsettles it. To put it in terms that flirt with the sort of nihilism or, at least, skepticism[35] to which, as we have said, he is sometimes subject, in *Moby-Dick* Melville realizes he must give over writing as the *Pequod's* carpenter lives, as "an unfractionated integral . . . without premeditated reference to this world or the next." He knows that to write not "by reason or by instinct . . . but merely by a kind of . . . spontaneous literal process" is, in the condition of his alienation, of the not pleasing of his reader, not an achievement but a kind of denial, even "a sort of unintelligence" (2.1293). Melville, as we might say, has fallen into intelligence. He has fallen from action into cognition, from writing into the condition of being a writer, into that "*Being* of the matter,*" in fact, as he put it in a letter to Hawthorne, where "lies the knot with which we choke ourselves." He knows that "as soon as you say *me,* a *God,* a *Nature,* so soon you jump off from your stool and hang from the beam."[36] That is, he knows that as an object given over to cognition he must disappear as cognizer and so, finally, as cognized as well. And yet he knows too, as nihilism does not, that such a disappearance might also be written. He knows that "he" can reassert himself *in* his disappearance. And so he rather reassembles his fractions, *re*meditates the relation of the literal to the referential. He passes *through* Being, not avoiding hanging, but writing it too, and writing it over and over again.

For example, he describes the whiteness of the whale:

> Though in many natural objects, whiteness refiningly en-
> hances beauty, as if imparting some special virtue of its own, as in
> marbles, japonicas, and pearls; and though various nations have
> in some way recognised a certain royal pre-eminence in this hue;
> even the barbaric, grand old kings of Pegu placing the title "Lord
> of the White Elephants" above all their other magniloquent
> ascriptions of dominion; and the modern kings of Siam unfurling
> the same snow-white quadruped in the royal standard; and the
> Hanoverian flag bearing the one figure of a snow-white charger;
> and the great Austrian Empire, Caesarian, heir to overlording
> Rome, having for the imperial color the same imperial hue . . .
> and though, besides all this, whiteness has been even made sig-
> nificant of gladness, for among the Romans a white stone marked
> a joyful day; and though in other mortal sympathies and sym-

bolizings, this same hue is made the emblem of many touching, noble things—the innocence of brides, the benignity of age; though among the Red Men of America the giving of the white belt of wampum was the deepest pledge of honor; though in many climes, whiteness typifies the majesty of Justice in the ermine of the Judge, and contributes to the daily state of kings and queens drawn by milk-white steeds; though even in the higher mysteries of the most august religions it has been made the symbol of the divine spotlessness and power; by the Persian fire worshippers, the white forked flame being held the holiest on the altar; and in the Greek mythologies, Great Jove himself being made incarnate in a snow-white bull . . . yet for all these accumulated associations, with whatever is sweet, and honorable, and sublime, there yet lurks an elusive something in the innermost idea of this hue, which strikes more of panic to the soul than that redness which affrights in blood. (2.993–94)

This is the typical style of the book. A doubtful consensus is established. That is, a consensus so well established already that it is beyond the need for further establishment—that whiteness signifies purity—is founded on material so dubious and, as it were, supererogatory that it is called into question *by* its founding. And yet this questionableness is not given the final word either, for it is then used as proof of its less acceptable opposite, that whiteness is terrifying. Here, the accepted and the not accepted merge. However unassented to the proposition of whiteness' terror, it becomes, now, the consensus' equivalent. In the community he creates with his reader, Melville moves beyond the opposition of agreement and disagreement. Neither can quite be isolated. The either/or of propositional logic becomes a kind of not/and. Indeed, the *ands* subordinate to the one side of the either/or—the "marbles, japonicas, and pearls," say, which demonstrate whiteness' beauty, or the practice of the "grand old kings of Pegu . . . and the modern kings of Siam . . . and the great Austrian Empire"— leach across their opposition to the side of whiteness' danger, becoming its very warrant. In linguistic terms, contiguity becomes a kind of analogy. Similarity is asserted in difference. Exclusion becomes a principle of inclusion. And Melville's eccentric opinions *in* their very eccentricity, his peculiar notions *in* their peculiarity, are socialized all the more.

As we might say more largely, the relation of the particular to the general is thoroughly recreated in *Moby-Dick*. A certain generalizing movement, the response to inauthority, is everywhere evident. No longer trusted, no longer what we called, in relation to Franklin, exemplary—that is, his actions taken no longer as independent instances provoking equally independent actions among his readers—Melville moves toward a kind of self-fictionalization or representativity that, deconstructively considered, might seem even to threaten the self. Thus in Plinlimmon's pamphlet in *Pierre,* for example, the horological or occasional self, seeking to regulate itself by the measure of absolute chronometry, denies itself and chronometry as well. The ease of the Franklinian relation between occasional and absolute has, under pressure, vanished. Gone is the insouciance we can find, say, even in such a passage as this from *Typee:*

> Lest the slightest misconception should arise from anything thrown out in this chapter, or indeed in any other part of the volume, let me here observe, that against the cause of missions in the abstract no Christian can possibly be opposed: it is in truth a just and holy cause. But if the great end proposed by it be spiritual, the agency employed to accomplish that end is purely earthly. . . . In short, missionary undertaking, however it may be blessed of Heaven, is in itself but human; and subject, like everything else, to errors and abuses. (1.233)

Here, both "abstract" Christianity and the "human" Christianity which Melville asserts it contradicts are both, almost naively, asserted as yet no contradiction. After *Typee,* Melville will no longer be able to remain quite so naive. And yet, in *Moby-Dick,* contradiction fully acknowledged does the work of naiveté. The self's loss of itself is asserted as the proof of self, and this in despite of such logic as would deny that such assertion *is* proof after all.[37]

This is the real function of *Moby-Dick*'s symbolism so called. For although many of Melville's commentators have mystified it, tak-

ing the symbol as the product of a self-idealization which skeptics
have, accordingly, read rather as the overthrow of the mystery of
self,[38] in *Moby-Dick* the symbol in fact rescues the self from idealization and its consequent demystification alike. Melville builds
up the objects of his attention. Would he interest the reader in an
ordinary American captain? It is because this captain has a scrip-
tural name, speaks in dramatic Quaker idiom, rules like a Scandinavian sea king, broods melancholically like a poetical pagan
Roman (2.872). Does he wish to write of a particular ship? It is
because the ship's complexion is dark as a French grenadier's, its
masts are cut in Japan, its decks worn like the flagstone in Canter-
bury, its rigging tricked out like a barbaric Ethiopian (2.867).
Nowhere can Melville quite recommend to us the things he is
interested in simply because he *is* interested in them. He must
justify his recommendation, analogize it, philosophize it, even
idealize it. But his justifications, so outrageous, are thus returned
to him. His authority, deflected outward as far as he can expand
it, is repossessed, its loss taken as the very warrant of its rec-
lamation.

Not even the whale itself, however it is expanded to fill the
book, quite escapes what we might call Melville's marked *rhetoric*
of expansion. There are, after all, so many whales in *Moby-Dick,*
and so many whale stories. There is the story of Job, the story of
Jonah, the story of Ahab. And though Ahab's whale story does
occupy more of the book than anyone else's, and that the last
portion too, we should be wary of constructing *Moby-Dick* as a plot
tending toward an end. For it is here with plot as with symbols.
No event or series of events quite expands to become *the* plot of the
book. No story bespeaking no self achieved beyond the difficulty
of its continuing life among other selves ever quite absorbs the
other stories into it. Neither Ahab, making all the crew the instru-
ments of his overweening will, nor Ishmael, squeezing himself
into other men's sperm, ever quite takes over. And Ahab and
Ishmael are only two of many characters in the book. For example, as indicated by the prominence of the "six-inch chapter,"
"The Lee Shore" (2.906), which Edward Rosenberry quite ac-
curately calls "famous" in *Moby-Dick* commentary, Bulkington

almost as fully engages Melville's energies as the many more chapters about Ahab himself.[39] Indeed, *Moby-Dick* is an epic in this sense, too. It asserts the equivalence of each chapter to all the chapters, of every part of the book to the whole book. It is only that the part, not itself quite whole—neither exemplary as in Franklin's epic, nor yet representative as in a nondemocratic epic—is rather what we might call an indexical part. That is, it is filed or indexed under the word *whale,* so that its arbitrariness is like that of "the letter H, which almost alone maketh up the signification of the word," as Melville ironically quotes Hackluyt in *Moby-Dick*'s "Etymology" section (2.781), or like the letter *w* in the phrase "in a whaler wonders soon wane" (2.1039), a not quite spurious epigrammatic proof of the believability of the Parsees' assimilation among the *Pequod*'s other crew members. The part is neither too arbitrary to form a whole nor so unarbitrary that the whole overwhelms the parts. Epic, in effect, has become anthology. The particular has become a reference. But the reference, thus, is neither typical nor isolate. It defines neither a transcendent consciousness nor none at all, but Melville still, a referencer, a "sub-sub-librarian" (2.782), a "consumptive usher to a grammar school" (2.780), whose ownership of reference, in his sub-subness and consumptiveness precisely, remains.[40]

Melville, as we might say, become Ishmael at the beginning of *Moby-Dick,* becomes Queequeg as *Moby-Dick* proceeds. He is alienated into his reference, into reference continually expanding away from him, like the hieroglyphics on Queequeg's body, which figure a totalizing cosmology. As the case of Queequeg shows, it is a cosmology which cannot really be understood, but can only be repeated. It is not Queequeg's cosmology, for he has been exiled from it, a prince in his kingdom no more. And yet, *by* repeating it, etching it into his coffin as it has been etched onto him, Queequeg lives on, a coffin only, perhaps, but saving the Ishmael who stands behind him and even the Melville who stands behind Ishmael. Queequeg, finally, alienated or idealized, is unreadable—by himself as well as by others. Yet offering this unreadability to his reader nevertheless—daring him not quite to read it, but to

"Read it if you can" (2.1165)—Melville will narrate it, narrate himself in all his unreadability, circulating himself, like the coffin in the whirlpool which carries it round and round, *to* his readership in his exile *from* his readership ever more intensely. As Martin Pops puts it, Melville's writing will become a kind of allegory of itself—in the modernist idiom, self-referential, more and more concerned with itself as writing.[41] But the writing which now becomes his subject is Melville reclaiming himself, passing through his own objectification to become a "subject," indeed, once more.

IV. Silence

Let us look at a passage from Melville's story of an exile proper, the opening of *Israel Potter*, subtitled *His Fifty Years of Exile*, to frame our discussion of the direction that Melville now will take. Melville is brooding about hieroglyphics or, more particularly, inscription, which is precisely the sort of self-referential hieroglyphics of which we have been speaking. He would write a biography of Israel Potter. Addressing the Bunker Hill Monument, he justifies writing about one who served at Bunker Hill but whose memory has passed with him:

> To His Highness the Bunker-Hill Monument . . . I am the more encouraged to lay this performance at the feet of your Highness, because, with a change in the grammatical person, it preserves, almost as in a reprint, Israel Potter's autobiographical story. Shortly after his return in infirm old age to his native land, a little narrative of his adventures, forlornly published on sleazy gray paper, appeared among the peddlers, written, probably, not by himself, but taken down from his lips by another. But like the crutch-marks of the cripple by the Beautiful Gate, this blurred record is now out of print. From a tattered copy, rescued by the merest chance from the rag-pickers, the present account has been drawn, which, with the exception of some expansions, and additions of historic and personal details, and one or two shiftings of scene, may, perhaps, be not unfitly regarded something in the light of a dilapidated old tombstone retouched. (3.425)

Now Melville's personal situation, standing, as it were, behind Is-rael Potter's, is clear. For the neglect accorded Potter, we may read the neglect accorded Melville after *Pierre*. For Potter's reception upon returning to "his native land," we may read Melville's reception, after turning from stories of the sea to stories of land. In his exaggerated description of the narrowness of the circulation of Potter's own tale—a book not quite so unknown as Melville claims—we may even read the exaggerated sense Melville had of the narrowness of circulation of his own works, despite the follow-ing he to some extent continued to have. Melville, contemplating the course of his career, is understandably bitter and projects himself onto the bitter career of another. And yet we should not too quickly read through Melville's projection and into his life which it would seem to signify. For forced into a life of significa-tion—fictionalized, as we have said, his living formalized *as* a career—what he represents, rather, is himself in the very grip of his representation. Folded onto Potter's, Melville's story is not the story of Potter but the story of the story of Potter, the story of how Potter has been turned into story. Accordingly, its speaker is not the Potter who cannot after all speak, nor a Melville speaking free and clear. Rather it is the Melville who may represent himself, now, only as he has become speechless.

To put it in other terms, it is *Israel Potter* that is Melville, not "Israel Potter," and its story is not quite an allegory *of* the story of Melville, but Melville's life, as we should say, become allegory itself. Melville, in the alienation of his authority for self-representa-tion, represents himself as an other. His "I" becomes, "with a change in the grammatical person," a "he." His autobiography becomes biography or, even, fiction, at any rate something objec-tified. His writing, once simply read, is now formalized as what must first be deciphered in order to be read. A "tattered copy rescued by the merest chance," a "blurred record . . . now out of print," it may even remind us of Hawthorne's *A,* as he presents it in "The Custom-House," a tattered rag folded in a blurred record, as well, which Hawthorne will imaginatively recreate, rescuing it from oblivion by a saving act of sympathy or ethical investment. Melville, however, does not need to invest it so, for he is so deeply implicated in it from the start that it does not require any further sympathy. Melville's relation to the language of his community is different from Hawthorne's. Coming down from no attic, not outside his audience or, rather, as we should say, his outsidedness inside it as well, he is too dispersed across the stories he finds to fix them as something he really can be said to find, as something external enough to grab hold of and recreate. The story is not his by direct recension. He does not inherit it, as Hawthorne conceived he did from Surveyor Pue, by the right of succession. Rather its recension is itself obscure. The voice of its telling is muffled beyond clarification, and repeating—even amplifying— its muffling is, accordingly, what he makes his mission. Melville does not take up a language outside him, but takes up outsided- ness itself, displaying it in a language that is his all the more. He writes not a self taking responsibility *for* its community, but a self, as it were, whose inability to make responsibility eventu- ate in anything beyond display he would have his community acknowledge.

To use the figure of the book, it is indeed an inscription on a "tombstone" that Melville would now write. Potter, who "well merits . . . tribute—a private of Bunker Hill, who for his faithful services was years ago promoted to a still deeper privacy under the ground," cannot write himself, and so Melville will. But what he would write is the "promotion" too, not just Potter's achievements but his passing from achievement. Melville addresses not Amer- ica, which Bunker Hill has made possible, but the Bunker Hill Monument. As he introduces his writing:

> Biography, in its purer form, confined to the ended lives of the true and brave, may be held the fairest meed of human virtue— one given and received in entire disinterestedness—since neither can the biographer hope for acknowledgment from the subject, nor the subject at all avail himself of the biographical distinction conferred. (3.425)

Writing, here, does not evidently accomplish anything. The self, denied, cannot through writing be made more than self as compensation. In effect, Melville's writing has become a kind of marker. It is the writing on a tombstone which can say but here am I, a tombstone only.[42] It is the voice of voicelessness, of the self whose communication of itself is static, stony, hemmed in. But, thus, marking is legitimated as a kind of communication nevertheless. The self remains neither more nor less than itself. For, writing it, the tombstone signifies not a self beyond signification, but the self signifying itself *as* signified, the self as it were incommunicado because it is caught *in* signification—and so beyond the dialectic of communication and silence, self and self-transcendence which we have seen open up after Franklin. As we might say, Melville conceives of noncommunication as communication too. Autobiographical or biographical, fact or factitious, his is no preexistent self, idealized or denied in a work mystifying it or deconstructing its mystification. Rather it is a self written, a self inscribed within the give-and-take of its relation to other nonpreexistent selves, the give-and-take of reader-writer relations, and it is only that the relation has changed that requires further noting. Past rather than before the dialectic, Melville's writing is no Franklinian letter but an inscription, precisely. The relation that in a letter is ever open to resignification has become limited by its enlistment under the general category of signification as such. The letter's circulation has contracted to a kind of monumental immobility. Melville's writing, as we have said, has been objectified. And yet the object, thus, is but subjectivity in its immobilization, subjectivity—the writer's difference let us even call it, though in the dead end of its inability, now, to make any difference—that Melville will render as the last sign of his democratic faith, still.

This is why, in the period after *Moby-Dick,* he turns to the new control and, even, inhibition of his short stories.[43] Melville, in a sense, reverses the pattern of Hawthorne. Taken as a whole, his career seems to move toward an ever greater impersonality, from a self imposing itself outward on the language of its community to a self not committing itself in language at all, speaking, as if alienated in the attic from which Hawthorne emerges, in a language which is the culture's that has alienated him rather than his.

Hiding himself in a job in the custom house of the sort that Hawthorne left, he publishes a self apparently ever less itself, a name commercialized, endlessly duplicated on sacks of imported goods, as Hawthorne had described it,[44] the autograph of a copyist or scrivener, in Melville's term. He grows increasingly less boisterous. His prose becomes less self-assertive, less *his* prose than prose in general, and, finally, in the thirty years of his well-known silence, it becomes a crudely imitational and largely unpublished verse, not so much verse, even, as not prose, a meditation on his inability to publish. In the third-person narratives that prior to the silence become his norm, Melville seems to give himself up. He renounces his hectic appealing to the reader, seeming to retreat into a kind of skepticism content with the possession of a bitter knowledge in effect above the self's appeals and their rejection.

And yet it is important to understand how little comfort Melville took in such skepticism after all, how much he offered it too to the world he had grown skeptical of. Melville does not give himself up and let it go at that, but asserts himself as one given up, all the more intensely. As Hawthorne put it, though he had "pretty much made up his mind to be annihilated," he did not "rest in that anticipation."[45] We might say that the knowledge which Melville now has carries with it its history, the writer's fall from action into knowledge, from autobiography into philosophy, of which we have spoken. Unauthorized, unassented to as he is, Melville cannot write himself. He writes *of* himself, of a self as object *to* be known or, rather, in the condition of its denial, of a self unknowable and so a sort of resting point or philosophical ground of nonassent, at last. Still, quite unphilosophically, Melville presents the necessity of appealing to such ungrounded grounds as a matter to be engaged autobiographically. As, for example, he does in *The Confidence-Man,* he lays himself out on the communal discourse. He disperses himself across it. The authorial voice is no longer an "I," not even a "we." The protagonist is not one man or even many, but indeterminate. And yet, we should say, the result is not the deconstruction of a selfhood Melville has formerly mystified, but the negotiation of what sorts of identities such grounds-

seeking selves may yet have. In the elaborated and often contradictory examples he gives of it, Melville does not undo, because he
never has promoted, "confidence," but lays out endlessly what
"we" are who are no "we," what we, who have no "confidence" in
each other, thereby might be said to mean by confidence, in all the
variety of our not quite listening to what we say.

To put it in other terms, Melville, under conditions that deny
all grounds of protest, protests still. He must give up the practical
hope of social reformation which he had entertained when he
criticized missionary activity in *Typee*. Franklinian amelioration,
as we have called it, the amendment of the generality by amendment of the particular, is impossible when the particular's only
standing is its reference *to* the generality. The individual cannot
rewrite the community by rewriting himself when the community
is constituted not *in* its individuals, but in their giving themselves
up to the community. In a sense, like Ahab, Melville finds the
world stacked up against him. He finds even his protest against
the world stacked against him, coopted because, in order to speak
it authoritatively, he must speak the very language he would protest against.[46] He refuses, however, the Ahabian dialectic, which
would deny cooption by claiming an undemocratic self-promotion
or transcendence of public discourse. He will not, as Ahab does,
take the world as a hieroglyphic to which he has the only key. He
will not read it as doubloon, imperialistically possessing it or,
nihilistically, projecting onto it the emptiness which he has become in his alienation from public hieroglyphics. He renounces
the Ahabian violence of imperialism and its reflux in nihilism.
Unlike both North and South, he chooses, in the era of the Civil
War, not to mystify the absence which is a community's nonassent
to each other as a presence which is truth beyond assent. He will
not elevate the inability to negotiate, which is writing unread, to
the Word which may be imposed because it is true beyond negotiation. Rather, he makes of nonreading the condition of his writing itself. He enters his silence into the public discourse, turning
the nonreading, or rejection, that produces silence back to the
rejecters as what they will find in him no matter how imperialistically they read. In effect he reminds his audience that there is

one who *has* been rejected. He challenges the coopting totalization of his society not on the basis of principles outside it, principles defined imperialistically, in their own turn, as a totality of a yet higher order, but on the basis of the society's own inability to assimilate one who, however caught up in it he is, cannot be made to affirm it. As we may say, Melville writes nonviolently a kind of civil disobedience, socially ineffective though civil disobedience which cannot persuade other members of society to join in it will, inevitably, be. But thus he upholds, against a seductive but totalitarian radicalism, a democracy triumphant, a democracy practicable because, indeed, he does practice it, even in the particular event of its failure. In the years of the Civil War and after, Melville's silence bespeaks a writer who preserves the faith against all odds. He is not silence*d*, but turns silence into a statement he publicly makes. And, indeed, that statement, his belief in democratic protest, is not so ineffective after all. For Melville's career ends not in silence but in its communication, so that failed as it was it may yet be heard, perhaps already has been, in a writing which has found its readership though after his death: the posthumous *Billy Budd.*

V. *Billy Budd*

Now *Billy Budd* is Melville's manuscript found in a drawer, even in a bottle, to invoke the bottle postal system Melville describes in *The Encantadas,* notes put in receptacles on sticks set up by wanderers in remote places to be retrieved and read years after their composition (3.817). Written shortly before his death, but not published until 1921, it is Melville's letter to the world that hardly wrote to him, his letter left, Hawthorne-like, as Hawthorne describes it in "The Custom-House," to a world he did not know, a dead letter, read at last. We might say—as critics have, indeed, said—that *Billy Budd* is Melville's last will and testament, a sort of authoritative text of his life, expressing his final intention about the variety of his earlier concerns, for all of Melville's old interests can be found summed up here.[47] We have, once again, a tale of the seas, once again a meditation on innocence and evil, chronometricals and horologicals. And yet a testament *as* summation, we should note, this text, like Bartleby, expresses hardly any "will" at all. It is more like a preference, not really intending anything, not settling any of the old problems, but marking them *as* his problems, the seas he has, with a certain preference or partiality, been navigating in a writing that has not reached any ending we might call such after all. Melville returns American letters *to* the letter, we should say, and this letter, now an inscription of the tombstone sort we have been discussing, reveals not Melville at last at the end of writing, not Melville, in Father Mapple's words, "stand[ing] forth his own inexorable self" (2.845), but a self still bound up in its writing, still defining itself in relation to a reader, only in the condition of nonrelation that a posthumous writing makes all the more evident.

As in *The Confidence-Man,* accordingly, Melville does not so much declare himself as lay himself out in the terms which, since his alienation, any declaration must assume. He raises the old cognitive issues which the alienation of the writer from his writing brings into being. He poses the old questions of knowledge, whose settling, presumably, would be a kind of self-knowledge as well. Only he does so not to *im*pose upon them, not to assert some univocal answer on which he may rest himself, but to accept a sort of restless moving through them as the very language of self. What "I's" may exist among what "we's" remains his question. Or better, negotiating the relation of "I's" and "we's" remains his activity, for to ask what one knows cannot be answered is not really to ask but to live, though in the condition of a certain inachievement, one's writing still. Why does Claggart hate Billy?

> Now to invent something touching the more private career of Claggart, something involving Billy Budd, of which something the latter should be wholly ignorant, some romantic incident implying that Claggart's knowledge of the young bluejacket began at some period anterior to catching sight of him on board the seventy-four—all this, not so difficult to do, might avail in a way more or less interesting to account for whatever of enigma may appear to lurk in the case. But in fact there was nothing of the sort. And yet the cause necessarily to be assumed as the sole one assignable is in its very realism as much charged with that prime element of Radcliffian romance, the mysterious, as any

> that the ingenuity of the author of *The Mysteries of Udolpho* could devise. For what can more partake of the mysterious than an antipathy spontaneous and profound such as is evoked in certain exceptional mortals by the mere aspect of some other mortal, however harmless he may be, if not called forth by this very harmlessness itself. (3.1381)

Here mystery is the very circumstance of life. Melville might invent something to explain it. He might build Claggart and Billy and, no doubt, himself upon it as, in effect, being that explanation. Yet sooner or later, as Melville now knows even before attempting it, what he builds will grow shaky, and so he builds in a different way. As we might say, every explanation, as he now understands, is finally mysterious itself, and so Melville will explain only so much from the very beginning.[48] He will ask himself questions not as if they were external to him, as if he were some internality who might come to know himself in answering them, but in a denial of the opposition of internal and external as itself the answer.

Why, for example, doesn't Billy kick when he is hanged?

> "You admit, then, that the absence of spasmodic movement was phenomenal" [the Purser asks the surgeon].
> "It was phenomenal, Mr. Purser, in the sense that it was an appearance the cause of which is not immediately to be assigned." (3.1428)

Or, again, how can the master-at-arms both love and hate the handsome sailor?

> Now envy and antipathy, passions irreconcilable in reason, nevertheless in fact may spring conjoined like Chang and Eng in one birth. (3.1384)

Nothing stands behind phenomena here. Though events may be difficult to explain, no deeper explanation lies buried somewhere beneath them. No ultimate cause will reconcile them. And because it will not, the events begin to lose their character of opposites in need of reconciliation. The contradiction of one event by another is not such a contradiction after all. The dialectic of Chang and Eng becomes a diacritic, the diacritic but a difference. The knowledge that the self would know is redefined, requiring not the insight to penetrate the vagaries of existence, but the sensitivity to experience them. A new multiplicity opens up, the possibility of explanation not at the level of Ahab's "little lower layer" (2.967), but as a demarcation of the events as they appear, a categorization not symbolic, nor even quite indexical, but phenomenal precisely, a matter not of fixed essences calling us to fix ourselves in understanding, but of shadings and shifting differentials requiring the flexibility to shade and to differentiate.

As Melville puts the general case, debating with himself Claggart's sanity or insanity:

> Who in the rainbow can draw the line where the violet tint ends and the orange tint begins? Distinctly we see the difference of the colors, but where exactly does the one first blendingly enter into the other? (3.1407)

This passage may remind us of *Moby-Dick*'s description of the whiteness of the whale, "the visible absence of color, and at the same time the concrete of all colors," the "colorless, all-color of atheism" (2.1001). It is only that the all-or-nothing quality of the meditation in *Moby-Dick* has been reconfigured. Opposition has yielded to discrimination. As Melville puzzles it out, as he puzzles out the meaning of everything in *Billy Budd,* he looks not to overwhelm it with his one truth, but to overdetermine it, to provide us with an array of truths any one of which we may choose. Why does the Dansker offer Billy such "smoky" ideas (3.1380)? Why is smokiness his epithet?

> As one of a boarding party from the *Agamemnon* he had received a cut slantwise along one temple and cheek leaving a long pale scar like a streak of dawn's light falling athwart the dark visage. It was on account of that scar and the affair in which it was known that he had received it, as well as from his blue-peppered complexion,

that the Dansker went among the *Bellipotent*'s crew by the name of "Board-Her-in-the-Smoke." (3.1377)

Cause and effect are equivalent here. And the cause—the scar, the affair, and the complexion—is a simultaneously plausible and arbitrarily differentiated threefold cause. Indeed, so many causes—and throughout the book—seem both arbitrary and plausible. Vere is "starry Vere" negatively, because of "a certain dreaminess of mood" (3.1369), and positively, because of his brilliant activity in a certain naval engagement (3.1370). He decides to execute Billy because the king's law demands it (3.1414–15); because not to execute him—king's law or no—might result in the crew's mutiny (3.1416–17); because to defer execution to a higher tribunal would be an abdication of his personal responsibility (3.1408–9). For some or all of these reasons Vere acts, and it may appear that the reasons do not line up, that they are not opposite, or complementary, or even, exactly, related. And yet their non-relation is exactly the point, for Melville renounces the dangerous and totalitarian will which would be required to say which reasons really matter and in what order. He returns the dialectic into which the American writer has fallen to its state prior to his fall. He writes what he would, giving such reasons for his writing as appear to him fit, nondialectically, *in* their appearance to him. It is only that "he" is no longer authoritative. As we might say, the either/or which, as we have discussed, *Moby-Dick* converted into an antidialectical not/and, has become in *Billy Budd* an either/and beyond dialectic. That is, the writer's explanation of events, not right or wrong, is but his explanation. And yet his explanation, no longer simply granted because it *is* his, is no longer simply sufficient either, but—an either/and, precisely—*unnecessary* and sufficient. The proliferation of Melville's reasons—his dispersion, as we have called it—describe a writer appealing for authority to an audience which regards his appeal *as* dispersed. As we may say, it is a kind of stutter. Melville has become a stutter. And "Billy Budd," the stuttering "spokesman" of his community, as Melville yet calls him (3.1354), *Billy Budd*—once more, the person and the book—is, accordingly, the story not of one who cannot quite communicate, who, standing somehow behind what he cannot say, tries to communicate himself unsuccessfully, but of the stutter which the self has now become.

Here how active Melville's thirty years of silence have been is especially evident. Beyond *The Confidence-Man,* Melville has learned to write his silence. Beyond *The Confidence-Man,* he holds nothing back from writing. In *Billy Budd* there are none of *The Confidence-Man*'s mild but still violent enough shifts from person to person, story to story, explanation to explanation. There is no story of China Aster or tale of an Indian Hater, what we called in relation to Brockden Brown independently dependent tales, unintegrated into the totality of the novel as if still struggling against totalization. There is no space between explanations or tales, emptinesses waiting to be idealized in a dialectic of faith and skepticism which still dominates readings of *The Confidence-Man.* Rather Melville is beyond dialectic and its struggle. As we might say, beyond *The Confidence-Man,* Melville works no longer to assert himself, but to narrate nonassertion *as* himself. Billy, indeed, is a tissue of nonself-assertion. There is Billy as nature: "welkin-eyed" (3.1354), a "singing bird" (3.1426), a St. Bernard (3.1361). There is Billy as Adam (3.1400). There is Billy as Christ. There is Billy as anything a community not authorizing Billy to be himself might make him, an "inside story," as the subtitle has it, of one become an outside alone. And yet, an outside as inside, precisely, this is Billy all the more.

Such a Billy is beyond the irony we have described as well. As Melville explains it, speaking of Billy's salute when he is being impressed, his "good-bye to you too, old *Rights-of-Man*": "if satire it was in effect, it was hardly so by intention" (3.1358). Billy cannot satirize. He cannot, in the condition of his inauthority, say, even in this way, I am Billy. He cannot, over and against his community, declare himself—a nature or man or God. And yet, in this non-declaration, is he not established more firmly than Vere—who does declare himself—and as the representative of his community at that? Is he not established more firmly than Vere, who, though a man, arrogating to himself, with his decision concerning Billy, the power of God, dies in a battle with the *Atheist,* caught in the dynamic of God and atheism once again? For Billy, declaring only the impenetrable, the satiric beyond satire "God Bless Captain Vere," declares a struggle yet continuing beyond struggle. As we should say, it is a declaration of civil disobedience reduced to witnessing. But it is civil disobedience still. It is silence in words. And, indeed, in the words of the sailors who echo it—or, even more, in the words of the sailor, "another foretopman" (3.1434), who writes Billy's story in "Billy in the Darbies," the little verse that concludes *Billy Budd*—do we not hear Melville's years of silence which the verses he wrote during them might be said to invoke?[49] Do we not hear Melville's silence, loud and clear, at last?

Notes
Index

Notes

Introduction

1. Henry David Thoreau, *Walden,* ed. J. Lyndon Shanley (Princeton: Princeton Univ. Press, 1971), p. 324. The force of Thoreau's "waking," in this sense, is the theme of Stanley Cavell in *The Senses of Walden,* Expanded Edition (San Francisco: North Point Press, 1981), especially in the section entitled "Sentences," pp. 36–69.

2. Immanuel Kant, *The Critique of Pure Reason,* trans. J. M. D. Meiklejohn (London: Dent, 1934), p. 454: "I term all that is possible through free will, practical. . . . [R]eason can have only a regulative, and not a constitutive, influence upon it. . . ."

3. See, for example, John R. Searle, "Reiterating the Differences: A Reply to Derrida," *Glyph,* 1 (1977), 198–208, and, even more polemically, "The Word Turned Upside Down," *New York Review of Books,* 27 Oct. 1983, pp. 74–79, his savage review of Jonathan Culler, *On Deconstruction: Theory and Criticism after Structuralism* (Ithaca: Cornell Univ. Press, 1982). Searle conceives of himself as an exponent of Austin's speech acts. But his position, in that case, is an extremely dogmatic Austinism or, as we might call it, a sort of weak Wittgensteinianism, in which Wittgenstein's arguments against the notion of a private language, *Philosophical Investigations,* trans. G. E. M. Anscombe (New York: Macmillan, 1953), pp. 88–104 [sections 243–315], become an argument Wittgenstein never makes *for* a public—and therefore, presumably, perspicuous—language instead. Searle, we should say, misses the interrogative note of Austin's *How to Do Things with Words* (London: Oxford Univ. Press, 1962), taking as prescriptive what Austin means as explanatory.

4. Stanley Fish, *Is There a Text in This Class: The Authority of Interpretive Communities* (Cambridge: Harvard Univ. Press, 1980). Fish's turn from his earlier deconstructive posture, as enunciated, say, so infamously in "Literature in the Reader: Affective Stylistics," *New Literary History*, 2 (1970), 123–62, is representative of the process. It helps a little to argue, as Fish has more recently in "With the Compliments of the Author: Reflections on Austin and Derrida," *Critical Inquiry*, 8 (1982), 693–721, that deconstruction and the "common sense" tradition are closer than it might at first seem. If this is so, however, common sense should include a certain skepticism about community equivalent to deconstruction's epistemological skepticism. I think it is fair (somewhat deconstructively) to say that the very strength of Fish's writing derives, on the contrary, from his taking his own practice as so normative for the practice of literary critics in general that it precludes the possibility of his taking such skepticism very seriously.

5. Perry Miller, *Errand into the Wilderness* (Cambridge: Belknap Press, 1956), especially "From Edwards to Emerson," pp. 184–203; Sacvan Bercovitch, *The Puritan Origins of the American Self* (New Haven: Yale Univ. Press, 1975); Charles Feidelson, *Symbolism and American Literature* (Chicago: Univ. of Chicago Press, 1953).

The argument that the history of literature is a descent from the sacred is powerful and widespread and, accordingly, has become a perfect target for deconstruction, as in much of the negative response to Northrop Frye, *The Great Code: The Bible and Literature* (New York: Harcourt Brace Jovanovich, 1982). For a brilliant such deconstruction using Wordsworth as prooftext, see Joshua Wilner, "Romanticism and the Internalization of Scripture," in *Midrash and Literature*, ed. Geoffrey H. Hartman and Sanford Budick (New Haven: Yale Univ. Press, 1986), pp. 237–51. For a discussion of a related problem, see my "The Bible as Literature: Reading like the Rabbis," *Semeia*, 31 (1985), 27–48.

Partially in an attempt to bypass the argument altogether, to start with a positive assertion rather than a negation, I begin my own history in this book with Benjamin Franklin, rather than the Puritans. If pressed about the Puritans, however, I should say that what they offered *as Americans* was a covenant, not a kerygma, that like later generations they were immigrants too.

6. Mikhail Bakhtin, *The Dialogic Imagination: Four Essays*, ed. Michael Holquist (Austin: Univ. of Texas Press, 1981); Leslie Fiedler, *Love and Death in the American Novel*, rev. ed. (New York: Stein and Day, 1966). For a fuller discussion, see the chapter on Cooper, below.

1: Benjamin Franklin and the Idea of Authorship

1. For a reproduction see Charles C. Sellers, *Benjamin Franklin in Portraiture* (New Haven: Yale Univ. Press, 1961), plate 10. Sellers gives a lucid account of the history of Franklin medallions. For reproductions of the others in the series see A. Storelli, *Jean Baptiste Nini: Sa Vie, Son Oeuvre, 1717–1786* (Tours, 1896).

2. Henry James, *Hawthorne* (1887; rpt. New York: AMS Press, 1968), p. 43.

3. D. H. Lawrence, *Studies in Classic American Literature* (New York: Thomas Seltzer, 1923), pp. 20–21.

4. Ibid., pp. 29, 30.

5. See Ralph Waldo Emerson, *The Journals and Miscellaneous Notebooks,* Vol. 2, ed. William H. Gilman, Alfred R. Ferguson, and Merrell R. Davis (Cambridge: Belknap Press, 1961), pp. 222–23. Melville's characterization appears in *Israel Potter: His Fifty Years of Exile,* especially chaps. 8 and 9.

6. See, especially, William Charvat in his classic *The Origins of American Critical Thought, 1810–1835* (Philadelphia: Univ. of Pennsylvania Press, 1936).

7. George Lukács, *The Theory of the Novel: A Historico-Philosophical Essay on the Forms of Great Epic Literature,* trans. Anna Bostock (London: Merlin Press, 1971), esp. pp. 46–55.

8. Leonard W. Labaree, Ralph L. Ketcham, Helen C. Boatfield, and Helene H. Fineman, eds., *The Autobiography of Benjamin Franklin* (New Haven: Yale Univ. Press, 1964), p. 133n. All references are to this edition.

9. Perry Miller, "From Edwards to Emerson," *Errand into the Wilderness* (Cambridge: Belknap Press, 1956), especially pp. 184–203.

10. Frank Kermode, *The Sense of an Ending: Studies in the Theory of Fiction* (New York: Oxford Univ. Press, 1967).

11. Jonathan Edwards, *Representative Selections,* ed. Clarence H. Faust and Thomas H. Johnson, rev. ed. (New York: Hill and Wang, 1962), p. 57.

12. *Edward Gibbon: Memoirs of My Life,* ed. Georges A. Bonnard (London: Thomas Nelson and Sons, 1966), pp. 3, 153–54.

13. I have used the Loeb Classical Library edition, A. T. Murray, trans., *Homer: The Iliad* (London: William Heineman, 1942). The passages concerning Thersites quoted below are in 3.211–24.

14. The edition is that of Rolfe Humphries, *The Aeneid of Virgil: A Verse Translation* (New York: Scribners, 1951).

15. Lukács, *Theory of the Novel*, p. 49.

16. Herman Melville, *Moby-Dick;* Nathaniel Hawthorne, *The Scarlet Letter;* Henry David Thoreau, *Walden;* Mark Twain, *The Adventures of Huckleberry Finn.*

17. "What Is an American" is the title of the famous Letter 3. The text quoted is Hector St. John de Crèvecoeur, *Letters from an American Farmer* (1782; London: Dent and Sons, 1912), pp. 14, 20.

18. John Bach McMaster, *Benjamin Franklin as a Man of Letters* (Boston, 1887).

19. See Cedric H. Whitman, *Homer and the Heroic Tradition* (Cambridge: Harvard Univ. Press, 1958), chap. ii, "The Geometric Structure of the *Iliad*," pp. 249–84.

2: Charles Brockden Brown and the Profession of Authorship

1. Quoted in Harry R. Warfel, *Charles Brockden Brown: American Gothic Novelist* (Gainesville: Univ. of Florida Press, 1949), p. 222. Brown biography presents vexing difficulties whose significance is discussed in Section 3. Most of the more certain details, however, have been taken from Warfel and from David Lee Clark, *Charles Brockden Brown: Pioneer Voice of America* (Durham: Duke Univ. Press, 1952), still the two, admittedly problematical, standards.

2. The romantic view begins at least as early as John Neal, writing for *Blackwood's Magazine* in 1824, and extends in a long tradition through Leslie Fiedler, *Love and Death in the American Novel*, rev. ed. (New York: Stein and Day, 1966), pp. 145–61. The realist position, antedating—but given especial currency in—the rise of realism to critical prominence, survives especially in the still frequent praise for Brown's rendering of the yellow fever epidemic in *Arthur Mervyn*. For a good summary, see Paul Witherington, "Charles Brockden Brown: A Bibliographical Essay," *Early American Literature,* 9 (1974), 164–87.

3. The claim seems to begin with William Dunlap, *The Life of Charles Brockden Brown* (Philadelphia, 1815), 2.12. It has been assumed by virtually every writer on Brown since. For a fuller discussion, see Bernard Rosenthal, ed., *Critical Essays on Charles Brockden Brown* (Boston: G. K. Hall, 1981), pp. 2ff.

4. Smith was a poet and noted physician, founder of the *Medical Repository,* America's first scientific journal. Adams was the son of President Adams. Kent, a close friend of Alexander Hamilton, was

chief justice of the New York State Supreme Court. All were members, with Brown, of the New York Friendly Club. See David Lee Clark, "Brockden Brown's First Attempt at Journalism," *University of Texas Studies in English,* 7 (1927), 155–74.

5. Paul Allen, *The Life of Charles Brockden Brown,* ed. Charles E. Bennett (1815, as Dunlap, *Life* [v. note 3]; Delmar, N.Y.: Scholars' Facsimile and Reprints, 1975), pp. 67–69. Dunlap evidently finished what Allen began, publishing the whole under his own name. The situation is very complicated, however, and the confusion over the authorship of the biography thus may be said to mirror the confusion over Brown's own authorship. See Bennett's Introduction, pp. v–xxiv, for a detailed account.

6. F. Scott Fitzgerald, *The Great Gatsby* (New York: Scribners, 1925), p. 182; Richard Poirier, *A World Elsewhere: The Place of Style in American Literature* (New York: Oxford Univ. Press, 1966). Note the beautiful nostalgia of both works in constructing America *as* a dream, just precisely the status that Brown, still too practical, however, will not yet allow it to have.

7. Cf. Edwin Sill Fussell, "*Wieland:* A Literary and Historical Reading," *Early American Literature,* 18 (1983), 172: "Writing was the imaginable source of woe, yet still more writing was the only exit from woe." Fussell's New Historical rendering of the situation of the writer in postrevolutionary America is illuminating throughout.

8. Charles Brockden Brown, *Wieland or The Transformation: An American Tale,* Bicentennial Edition, *The Novels and Related Works of Charles Brockden Brown,* ed. Sydney J. Krause and S. W. Reid, 5 vols. (Kent, Ohio: Kent State Univ. Press, 1977–86), 1.221. Except where otherwise noted, all quotations are from the Kent State edition, cited by volume and page number.

9. Warfel, *Charles Brockden Brown,* p. 91.

10. Ibid., pp. 75–76.

11. Clark, *Charles Brockden Brown,* pp. 53–107.

12. Eleanor M. Tilton, "'The Sorrows' of Charles Brockden Brown," *PMLA,* 69 (1954), 1304–8.

13. Herbert Brown, "Charles Brockden Brown's 'The Story of Julius': Rousseau and Richardson 'Improved,'" in *Essays Mostly on Periodical Publishing in America,* ed. James Woodress (Durham: Duke Univ. Press, 1973), pp. 39, 52, 50. Also Clark, *Charles Brockden Brown,* p. 28.

14. Warfel, *Charles Brockden Brown,* pp. 63–64.

15. Ibid., p. 60.

16. Ibid., pp. 57–59.

17. Herbert Brown, "The Story of Julius," p. 39.

18. It is possible, however, that Brown had read only the first volume of Rousseau and was comparing size with this.

19. The primary text here is Harold Bloom, *The Anxiety of Influence* (New York: Oxford Univ. Pres, 1973), which has been largely read, and not without reason, as a sort of romanticized Derrideanism. It should be noted, however, that Bloom's very commitment to romanticism, gnosticism, and other such mystifications, as a good Derridean would call them, has engaged him even more than his poets in a battle against the deconstructive logic in which he is caught up. This battle antedates the appearance of Derrida on the American scene—hence "anticipates"—and has continued since. See, for example, the first chapter of *Poetry and Repression* (New Haven: Yale Univ. Press, 1976), where the poet, still bound to a precursor, yet seems to have the (self-generated?) power to establish him as such.

20. William Godwin, *Caleb Williams,* ed. David McCracken (1794; London: Oxford Univ. Press, 1970), p. 4.

21. James Brown, cited by Brown in a letter, in Clark, *Charles Brockden Brown,* p. 181.

22. The complaints are already present in the first full-length study, Martin S. Vilas, *Charles Brockden Brown: A Study of Early American Fiction* (Burlington, Vt.: Free Press Association, 1904). The most recent and best of the nativists is Alan Axelrod, *Charles Brockden Brown: An American Tale* (Austin: Univ. of Texas Press, 1983).

23. See, e.g., the Preface to the New York Edition of *The American,* conveniently reprinted in *The Art of the Novel: Critical Prefaces by Henry James,* ed. Richard P. Blackmur (New York: Scribners, 1934), pp. 33–34: "The balloon of experience is in fact of course tied to the earth, and under that necessity we swing, thanks to a rope of remarkable length, in the more or less commodious car of the imagination; but it is by the rope we know where we are, and from the moment that cable is cut we are at large and unrelated: we only swing apart from the globe—though remaining as exhilarated, naturally, as we like, especially when all goes well. The art of the romancer is, 'for the fun of it,' insidiously to cut the cable, to cut it without our detecting him."

24. Thomas Love Peacock, *Memoirs of Shelley and Other Essays and Reviews,* ed. Howard Mills (New York: New York Univ. Press, 1970), p. 43.

25. The most exquisitely poised passage along these lines occurs in

Wieland, when Pleyel, praising Clara's deportment, even to "the colour of a shoe, the knot of a ribband, or your attitude in plucking a rose," calls upon his fiancée, "as she wished to secure and enhance my esteem," to study them as "a model of assiduous study, and indefatigable imitation" (1.123).

26. Russel B. Nye, "The Early Novel: Charles Brockden Brown's American Gothic," *American Literary History, 1607–1830* (New York: Alfred A. Knopf, 1970), pp. 241–44. Fred Lewis Pattee, ed., *Wieland or The Transformation, together with Memoirs of Carwin the Biloquist: A Fragment* (New York: Harcourt, Brace and World, 1926), pp. ix–xlvi, makes, perhaps, the broadest claim.

27. As Frederick S. Frank, *Guide to the Gothic: An Annotated Bibliography of Criticism* (Metuchen, N.J.: Scarecrow Press, 1984), p. xii, summarizes it: "If there is a dominant trend in twentieth-century criticism of the Gothic, it is probably the developing outlook that the Gothic, like the tragic, is preoccupied thematically with problems of identity and mysteries of the self." This is the position powerfully argued, especially in relation to *Edgar Huntly,* by Leslie Fiedler and by Richard Slotkin, *Regeneration through Violence: The Mythology of the American Frontier, 1600–1860* (Middletown, Conn.: Wesleyan Univ. Press, 1973), pp. 382–90.

Undeniably some sort of prepsychological expression is at work in the gothic. The psyche, however, discovers itself only in its opposition to already formalized explanations of identity—the sorts of explanation, for example, elaborated in Tzvetan Todorov, *The Fantastic: A Structural Approach to a Literary Genre,* trans. Richard Howard (Cleveland: Case Western Reserve Univ. Press, 1973)—and it is this opposition that undoes identity after all. For an attempt to save identity, nevertheless, as that which experiences undoing, see Francis Russell Hart, "The Experience of Character in the English Gothic Novel," in *Experience in the Novel: Selected Papers from the English Institute,* ed. Roy Harvey Pearce (New York: Columbia Univ. Press, 1968), pp. 83–105. But in Brown, we are a stage before Hart, as well.

Horace Walpole's *The Castle of Otranto* (1764) is generally credited with initiating the mode, Ann Radcliffe with providing its classic form, and so I use these two as termini for my discussion.

28. Compare the treatment of incest in William Hill Brown, *The Power of Sympathy* (1789), arguably the "first" American novel. Here too the arbitrariness of incest is a theme. But it is so arbitrary that its force, and the force of the family in general, is almost denied altogether.

29. Paul de Man, "The Rhetoric of Temporality," in *Interpretation:*

Theory and Practice, ed. Charles S. Singleton (Baltimore: Johns Hopkins Univ. Press, 1969), pp. 197–98.

30. Representative is Nina Baym, "A Minority Reading of *Wieland,*" in *Critical Essays on Charles Brockden Brown,* p. 88, who accuses Brown of "carelessness, haste, forgetfulness, and changing intention." Rosenthal's rejoinder, "The Voices of Wieland," pp. 104–21, offers the best defense, perceptively arguing a "deeper" thematic coherence for anomalies which, he maintains, are only structural. Still, the question remains, why do these anomalies seem to appear in the first place? See the discussion following.

31. Ralph Waldo Emerson, "The Poet," *Essays: Second Series* (1844), *The Collected Works of Ralph Waldo Emerson,* Vol. 3, ed. Joseph Slater, Alfred R. Ferguson, and Jean Ferguson Carr (Cambridge: Belknap Press, 1983), p. 15.

32. Donald A. Ringe, *Charles Brockden Brown* (New York: Twayne, 1966), p. 44, catalogues the difficulties succinctly.

33. See, e.g., Warner B. Berthoff, "Adventures of the Young Man: An Approach to Charles Brockden Brown," *American Quarterly,* 9 (1957), 421–34. Also Paul Witherington, "Brockden Brown's Other Novels: *Clara Howard* and *Jane Talbot,*" *Nineteenth-Century Fiction,* 29 (1974), 257–72.

34. Fiedler, *Love and Death,* pp. 157–58.

35. For a full account see S. W. Reid, "Textual Essay," in the Bicentennial Edition, 3.476–89.

36. William Spengemann, *The Adventurous Muse: The Poetics of Americ..n Fiction, 1789–1900* (New Haven: Yale Univ. Press, 1977), p. 99. See also Paul Witherington, "Benevolence and the 'Utmost Stretch': Charles Brockden Brown's Narrative Dilemma," *Criticism,* 14 (1972), 175–91.

37. See Donald A. Ringe, "Historical Essay," in the Bicentennial Edition, 5.433–74, for a detailed account of the criticism from Brown's time until the present. For nearly the only two opposing views see Sydney J. Krause, "*Clara Howard* and *Jane Talbot:* Godwin on Trial," in *Critical Essays on Charles Brockden Brown,* pp. 184–211, and Witherington, "Brockden Brown's Other Novels."

38. Warfel, *Charles Brockden Brown,* pp. 70, 72.

39. Warner Berthoff, "Charles Brockden Brown's Historical 'Sketches': A Consideration," *American Literature,* 28 (1956), 154.

3: Cooper's Myth

1. Pending the completion of the State University of New York at Albany edition, no authoritative Cooper exists. For the novels, the

F. O. C. Darley Edition (New York: W. A. Townsend, 1859), which I have used, is perhaps the most generally available and has the added attraction of Darley's splendidly irrelevant illustrations. Still, as no textual problems relevant for this study arise, it seems preferable to indicate references by chapter.

2. Given greatest currency at the Cooper Memorial of 1852 by William Cullen Bryant in his commemorative discourse, published in *Prose Writings of William Cullen Bryant,* ed. Parke Godwin (New York: D. Appleton, 1884), 1.229–30.

3. The remarks of Melville, Parkman, and Simms are reprinted in George Dekker and John P. McWilliams, eds., *Fenimore Cooper: The Critical Heritage* (London: Routledge and Kegan Paul, 1973), pp. 244, 249, 227. For Whitman, see Horace Traubel, *With Walt Whitman in Camden,* Vol. 4, ed. Sculley Bradley (Philadelphia: Univ. of Pennsylvania Press, 1953), p. 62.

4. Thus, e.g., Robert Spiller, *Fenimore Cooper: Critic of His Times* (New York: Minton, Balch, 1931), pp. 100–101, who notes Cooper's own citation of a remark by Thomas Jefferson, that "no American should leave his country for more than five years lest he get behind it." Most of the details of Cooper's European experience are taken from Spiller.

5. The loci classici are, for Irving, Vernon Louis Parrington, *Main Currents in American Literature* (New York: Harcourt, Brace, 1930), 2.203–12; for James, Van Wyck Brooks, *The Pilgrimage of Henry James* (New York: E. P. Dutton, 1925); and, for Hawthorne, quite wonderfully, James himself, *Hawthorne* (1887; rpt. New York: AMS Press, 1968).

6. Quoted in Stephen Railton, *Fenimore Cooper: A Study of His Life and Imagination* (Princeton: Princeton Univ. Press, 1978), p. 126.

7. Quoted in Spiller, *Fenimore Cooper,* p. 192.

8. Bryant, *Prose Writings,* 1.230; Longfellow, in *Fenimore Cooper: The Critical Heritage,* p. 246.

9. Cooper's strenuous defense of property rights, and in particular of his own title to "Three-Mile Point," the parkland of his inherited estate in Cooperstown which had been appropriated by the townspeople to public use, is of especial interest in this connection. See Spiller, *Fenimore Cooper,* pp. 252–69. As Cooper argues in the rent-strike trilogy, *Satanstoe, The Chainbearer,* and *The Redskins,* these lands are his because his ancestors once worked hard to get them, the hard work of the current renters constituting, presumably, a somehow lesser claim. Cf. the scene in *The Prairie* where the trapper struggles to distinguish Ishmael Bush's lawless disregard of property from his own more high-minded disregard: " 'I cannot say that you are wrong,' returned the

trapper, whose opinions on this important topic, though drawn from very different premises, were in singular accordance with those of his companion, 'and I have often thought and said as much when and where I have believed my voice could be heard. But your beasts are stolen by them who claim to be masters of all they find in the deserts' " (chap. 5).

10. And, indeed, as Roy Harvey Pearce argues, in a well-known article, "The Leatherstocking Tales Re-Examined," *South Atlantic Quarterly,* 46 (1947), 524–36, Cooper's social concerns threaten the western novels as well. Wayne Franklin, *The New World of James Fenimore Cooper* (Chicago: Univ. of Chicago Press, 1982), p. 24, speaking of *Precaution,* puts it finely: "as the work stands, it hints, among other things, at Cooper's perennial distrust of the social occasion as a moment of truth."

11. For a study of *Precaution's* relation to Austen's *Persuasion,* see George E. Hastings, "How Cooper Became a Novelist," *American Literature,* 12 (1940), 20–51. For a representative though not unsympathetic evaluation of the place of *Precaution* in Cooper's canon, see Donald Ringe, *James Fenimore Cooper* (New York: Twayne, 1962), pp. 23–25.

12. And *The Monikins,* as a blatant fable, is the exception that proves the rule. Appropriating reference away from itself into itself as the very condition of its legibility, it assumes, we might say, the categorical beyond any further need to invoke it.

13. Robert Grossman, *James Fenimore Cooper* (1949; Stanford: Stanford Univ. Press, 1967), pp. 36–37.

14. Mark Twain, "Fenimore Cooper's Literary Offenses" (1895), in *The Shock of Recognition: The Development of Literature in the United States Recorded by the Men Who Made It,* ed. Edmund Wilson, 2d ed. (New York: Grosset and Dunlop, 1955), p. 587.

15. Railton, *Fenimore Cooper,* p. 19.

16. Spiller, *Fenimore Cooper,* pp. 226–30; Dorothy Waples, *The Whig Myth of James Fenimore Cooper* (New Haven: Yale Univ. Press, 1938), pp. 143–56, 164–65.

17. Alexis de Tocqueville, *Democracy in America* (1835), the Henry Reeve text, ed. Phillips Bradley (1838; New York: Knopf, 1945).

18. James Fenimore Cooper, *The American Democrat, or Hints on the Social and Civic Relations of the United States of America* (Cooperstown, 1838), p. 4.

19. Cooper, *The American Democrat,* pp. 17–27.

20. For a brilliant account of Twain's struggle to authorize himself,

see Warwick Wadlington, *The Confidence Game in American Literature* (Princeton: Princeton Univ. Press, 1975), pp. 174–284.

21. John Pendleton Kennedy, *Horse-Shoe Robinson,* ed. Ernest E. Leisy (1835; 2d ed. 1852; New York: American Book Co., 1937).

22. William Gilmore Simms, *The Yemassee,* ed. Alexander Cowie (1835; rev. 1853; New York: American Book Co., 1937).

23. Simms, *The Yemassee,* pp. 188–200.

24. And not only pejoratively, as here, but positively and throughout the Leatherstocking tales.

25. George Dekker, *James Fenimore Cooper: The American Scott* (New York: Barnes and Noble, 1967), p. 82.

26. The European novels are *The Bravo, The Heidenmauer,* and *The Headsman.* Cooper's projection and abandonment of the thirteen-novel series is reported by his daughter, Susan F. Cooper, *Pages and Pictures from the Writings of James Fenimore Cooper* (New York, 1861), pp. 101–2.

27. In addition to Spiller and Waples see, e.g., John P. McWilliams, Jr., *Political Justice in a Republic* (Berkeley: Univ. of California Press, 1972).

28. Leslie Fiedler, *Love and Death in the American Novel,* rev. ed. (New York: Stein and Day, 1966); D. H. Lawrence, *Studies in Classic American Literature* (New York: Thomas Seltzer, 1923).

29. Leon Howard, Introduction, *The Pioneers* (New York: Holt, Rinehart and Winston, 1959).

30. A survey of the problem from a somewhat different angle and an attempt to resolve it may be found in Allen M. Axelrad, "The Order of the Leatherstocking Tales: D. H. Lawrence, David Noble, and the Iron Trap of History," *American Literature,* 54 (1982), 189–211.

31. As Marius Bewley with poignant but misplaced sympathy puts it in *The Eccentric Design: Form in the Classic American Novel* (New York: Columbia Univ. Press, 1959), p. 98, the scene's greatness is its "registering, both with tenderness and surgical realism, the tensions of a highly developed and refined moral consciousness under the shock of a brutal necessity." The reading of *The Deerslayer* as the culmination of a kind of mythic ascent was first proposed by D. H. Lawrence, *Studies in Classic American Literature,* who still seems convincing to me. For a good argument, however, that *The Deerslayer,* rather, debunks myth, see William P. Kelly, *Plotting America's Past: Fenimore Cooper and the Leatherstocking Tales* (Carbondale: Southern Illinois Univ. Press, 1983), pp. 159–87.

32. Though exhibiting, still, strong marks of politically motivated

distemper, the general reception of *The Pathfinder* was almost grateful: "We are sorry for what we deem [have earlier been] his deviations from his true course as a novelist. . . . We congratulate Mr. Cooper and the public . . . upon his return to his old ground of romance." Quoted in *The Pathfinder,* ed. Richard Dilworth Rust (Albany: SUNY Press, 1979), p. xxi.

33. Most complete is Blake Nevius, *Cooper's Landscapes: An Essay on the Picturesque Vision* (Berkeley: Univ. of California Press, 1976).

34. Terence Martin, "From the Ruins of History: *The Last of the Mohicans,"* *Novel,* 2 (1969), 221–29, offers an especially interesting reading along these lines.

35. Cf. Wayne Franklin, *New World of James Fenimore Cooper,* p. 244: "The 'shrieks, groans, exhortations, and curses' which arise during this 'jubilee of the devils,' as Gamut calls the massacre, are 'real' sounds in their own way. But in them, as in the persistent yells which ring through the tale as a whole . . . we may hear, I think, the accent of Cooper's own increasingly disordered voice. For the nightmare of *The Last of the Mohicans* is the author's; it is his sensibility which dreams the dream of its action."

36. See Henry Nash Smith, Introduction to *The Prairie* (New York: Holt, Rinehart and Winston, 1950), pp. xii–xvi.

37. See Mikhail Bakhtin, *The Dialogic Imagination: Four Essays,* ed. Michael Holquist (Austin: Univ. of Texas Press, 1981).

38. Even the otherwise generally respectful Middleton and Paul can sometimes not stand Natty's wise talk. As Cooper describes them, bound at the stake and forced to endure Natty lecturing instead of acting when a diversion offers opportunity for escape: "'Harkee, old trapper,' shouted Paul, whose patience could no longer maintain itself under the calculating and prolix explanations of the other, 'suppose you cut two things I can name, short off. That is to say, your conversation, which is agreeable enough over a well-baked buffalo's hump, and these damnable thongs of hide, which, according to my experience, can be pleasant nowhere. A single stroke of your knife would be of more service just now than the longest speech that was ever made in a Kentucky courthouse'" (chap. 29).

4: Poe and Plagiarism

1. *The Complete Works of Edgar Allan Poe,* Virginia Edition, 17 vols., ed. James A. Harrison (1902; New York: AMS Press, 1965), 16.183. Al-

though it has been superseded in part, the Virginia Edition is still the most complete collection of Poe yet published. References will be given in parentheses in the text.

2. Complete biographical details may be found in Arthur Hobson Quinn, *Edgar Allan Poe: A Critical Biography* (New York: Appleton-Century-Crofts, 1941).

3. From Baudelaire on, this has, in effect, been the authorized French view. As Mallarmé in his memorial, "Le Tombeau d'Edgar Poe," put it, Poe's "voix étrange" gave "un sens plus pur aux mots de la tribu." Rpt. in Célestin Pierre Cambiaire, *The Influence of Edgar Allan Poe in France* (1927; New York: Haskell House, 1970), p. 130. For a fuller discussion of the French Poe see Cambiaire and, especially, Patrick F. Quinn, *The French Face of Edgar Poe* (Carbondale: Southern Illinois Univ. Press, 1957).

4. *Eureka*, 16.311: "On the Universal agglomeration and dissolution, we can readily conceive that a new and perhaps totally different series of conditions may ensue—another creation and irradiation, returning into itself . . . a novel Universe swelling into existence, and then subsiding into nothingness, at every throb of the Heart Divine. And now—this Heart Divine—what is it? *It is our own.*"

5. *The Poetical Works of William Wordsworth*, ed. Thomas Hutchinson (London: Oxford Univ. Press, 1936), p. 149.

6. See the summary and evaluation of readings by Cleanth Brooks and F. W. Bateson in E. D. Hirsch, Jr., "Objective Interpretation," *PMLA*, 75 (1960), 463–79, rpt. in *Validity in Interpretation* (New Haven: Yale Univ. Press, 1967), pp. 209–44.

7. Elizabeth Sewell, *The Field of Nonsense* (London: Chatto and Windus, 1952), pp. 44–54.

8. James's remarks, rpt. in I. M. Walker, ed., *Edgar Allan Poe: The Critical Heritage* (London: Routledge and Kegan Paul, 1986), p. 53, appear in a review of Baudelaire. The full comment of Lowell, rpt. Walker, p. 17, from *Fable for Critics* (1848), is "There comes Poe, with his raven, like Barnaby Rudge, / Three-fifths of him genius and two-fifths sheer fudge, / Who talks like a book of iambs and pentameters, / In a way to make people of common sense damn meter, / Who has written some things quite the best of their kind, / But the heart somehow seems all squeezed out by the mind."

9. For Poe's relation to his critics see Sidney P. Moss, *Poe's Literary Battles: The Critic in the Context of His Literary Milieu* (Durham, N.C.: Duke Univ. Press, 1963). Also Perry Miller, *The Raven and the Whale: The*

War of Words and Wits in the Era of Poe and Melville (New York: Harcourt, Brace, 1956).

10. Carl L. Anderson, *Poe in Northlight: The Scandinavian Response to His Life and Work* (Durham, N.C.: Duke Univ. Press, 1973); Joan Delaney Grossman, *Edgar Allan Poe in Russia: A Study in Legend and Literary Influence* (Wurzburg: Jal-Verlag, 1973); André Karatson, *Edgar Allan Poe et le Groupe des Ecrivains du "Nyugat" en Hongrie* (Paris: Presses Universitaires de France, 1971).

Tate, "Our Cousin, Mr. Poe," rpt. in *Poe: A Collection of Critical Essays,* ed. Robert Regan (Englewood Cliffs, N.J.: Prentice-Hall, 1967), pp. 38–50. As Tate puts it succinctly, p. 41: "If he was a madman he was also a gentleman."

11. The infamous Rufus Wilmot Griswold, in his "Ludwig" review, rpt. in *The Recognition of Edgar Allan Poe: Selected Criticism since 1829,* ed. Eric W. Carlson (Ann Arbor: Univ. of Michigan Press, 1966), pp. 28–35, spoke for a generation. For an early response and survey by way of refutation, see Poe's one-time fiancée, Sarah Helen Whitman, *Edgar Poe and His Critics* (1860; New York: AMS Press, 1966), and the "Account of His Death, by His Attending Physician," John J. Moran, *A Defense of Edgar Allan Poe: Life, Character and Dying Declarations of the Poet* (1885; New York: AMS Press, 1966).

12. Marie Bonaparte, *The Life and Works of Edgar Allan Poe: A Psycho-Analytic Interpretation,* trans. John Rodken (London: Imago Publishing Co., 1949).

13. Joseph Wood Krutch, *Edgar Allan Poe: A Study in Genius* (New York: Knopf, 1926).

14. See, especially, the immensely powerful David Halliburton, *Edgar Allan Poe: A Phenomenological View* (Princeton: Princeton Univ. Press, 1973). Georges Poulet, *Studies in Human Time,* trans. Elliott Coleman (Baltimore: Johns Hopkins Univ. Press, 1956), pp. 330–34, and *The Metamorphosis of the Circle,* trans. Carley Dawson and Elliott Coleman (Baltimore: Johns Hopkins Univ. Press, 1966), pp. 182–202, is also of interest. In Poulet's case, however, the "I" for whom the critic speaks seems universalized so completely from the start that the otherness which Halliburton must work to transform vanishes altogether. As we might be inclined to say, Poulet's Poe is difficult to particularize as "Poe" altogether. See n. 19 below. And cf. the general criticism of Poulet's phenomenology in Geoffrey Hartman, *Beyond Formalism: Literary Essays, 1958–1970* (New Haven: Yale Univ. Press, 1970), pp. 51–56.

15. Daniel Hoffman, *Poe Poe Poe Poe Poe Poe Poe* (New York: Doubleday, 1972).

16. Louis Renza, "Poe's Secret Autobiography," in *The American Renaissance Reconsidered,* Selected Papers from the English Institute, 1982–83, ed. Walter Benn Michaels and Donald E. Pease (Baltimore: Johns Hopkins Univ. Press, 1985), p. 58. Insisting on what he calls the "materiality" of Poe's language, Renza resolutely refuses not only the traditional positivist, but also the more sophisticated deconstructive, evasions of Poe all too common in current criticism.

17. Patrick F. Quinn, *French Face of Edgar Poe.*

18. The line is from his introductory poem, "Au Lecteur," in *Les Fleurs du Mal* (Paris, 1857). For a handy translation of Baudelaire's various critical prefaces to his translations of Poe see *Baudelaire on Poe,* trans. Lois Hyslop and Francis E. Hyslop, Jr. (State College, Pa.: Bald Eagle Press, 1952).

19. Thus Jacques Lacan, "Seminar on 'The Purloined Letter,'" in "French Freud: Structural Studies in Psychoanalysis," *Yale French Studies,* 48 (1972), 38–72, and the response of Jacques Derrida, "Le Facteur de la Vérité," *Poétique,* 21 (1975), 96–147. These are interpretations in only the most limited way. More properly, using Poe as a kind of after-the-fact authorization for a deconstruction they assume in advance, they signify the assimilation of Poe into French as a fait "always already," to use Derrida's phrase, accompli.

20. Most pointed and most amusing is Aldous Huxley, "Vulgarity in Literature," rpt. in *Poe: A Collection of Critical Essays,* pp. 31–37. Huxley renders a famous passage in Milton's *Paradise Lost* in Poe-ese. Thus Milton:

> Like that fair field
> Of Enna, where Proserpine gathering flowers,
> Herself a fairer flower, by gloomy Dis
> Was gathered, which cost Ceres all that pain
> To seek her through the world.

And Poe:

> It was noon in the fair field of Enna,
>   Where Proserpina gathering flowers—
>   Herself the most fragrant of flowers,

Was gathered away to Gehenna
  By the Prince of Plutonian powers;
Was borne down the windings of Brenner
  To the gloom of his amorous bowers—
Down the tortuous highway of Brenner
  To the God's agapeminous bowers.

21. *Edgar Allan Poe: Essays and Reviews,* ed. G. R. Thompson (New York: Library of America, 1984), p. 1025.

22. See, especially, Moss, *Poe's Literary Battles.*

23. For a review of the charges against Coleridge and a defense of his plagiarism as a method of (romantic) composition, see Thomas McFarland, *Coleridge and the Pantheist Tradition* (Oxford: Clarendon Press, 1969), "The Problem of Coleridge's Plagiarism," pp. 1–52.

24. John Livingston Lowes, *The Road to Xanadu: A Study in the Ways of the Imagination* (Boston: Houghton Mifflin, 1927).

25. Burton Pollin, *Discoveries in Poe* (Notre Dame, Ind.: Univ. of Notre Dame Press, 1970).

26. Halliburton, *Edgar Allan Poe,* p. 369.

27. There are various titles for the various editions of the story. See the notes in Thomas Ollive Mabbott, ed. *The Collected Works of Edgar Allan Poe,* Vol. 2 (Cambridge: Belknap Press, 1978), pp. 336, 347.

28. *Tales of the Grotesque and Arabesque* (Philadelphia, 1840) is the name Poe gave to his first collection of stories.

29. Quoted in Hoffman, *Poe Poe Poe Poe Poe Poe Poe,* p. 119.

30. Quoted in N. Bryllion Fagin, *The Histrionic Mr. Poe* (Baltimore: Johns Hopkins Univ. Press, 1949), p. 207.

31. "Ars Poetica," in *The Collected Poems of Archibald MacLeish* (Boston: Houghton Mifflin, 1962), pp. 50–51. For a fine reading of the place of Poe's aesthetics in the history of formalism see Frank Lentricchia, "Four Types of Nineteenth-Century Poetic," *Journal of Aesthetics and Art Criticism,* 26 (1968), 351–66.

32. Thus, e.g., on "The Fall of the House of Usher," Vincent Buranelli, *Edgar Allan Poe* (New York: Twayne, 1961), p. 138: "Poe is *not* Roderick Usher. He is the creator of Roderick Usher." Similarly, James W. Gargano, "The Question of Poe's Narrators," *College English,* 25 (1963), 177–81.

33. For a further development of this point, see my "The Problem of Poe," *Georgia Review,* 32 (1978), 645–57.

34. This tendency was first noticed by Kenneth Burke, " 'The Principle of Composition,' " *Poetry,* 99 (1961), 46–53.

35. Sharon Cameron, *The Corporeal Self: Allegories of the Body in Melville and Hawthorne* (Baltimore: Johns Hopkins Univ. Press, 1981).

36. For a discussion of Coleridge, synecdoche, symbolism, and the American tradition, see Charles Feidelson, Jr., *Symbolism and American Literature* (Chicago: Univ. of Chicago Press, 1953), especially pp. 44–76.

37. Constance Rourke, *American Humor: A Study of the National Character* (1931; Garden City, N.Y.: Doubleday, 1953), p. 45: "Of all American writers Poe has become a symbol for the type of genius which rises clear from its time, nourished mainly from hidden inner sources. Poe himself would have delighted in that theory, for he fostered the conviction that he ranged over only the rarest and most esoteric materials. But Poe came from that Scotch-Irish stock with its heritage of unsettlement from which were drawn the scouts and myth-makers and many strollers of the West; the theatrical strain that had been strong among them was his by birth; and he began to write at the end of the '20's when American myth-making was passing into its great popular diffusion." For Poe the journalist, see David K. Jackson, *Poe and "The Southern Literary Messenger"* (1934; New York: Haskell House, 1970).

38. T. S. Eliot, "From Poe to Valéry," rpt. in *The Recognition of Edgar Allan Poe,* pp. 205–19.

39. T. S. Eliot, *Selected Essays,* New Edition (New York: Harcourt, Brace, 1950): "Hamlet and His Problems," pp. 121–26; "The Metaphysical Poets," pp. 241–50; "Tradition and the Individual Talent," pp. 3–11. The remark on stealing is in "Philip Massinger," p. 182.

40. Ralph Waldo Emerson, "Nature," in *The Collected Works of Ralph Waldo Emerson,* Vol. 1, ed. Alfred R. Ferguson and Robert E. Spiller (Cambridge: Belknap Press, 1971), p. 13. Poe as naysayer to Emersonian transcendentalism has been a commonplace at least since Harry Levin, *The Power of Blackness: Hawthorne, Poe, Melville* (New York: Knopf, 1967). A better formulation, however, would be that Poe says no and yes simultaneously, that, transcendentalizing death, he yet does not transcend it. For a similar reading of Emerson himself see Harold Bloom, *Figures of Capable Imagination* (New York: Seabury Press, 1976), pp. 46–64, 67–88. And, especially, for a radically revisionist reading which presents Emerson in a context too unideal to have an opposite altogether, see Stanley Cavell's two articles, "Thinking of Emerson" and "An Emerson Mood," conveniently printed in the Expanded Edi-

tion of *The Senses of Walden* (San Francisco: North Point Press, 1981), pp. 123–38, 141–60.

41. Henry David Thoreau, *Walden,* ed. J. Lyndon Shanley (Princeton: Princeton Univ. Press, 1971), p. 318.

42. Mabbott, *Collected Works of Edgar Allan Poe,* 2.521.

43. See Hoffman, *Poe Poe Poe Poe Poe Poe Poe,* pp, 112–13, for a fine discussion of this point.

5: Hawthorne and the Responsibility of Outsidedness

1. *The Centenary Edition of the Works of Nathaniel Hawthorne,* ed. William Charvat, Roy Harvey Pearce, Claude M. Simpson, and Thomas Woodson (Columbus: Ohio State Univ. Press, 1962–), 10.360. Except where noted, all references are to this edition.

2. Frederick Crews, *The Sins of the Fathers: Hawthorne's Psychological Themes* (London: Oxford Univ. Press, 1966), pp. 80–95.

3. Michael Colacurcio, *The Province of Piety: Moral History in Hawthorne's Early Tales* (Cambridge: Harvard Univ. Press, 1984), pp. 107–30.

4. Ibid., p. 112. "The necessity of his own historicism" is, at first blush, perhaps not quite fair. Colacurcio insists on freedom of choice throughout. His point about history is not that it determines people's actions, but that unless people give over mythological evasions, they will be unable to determine the course of such history as they may hope to have in the future. Still, since he has seen fit to exaggerate my own position, I may as well exaggerate his. For Hawthorne does not, as it seems to me, think that history and mythology are so very easily distinguishable as Colacurcio, confirmed historicist that he is, does. Or better, even where he does distinguish, he is not so ready to give up the mythology he has exposed, for that would be to give up himself, as mythologizer, as well. Colacurcio would appear to believe that to get the facts right is to be saved. As he puts it, p. 130, "To study the relevant history is to learn to construe the text." As we might say, however, for Hawthorne, to construe one text is also to establish another, and what he insists upon is that to do the former does not exonerate one from the consequences of doing the latter.

5. Lionel Trilling, "Our Hawthorne," in Roy Harvey Pearce, ed., *Hawthorne Centenary Essays* (Columbus: Ohio State Univ. Press, 1964), pp. 429–58.

6. E.g., Newton Arvin, *Hawthorne* (Boston: Little, Brown, 1929). In

more metaphysical terms the tradition begins as early as Melville's famous piece, "Hawthorne and His Mosses," in *Pierre, The Piazza Tales, The Confidence Man, Uncollected Prose, Billy Budd, Sailor,* ed. Harrison Hayford (New York: Library of America, 1984), pp. 1154–71.

7. Thus, e.g., Lawrence Sargent Hall, *Hawthorne: Critic of Society,* Yale Studies in English, 99 (New Haven: Yale Univ. Press, 1944).

8. Randall Stewart, *Nathaniel Hawthorne: A Biography* (New Haven: Yale Univ. Press, 1948). For the reclusive Hawthorne, see Arvin. Nor is my point some compromise between the two, as in Mark Van Doren, *Nathaniel Hawthorne* (1949; rpt. New York: Viking Press, 1957). Rather, the idea of reclusiveness needs to be reformulated altogether.

9. This is Melville's reading, speaking of Hawthorne's "power of blackness," in "Hawthorne and His Mosses," p. 1159. Melville, on the brink of a readership crisis, keeps his faith by searching out a soulmate. Influential academic readings in the same vein are Roy Male, *Hawthorne's Tragic Vision* (Austin: Univ. of Texas Press, 1957), and Richard Harter Fogle, *Hawthorne's Fiction: The Light and the Dark* (Norman: Univ. of Oklahoma Press, 1952).

10. Thus Crews's manifestly subversive intent. "Subversion," however, may be but the name we give to glorify what is already as acceptable as official doctrine. What is proposed as subversive, that is, must already have been accepted in advance if it is to be felt as subversive rather than ignored as merely eccentric. Note the wide and almost immediate acclaim of Crews's work compared with the relative lack of notice of a fine precursor, Rudolph Von Abele's *The Death of the Artist: A Study of Hawthorne's Disintegration* (The Hague: Martinus Nijhoff, 1955).

11. Quoted in Hubert H. Hoeltje, *Inward Sky: The Mind and Heart of Nathaniel Hawthorne* (Durham, N.C.: Duke Univ. Press, 1962), p. 79. Cilley stands in perfect contrast to Hawthorne in this regard. As Hawthorne describes him, in "Jonathan Cilley," *Nathaniel Hawthorne: Tales and Sketches,* ed. Roy Harvey Pearce (New York: Library of America, 1982), p. 608: "There was a singular contrast between the flow of thoughts from his lips, and the coldness and constraint with which he wrote; and though, in maturer life, he acquired a considerable facility in exercising the pen, he always felt the tongue to be his peculiar instrument." The pen, as we might put it, was rather Hawthorne's peculiar instrument, and he had to learn to acquire facility, instead, with the tongue. Compare our discussion of writing in section 2, below.

12. Yvor Winters, "Maule's Curse, or Hawthorne and the Problem of

Allegory," *Maule's Curse: Seven Studies in the History of American Obscuran-
tism,* in *In Defense of Reason* (Denver: Alan Swallow, 1947), pp. 157–75.

13. Hawthorne's family name was originally Hathorne, without the
w, though a "Hawthorne" variant evidently already existed. For the
details see Arlin Turner, *Nathaniel Hawthorne: A Biography* (New York:
Oxford Univ. Press, 1980), pp. 395–96.

14. An early argument of this sort is Frank Kermode, "Hawthorne's
Modernity," *Partisan Review,* 41 (1974), 428–41. More sophisticated and
incisive is John Carlos Rowe, *Through the Custom-House: Nineteenth-Century American Fiction and Modern Theory* (Baltimore: Johns Hopkins Univ.
Press, 1982), his chapter on *The Blithedale Romance,* pp. 52–90.

15. See the penetrating account of Jonathan Arac, "The Politics of
The Scarlet Letter," in *Ideology and Classic American Literature,* ed. Sacvan
Bercovitch and Myra Jehlen (Cambridge: Cambridge Univ. Press,
1986), pp. 247–66. Arac charges Hawthorne with a mystification of
passivity over action in relation to slavery and other political issues of
the mid-century. And, indeed, Hawthorne was passive. I do not, however, think he mystified anything. He made his choice—not to act—
which, he decided, was a better choice than war and for which I do not
think he held himself anything less than fully accountable.

For a related account, see Eric J. Sundquist, "Slavery, Revolution,
and the American Renaissance," in *The American Renaissance Reconsidered,* Selected Papers from the English Institute, 1982–83, ed. Walter
Benn Michaels and Donald E. Pease (Baltimore: Johns Hopkins Univ.
Press, 1985), pp. 11–12.

16. And, similarly, over his publisher's objection, he dedicates *Our
Old Home* to Pierce, despite the danger to sales that, in the midst of the
Civil War, such a dedication presented. Hawthorne sacrificed, perhaps, the aims of the war to his friendship. But, then, sacrificing his
friendship to the war would have been for him a sacrifice too. For a full
account, see Claude M. Simpson's Introduction to the Centenary Edition text, 5.xxv–xxix.

17. Cf. Hawthorne's remarks about Indian tales in "Sketches from
Memory" (10.428–29): "The hearts of the pale-faces would not thrill to
these superstitions of the red men, though we spoke of them in the
centre of their haunted region. The habits and sentiments of that
departed people were too distinct from those of their successors to find
much real sympathy. It has often been a matter of regret to me, that I
was shut out from the most peculiar field of American fiction, by an
inability to see any romance, or poetry, or grandeur, or beauty in the

Indian character, at least, till such traits were pointed out by others. I do abhor an Indian story. Yet no writer can be more secure of a permanent place in our literature, than the biographer of the Indian chiefs. His subject, as referring to tribes which have mostly vanished from the earth, gives him a right to be placed on a classic shelf, apart from the merits which will sustain him there." As discussed below, if Cooper's myth is the discourse of the other, then for Hawthorne, Indian tales in the manner of Cooper are too other to be "his" myth, altogether.

18. Immanuel Kant, *The Critique of Pure Reason,* trans. J. M. D. Meiklejohn (London: Dent, 1934), p. 454. See Introduction, n. 2, above.

19. Mikhail Bakhtin, *The Dialogic Imagination: Four Essays,* ed. Michael Holquist (Austin: Univ. of Texas Press, 1981).

20. For a chronology and a discussion of the proposed volumes and their probable contents, see Elizabeth Lathrop Chandler, "A Study of the Sources of the Tales and Romances Written by Nathaniel Hawthorne before 1853," *Smith College Studies in Modern Languages,* 7 (July 1926).

21. "Fragments from the Journal of a Solitary Man" was published but uncollected. "Passages from a Relinquished Work" was reprinted in *Mosses from an Old Manse.* Note, also, "The Christmas Banquet," which is subtitled "From the Unpublished Allegories of the Heart," collected in *Mosses,* and "Ethan Brand," subtitled "A Chapter from an Abortive Romance," collected in *The Snow-Image.* In "The Custom-House," Hawthorne insists on speaking of *The Scarlet Letter* as if it were one of a volume of stories even after he knows it has expanded to the size of a novel and is to be published alone (1.43). The story both is and is not Hawthorne's. It is and is not a formal whole.

22. Cf. my *Rediscovering Hawthorne* (Princeton: Princeton Univ. Press, 1977), where the progress of this investment is treated in somewhat different language over the length of Hawthorne's career.

23. When Hawthorne, accordingly, asked his friends to return or destroy their copies of *Fanshawe,* he was acting out of more than embarrassment at a juvenile work. Or rather, to define it in rhetorical terms, embarrassment is finding what is not the self being taken *for* the self. As Roy Harvey Pearce puts it in his Introduction to the Centenary text, 3.39: "Despite the destruction of Elizabeth Hawthorne's and Horatio Bridge's copies, the weight of the evidence is that Hawthorne wished not necessarily to suppress *Fanshawe,* but rather his connection with it." For a complete account, see Pearce.

24. My reading of "Wakefield" is heavily indebted to Herbert Per-luck's wonderfully sensitive "The Artist as 'Crafty Nincompoop': Hawthorne's 'Indescribable Obliquity of Gait' in 'Wakefield,' " *Nathaniel Hawthorne Journal, 1978,* ed. C. E. Frazer Clark, Jr. (Detroit: Gale Research Co., 1984), pp. 181–94.

25. Cf. Stanley Cavell's meditation on Emerson's proclamation of his "Self-Reliance," "I would write on the lintels of the door-post, *Whim,*" in "An Emerson Mood," rpt. in *The Senses of Walden,* Expanded Edition (San Francisco: North Point Press, 1981), p. 154: "The call of one's genius presents itself with no deeper authority than whim. And what presents itself in the form of whim is bound sometimes to be exactly whim and nothing more." We might say that whim is sometimes but "whim-wham" and that the difference is a matter precisely of deliberation or decision. For a beautiful treatment along these lines of Thoreau's insistence on deliberation, see John M. Dolan, "The Distant Drum in *Walden,*" *Thoreau Quarterly,* 14 (1982), 71ff.

26. The Virginia Edition, 13.148.

27. See chap. 4, n. 36, above. For application to Hawthorne, see Charles Feidelson, Jr., *Symbolism and American Literature* (Chicago: Univ. of Chicago Press, 1953), pp. 6–16.

28. "Unpardonable sin" is the term Hawthorne uses explicitly in "Ethan Brand" (11.87), where Brand's pursuit of the knowledge of sin is itself declared sinful. As we might say of man's fall, Adam, in Hawthorne's understanding of him, did not so much come into a knowledge of good and evil as it existed prior to him, as establish good and evil through his very desire to know them.

29. Hyatt H. Waggoner, *Hawthorne: A Critical Study* (Cambridge: Belknap Press, 1955), pp. 51–52, who ranks it "among the greatest stories in the language," is typical.

30. Tableau-vivant-like devices are among Hawthorne's favorites. They appear explicitly in *The Blithedale Romance,* 3.106–7, organized by Zenobia and having the effect of pointing out the unreality of these Boston intellectuals doing farm work in their "arcadia." But throughout his novels, a tendency toward static staging is evident, as noted, e.g., by Malcolm Cowley, "Five Acts of *The Scarlet Letter,*" *College English,* 19 (1957), 11–16. I would suggest the cause was Hawthorne's constant temptation to freeze life and have done with it once and for all. And, indeed, his finally having done with it may account for the unfinished romances with their attempted organization around frozen images that Hawthorne himself cannot believe. Thus he meditates on a

character in *Doctor Grimshawe's Secret:* "Shall he be preternatural? . . . A man with a mortal disease?—a leprosy?—a eunuch?—a cork leg?—a golden touch?—a dead hand?—a false nose?—a glass eye? . . . Some damn'd thing is the matter." Quoted in Edward Hutchins Davidson, *Hawthorne's Last Phase* (New Haven: Yale Univ. Press, 1949), p. 56.

31. For an index of the problem's intractability see Waggoner, *Hawthorne,* pp. 47–51, who in reading the laugh as focusing a pattern of laughter throughout the story is in effect driven to proliferate his difficulty even as he would solve it.

32. Crews, *Sins of the Fathers,* pp. 61–79. Colacurcio, *Province of Piety,* p. 563, nn. 62 and 67, reviews the historical criticism. See, also, Larzer Ziff, *Literary Democracy: The Declaration of Cultural Independence in America* (New York: Viking, 1981), pp. 144–45, who, stating both positions, winds up invoking what he himself calls "myth," precisely the evasion I describe below.

33. For a summary of the disagreement, see Michael Davitt Bell, *Hawthorne and the Historical Romance of New England* (Princeton: Princeton Univ. Press, 1971), p. 77.

6: Melville's Silence

1. For a good account of the history of *Moby-Dick*'s reception see Hershel Parker's contribution to the "Historical Note" of *Moby-Dick or The Whale,* Northwestern-Newberry Edition (Evanston, Ill.: Northwestern Univ. Press and The Newberry Library, 1988), 6.689–754. *Moby-Dick as Doubloon: Essays and Extracts, 1851–1970,* ed. Parker and Harrison Hayford (New York: Norton, 1970), offers an exhaustive anthology of opinion and commentary.

2. On Ishmael, see Paul Brodtkorb, Jr., *Ishmael's White World: A Phenomenological Reading of "Moby-Dick"* (New Haven: Yale Univ. Press, 1965), pp. 102–39. Melville's skepticism is explored, with a variety of emphases, in studies that constitute a virtually canonic modern reading. Of particular note are Richard P. Blackmur, "The Craft of Herman Melville: A Putative Statement," rpt. in *Melville: A Collection of Critical Essays,* ed. Richard Chase (Englewood Cliffs, N.J.: Prentice-Hall, 1962), pp. 75–90, an as it were predeconstructive look at the slippage between various Melvillean discourses; James Guetti, *The Limits of Metaphor: A Study of Melville, Conrad, and Faulkner* (Ithaca: Cornell Univ. Press, 1967), who discusses linguistic problems; and Edgar Dryden, *Melville's Thematics of Form: The Great Art of Telling the*

Truth (Baltimore: Johns Hopkins Univ. Press, 1968), an influential study of Melville's epistemology.

3. *The Letters of Herman Melville,* ed. Merrell R. Davis and William H. Gilman (New Haven: Yale Univ. Press, 1960), p. 133.

4. Henry Sussman, "The Deconstructor as Politician: Melville's *Confidence-Man,"* *Glyph,* 4 (1978), 54. Cf. Rodolphe Gasché, "The Scene of Writing: A Deferred Outset," *Glyph,* 1 (1977), 150–71. Melville as modernist was formulated most extensively by Charles Feidelson, *Symbolism and American Literature* (Chicago: Univ. of Chicago Press, 1953), but it has been a dominant theme from almost the beginning of the Melville revival until now. See, e.g., Harold Beaver, "Melville and Modernism," *Dutch Quarterly Review of Anglo-American Letters,* 13 (1983), 1–15.

5. The literature is vast. Among the "old" historians see F. O. Matthiessen, *American Renaissance: Art and Expression in the Age of Emerson and Whitman* (New York: Oxford Univ. Press, 1941), pp. 369–514, and Richard Chase, *Herman Melville: A Critical Study* (New York: Macmillan, 1949). Notable among the new are Michael Paul Rogin, *Subversive Genealogy: The Politics and Art of Herman Melville* (New York: Knopf, 1983), and Carolyn L. Karcher, *Shadow over the Promised Land: Slavery, Race, and Violence in Melville's America* (Baton Rouge: Louisiana State Univ. Press, 1980). Milton R. Stern, "Melville, Society, and Language," in *A Companion to Melville Studies,* ed. John Bryant (Greenwood Press: New York, 1986), pp. 433–79, gives a finely integrated overview.

6. *Moby-Dick,* in *Redburn: His First Voyage; White-Jacket, or The World in a Man-of-War; Moby-Dick, or The Whale,* ed. G. Thomas Tanselle, (New York: Library of America, 1983), [2].795. All references are to the appropriate volume (number supplied) of the three-volume Library of America Edition, which largely reprints the official Northwestern-Newberry Edition in a convenient format. The other volumes are [1] *Typee, Omoo, Mardi,* ed. Tanselle (New York, 1982), and [3] *Pierre, Israel Potter, The Piazza Tales, The Confidence-Man, Uncollected Prose, Billy Budd, Sailor,* ed. Harrison Hayford (New York, 1984).

7. For a complete account, including the controversy which *Typee* engendered, see Hugh W. Hetherington, *Melville's Reviewers, British and American: 1846–1891* (Chapel Hill: Univ. of North Carolina Press, 1961), pp. 20–65. Especially good at placing Melville in relation to conventional portraits of the South Seas is T. Walter Herbert, Jr., *Marquesan Encounters: Melville and the Meaning of Civilization* (Cambridge: Harvard Univ. Press, 1980).

8. Quoted from the *American Review* (April 1846), in Hetherington, *Melville's Reviewers,* pp. 34–35.

9. Quoted from the London *Critic* (March 1846) and the London *Examiner* (March 1846), rpt. in *Melville: The Critical Heritage,* ed. Watson G. Branch (London: Routledge and Kegan Paul, 1974), pp. 56, 60.

10. Typical was George Washington Peck in the *Morning Courier and New York Enquirer* (April 1840), discussed in Hetherington, *Melville's Reviewers,* pp. 37–40.

11. From extracts of reviews included in the Harper and Brothers advertisements for *Typee* and *Omoo,* rpt. in *The Recognition of Herman Melville: Selected Criticism since 1846,* ed. Hershel Parker (Ann Arbor: Univ. of Michigan Press, 1967).

12. See, e.g., Merton M. Sealts, Jr., *Melville's Reading: A Check-List of Books Owned and Borrowed* (Madison: Univ. of Wisconsin Press, 1966). The wide reading that went into the composition of *Mardi* is mentioned, usually unfavorably, by almost all Melville's contemporaneous reviewers.

13. *Letters,* p. 130.

14. Richard Brodhead, *The School of Hawthorne* (New York: Oxford Univ. Press, 1986), pp. 17–47. Brodhead's rich discussion of Melville places him over and against a debilitating cult of domesticity exemplified in the works of Hawthorne's "scribbling women" and such male writers as N. P. Willis. He thus extends his earlier treatment of the romance/novel opposition, in *Hawthorne, Melville, and the Novel* (Chicago: Univ. of Chicago Press, 1976), to political and social grounds. More widely, however, the background to Brodhead is a buried, yet extended, controversy over whether Melville is best read in a line of popular writing, as favored by nativists like Constance Rourke, *American Humor: A Study of the National Character* (1931; Garden City, N.Y.: Doubleday, 1953), pp. 154–60, and Edward H. Rosenberry, *Melville and the Comic Spirit* (Cambridge: Harvard Univ. Press, 1955), or whether he is best seen as unappreciated highbrow or intellectual, as, e.g., in Raymond M. Weaver's founding *Herman Melville: Mariner and Mystic* (New York: Doran, 1921). In effect, Brodhead would resolve the controversy by establishing a high nativist tradition, but thus, in his very attempt at resolution, he grants a division between the writer and his culture, between self and society, which Melville could never accept and of which the division between high and low, popular and intellectual, romance and novel are mere epiphenomena. Melville, we should say, is not a self who might choose to belong to this or that readership

or, for that matter, a writer who might choose to write this or that sort of writing. Rather, there was for him (as, it seems to me, for all seriously democratic writers) one readership only, higher *and* lower than he, more and less intellectual, and this was the problem, beyond resolution, that he had to face *in* his writing—of whatever sort—over and over again. As Ann Douglas, *The Feminization of American Culture* (New York: Knopf, 1977), p. 320, puts it, "Melville's Americanness consisted in part in his awareness that he could not be significantly better than his culture. . . . If his readers are dispossessed, so is Melville." Similarly, see Carolyn Porter's excellent "Call Me Ishmael, or How to Make Double-Talk Speak," in *New Essays on "Moby-Dick,"* ed. Brodhead (Cambridge: Cambridge Univ. Press, 1980), pp. 73–108.

15. The major statement is Merrell R. Davis, *Melville's "Mardi": A Chartless Voyage* (New Haven: Yale Univ. Press, 1952). Such a work as Maxine Moore, *That Lonely Game: "Mardi" and the Almanac* (Columbia: Univ. of Missouri Press, 1975), with its fantastic claim of an esoteric key which unlocks the novel, only proves the point. *Mardi* is impossible to grasp except as expounding its own impossibility.

16. *Letters,* p. 71. "Unreadable" is the judgment of the reviewer in the London *Morning Chronicle* (May 1849), quoted in Jay Leyda, ed., *The Melville Log: A Documentary Life of Herman Melville, 1819–1891, With a New Supplementary Chapter* (1951; New York: Gordian Press, 1969), 1.304, and, in similar words, most others.

17. E. L. Grant Watson, "Melville's Testament of Acceptance: *Billy Budd,*" *New England Quarterly,* 6 (1933), 319–27, and, for a review of the refutations with an extension of his own, Paul Withim, *"Billy Budd:* Melville's Testament of Resistance," *Modern Language Quarterly,* 20 (1959), 115–27.

18. A good survey of the literature on the subject is James C. Wilson, "The Hawthorne-Melville Relationship: An Annotated Bibliography," *American Transcendental Quarterly,* 45–46 (1980), 5–79.

19. *Letters,* p. 125.

20. *Letters,* p. 142.

21. The most powerful reading of Melville and homosexuality is Edwin Haviland Miller, *Herman Melville: A Biography* (New York: Braziller, 1975). See also Robert K. Martin, *Hero, Captain, and Stranger: Male Friendship, Social Critique, and Literary Form in the Sea Novels of Herman Melville* (Chapel Hill: Univ. of North Carolina Press, 1986).

22. *Letters,* p. 131.

23. Ralph Waldo Emerson, "Nature," in *The Collected Works of Ralph*

Waldo Emerson, Vol. 1, ed. Robert E. Spiller and Alfred R. Ferguson (Cambridge: Belknap Press, 1971), p. 10: "Standing on the bare ground,—my head bathed by the blithe air, and uplifted into infinite space,—all mean egotism vanishes. I become a transparent eye-ball. I am nothing. I see all. The currents of the Universal Being circulate through me; I am part or particle of God."

24. As Julian, Hawthorne's son, wrote of a late interview with Melville, *Log,* 2.782: "When I visited him in 1883 to ask whether he had letters from my father, in reply to those he had written him, he said, with a melancholy gesture, that they had all been destroyed long since, as if implying that the less said or preserved, the better!"

25. "It is curious, how a man may travel along a country road, and yet miss the grandest, or sweetest of prospects, by reason of an intervening hedge, so like all other hedges, as in no way to hint of the wide landscape beyond. So has it been with me concerning the enchanting landscape in the soul of this Hawthorne, this most excellent Man of Mosses. His 'Old Manse' has been written now four years, but I never read it till a day or two since. I had seen it in the book-stores—heard of it often—even had it recommended to me by a tasteful friend, as a rare, quiet book, perhaps too deserving of popularity to be popular. But there are so many books called 'excellent,' and so much unpopular merit, that amid the thick stir of other things, the hint of my tasteful friend was disregarded, and for four years the Mosses on the old Manse never refreshed me with their perennial green" (3.1154–55).

26. Consider, too, Melville's portrayal in *Clarel* of Vine, whom almost all critics take to be modeled on Hawthorne. For a brief but excellent analysis, see Walter E. Bezanson, Introduction to *Clarel: A Poem and Pilgrimage in the Holy Land* (New York: Hendricks House, 1960), pp. xc–xcix.

27. *Log,* 2.926, 1.459. And, similarly, *Log,* 2.925, in yet another letter of the same period: "He [Melville] told me he was naturally so silent a man, that he was complained of a great deal on this account; but that he found himself talking to Mr. Hawthorne to a great extent. He said Mr. Hawthorne's great but hospitable silence drew him out—that it was astonishing how *sociable* his silence was."

28. *Letters,* pp. 153–63.

29. Paul de Man, "The Rhetoric of Temporality," in *Interpretation: Theory and Practice,* ed. Charles S. Singleton (Baltimore: Johns Hopkins Univ. Press, 1969). pp. 173–209.

30. Dryden, *Melville's Thematics of Form,* p. 59.

31. *Letters,* pp. 146, 150.

32. Hawthorne, *The Letters, 1843–1853,* Centenary Edition (Columbus: Ohio State Univ. Press, 1985), 16.371.

33. Hence such a classic compendium as H. Bruce Franklin, *The Wake of the Gods: Melville's Mythology* (Stanford: Univ. of Stanford Press, 1963), or Dorothea Melitsky Finkelstein, *Melville's Orienda* (New Haven: Yale Univ. Press, 1961). On the confusion of levels of reality, William B. Dillingham, *Melville's Later Novels* (Athens: Univ. of Georgia Press, 1986), p. 28, is precise: "It is one thing to write a symbolic novel; it is something else to write a symbolic novel and claim repeatedly that it is pure realism, and that is what Melville has done."

34. "Mr. Melville has to thank himself only if his horrors and his heroics are flung aside by the general reader, as so much trash belonging to the worst school of Bedlam literature,—since he seems not so much unable to learn as disdainful of learning the craft of an artist." From a review by Henry F. Chorley, *Atheneum* (October 1851), rpt. in *Melville: The Critical Heritage,* p. 254. Similarly, the review in the *Brittania* (November 1851), the London *Morning Chronicle* (December 1851), and the *Southern Quarterly Review* (January 1852), in ibid., pp. 260–61, 284–88, 289, and others. For modern works, see the still authoritative Howard P. Vincent, *The Trying-Out of "Moby-Dick"* (Boston: Houghton Mifflin, 1949), and George R. Stewart, "The Two *Moby-Dick*s," *American Literature,* 25 (1954), 414–48.

35. To distinguish, nihilism is a positivization of skepticism. It installs in "Being" itself what properly is only a wariness about the act of approaching Being. We might say that nihilism belongs to ontology while skepticism belongs to epistemology, except that the traditional philosophical hierarchy of ontology and epistemology in effect gives up the game before it even begins, in the case of Melville propelling him into a self-negation which his understanding of self as a function of action prior to its definition as existent everywhere denies. For a philosophical attempt to reverse the order of philosophy—establishing, in his wonderful slogan, that "ethics is metaphysically prior to ontology"—see Emmanuel Levinas, especially *Totality and Infinity: An Essay on Exteriority,* trans. Alphonso Lingis (Pittsburgh: Duquesne Univ. Press, 1969).

36. *Letters,* p. 125.

37. Compare the lawyer's attempt in "Bartleby, the Scrivener," 3.664, to find grounds for Billy's eviction: "a vagrant is he? What! he a vagrant, a wanderer, who refuses to budge? It is because he will *not* be a vagrant, then, that you seek to count him *as* a vagrant. That is too

absurd. No visible means of support: there I have him. Wrong again: for indubitably he *does* support himself, and that is the only unanswerable proof that any man can show of his possessing the means so to do."

38. Thus Feidelson, who does both. See, especially, *Symbolism and American Literature*, chap. 5, "The Fool of Truth," pp. 162–212.

39. Edward Rosenberry, "Melville's Comedy and Tragedy," in *A Companion to Melville Studies*, p. 607.

40. Cf. James McIntosh, "The Mariner's Multiple Quest," in *New Essays on "Moby-Dick*," pp. 30–31: "ultimately one imagination travels on all these voyages. *Moby-Dick* has a kind of associative unity in that its various characters keep investigating the same phenomena and noumena—one whale, one White Whale. . . . The book is a many-headed representation of the soul engaged in a simple, if multifaceted, adventure. Hence one 'mariner' on a group of interrelated voyages, hence a 'multiple quest.' "

41. Martin Pops, *The Melville Archetype* (Kent, Ohio: Kent State Univ. Press, 1970), p. 144.

42. For a discussion of the language of tombstones in another context, see Geoffrey Hartman, "Wordsworth, Inscription, and Romantic Poetry," in *Beyond Formalism: Literary Essays, 1958–1970* (New Haven: Yale Univ. Press, 1970), pp. 206–30.

43. Particularly impressed by Melville's apparently new grasp of artistic craft are Warner Berthoff, *The Example of Melville* (Princeton: Princeton Univ. Press, 1962), and R. Bruce Bickley, Jr., *The Method of Melville's Shorter Fiction* (Durham, N.C.: Duke Univ. Press, 1975). Perhaps most interesting, however, is R. W. B. Lewis, "Melville after *Moby-Dick:* The Tales," rpt. in *Modern Critical Views: Herman Melville,* ed. Harold Bloom (New York: Chelsea House, 1980), pp. 77–90, who remarks of the stories that in them "Melville came to speak in all eloquence with what Scott Fitzgerald would call 'the authority of failure,' that, indeed, he learned to make expert shorter fiction out of the failure of his longer fiction."

44. *The Scarlet Letter,* Centenary Edition, 1.27.

45. *Log,* 2.529.

46. Cf. Donald E. Pease, "*Moby-Dick* and the Cold War," in *The American Renaissance Reconsidered,* ed. Walter Benn Michaels and Pease, Selected Papers from the English Institute, 1982–83 (Baltimore: Johns Hopkins Univ. Press, 1985), pp. 113–55. See, also, Pease's exceedingly fine *Visionary Compacts: American Renaissance Writings in Cultural Context* (Madison: Univ. of Wisconsin Press, 1987).

47. For a history of the manuscript of *Billy Budd,* see Harrison Hay-

ford and Merton M. Sealts, Jr., Editors' Introduction to their standard text, *Billy Budd (An Inside Narrative)* (Chicago: Univ. of Chicago Press, 1962), pp. 1–39. For critical treatment of *Billy Budd,* see above, n. 17.

48. Ludwig Wittgenstein, *Philosophical Investigations,* trans. G. E. M. Anscombe (New York: Macmillan, 1953), p. 3 [section 1]: "Explanations come to an end somewhere." Melville, like Wittgenstein, in Stanley Cavell's reading of him, *The Claim of Reason: Wittengstein, Skepticism, Morality, and Tragedy* (New York: Oxford Univ. Press, 1979), does not so much answer skepticism as give us a way to proceed *with* it. We might say that both attempt not so much to break with traditional writing or thinking as to offer, in the Kantian sense, a "critique" of writing that enables it to proceed.

49. And, in fact, "Billy in the Darbies" was evidently first composed for inclusion in *John Marr and Other Sailors,* one of the poetry volumes issued during Melville's silence. For details, see Merton M. Sealts, Jr., "Innocence and Infamy: *Billy Budd, Sailor*" in *A Companion to Melville Studies,* pp. 410–12.

Index